An Eye in the Storm

An Eye in the Storm

An American War Correspondent's
Experiences of the First World War
from the Western Front to Gallipoli
—and Beyond

Arthur Ruhl

LEONAUR

An Eye in the Storm: an American War Correspondent's Experiences of the First World War from the Western Front to Gallipoli—and Beyond
by Arthur Ruhl

Published by Leonaur Ltd

ISBN: 978-1-84677-343-3 (hardcover)
ISBN: 978-1-84677-344-0 (softcover)

http://www.leonaur.com

Publisher's Notes

Contents

The Germans Are Coming!   7

Paris at Bay   18

After the Marne   26

The Fall of Antwerp   36

Paris Again—and Bordeaux   56

"The Great Days"   79

Two German Prison Camps   97

In the German Trenches at La Bassée   104

The Road To Constantinople   118

The Adventure of the Fifty Hostages   137

With The Turks at the Dardanelles   153

Soghan-Dere and the Flier of Ak-Bash   169

A War Correspondents' Village   179

Cannon Fodder   186

East Of Lemberg   202

In the Dust of the Russian Retreat   219

CHAPTER 1

The Germans Are Coming!

The Germans had already entered Brussels, their scouts were reported on the outskirts of Ghent; a little farther now, over behind the horizon wind-mills, and we might at any moment come on them.

For more than a fortnight we had been hurrying eastward, hearing, through cable despatches and wireless, the far-off thunder of that vast grey tide rumbling down to France. The first news had come drifting in, four thousand miles away, to the little Wisconsin lake where I was fishing. A strange herd of us, all drawn in one way or another by the war, had caught the first American ship, the old St. Paul, and, with decks crowded with trunks and mail-bags from half a dozen ships, steamed eastward on the all but empty ocean. There were reservists hurrying to the colours, correspondents, men going to rescue wives and sisters. Some were hit through their pocketbooks, some through their imaginations—like the young women hoping to be Red Cross nurses, or to help in some way, they weren't sure how.

One had a steamer chair next mine—a pale, Broadway tomboy sort of girl in a boyish sailor suit, who looked as if she needed sleep. Without exactly being on the stage, she yet appeared to live on the fringe of it, and combined the slangy freedoms of a chorus girl with a certain quick wisdom and hard sense. It was she who discovered a steerage passenger, on the Liverpool dock, who had lost his wife and was bringing his four little children back to Ireland from Chicago, and,

7

while the other cabin passengers fumed over their luggage, took up a collection for him then and there.

"Listen here!" she would say, grabbing my arm. "I want to tell you something. I'm going to see this thing—d'you know what I mean?—for what it'll do to me—you know—for its effect on my mind! I didn't say anything about it to anybody—they'd only laugh at me—d'you know what I mean? They don't think I've got any serious side to me. Now, I don't mind things—I mean blood—you know—they don't affect me, and I've read about nursing—I've prepared for this! Now, I don't know how to go about it, but it seems to me that a woman who can—you know—go right with 'em—jolly 'em along—might be just what they'd want—d'you know what I mean?"

One Russian had said good-by to a friend at the dock, he to try to get through this way, the other by the Pacific and Trans-Siberian. The Englishman who shared my stateroom was an advertising man. "I've got contracts worth fifty thousand pounds," he said, "and I don't suppose they're worth the paper they're written on." There were several Belgians and a quartet of young Frenchmen who played cards every night and gravely drank bottle after bottle of champagne to the glory of France.

Even the Balkans were with us, in the shape of a tall, soldier-like Bulgarian with a heavy moustache and the eyes of a kindly and highly intelligent hawk. He was going back home—*to fight?*

"Yes, to fight."

"With Serbia?" asked some one politely, with the usual vague American notion of the Balkan states. The Bulgarian's eyes shone curiously.

"You have a sense of humour!" he said.

This man had done newspaper work in Russia and America, studied at Harvard, and he talked about our politics, theatres, universities, society generally. It was a pity, he said, and the result of the comparative lack of critical spirit in America that Mr. Roosevelt had been a hero so long. There were party papers mechanically printing their praise or blame—"and then, of course, the *New York Evening Post* and the *Springfield Republican* "—but no general intelligent criticism of ideas for a popular idol to meet and answer. "On the whole, he's a good influence—but in place of something better. It isn't good for a man to stand so long in the bright sunshine."

That it was impossible for the Mexicans to work out their own salvation he doubted. "I think of Bulgaria—surely our inheritance of Turkish rule was almost as bad, and of how the nation has responded, and of the intensive culture we had at a time when we were only a name to most western Europeans." He was but one of those new potentialities which every whisper from the now cloud-wrapped Continent seemed to be opening—this tall, scholar-fighter from the comic-opera land where Mr. Shaw placed his chocolate soldiers.

In a steamer chair a frail-looking young woman in a white polo coat looked nervously out on the sea. She was Irish and came of a fighting line—father, uncles, and brothers in army and navy, her husband in command of a British cruiser, scouting the very steamship lane through which we were steaming. Frail-looking, but not frail in spirit—a fighter born, with Irish keenness and wit, she was ready to prick any balloon in sight. She had chased about the world too long after a fighting family to care much about settling down now. They couldn't afford to keep a place in England and live somewhere else half the time—"and, after all, what is there in being a cabbage?" She talked little. "You can learn more about people merely watching them," and she lay in her steamer chair and watched.

She could tell, merely by looking at them in their civilian's clothes, which were army and which navy men, which "R. Ns" and which merchant- service men. We spoke of a young lieutenant from an India artillery regiment. "Yes—'garrison-gunner,'" she said. She was sorry for the German people, but the Kaiser was "quite off his rocker and had to be licked."

War suddenly reached out for us as we came up to Mersey Bar, and an officer in khaki bellowed from the pilot-boat: "Take down your wireless!" Down it came, and there the ship stayed for the night, while the passengers crowded about a volunteer town-crier who read from the papers that had come aboard, and, in the strange quiet that descends on an anchored steamship, asked each other how true it was that the German military bubble—a magazine article with that title had been much read on the way over—had burst.

Slowly next morning we crept up the Mersey, past a rusty tramp outward bound, crowded with khaki-clad men. All the shipping was tooting as she swept by, and the men cheering and waving their hats at the land they might never come back to. The regular landing-stages were taken by transports, tracks were held for troop-trains, and it was night before we got down to London, where crowds and buses stormed along as usual and baritone soloists in every music-hall were roaring defiance to the Kaiser and reiterating that Britannia ruled the waves.

Into the fog of war that covered the Continent an army of Englishmen had vanished, none knew where. Out of it came rumours of victories, but as I crossed the Strand that morning on the way to Charing Cross, a newsboy pushed an extra into the cab window—the Germans were entering Brussels! Yet we fought into the boat train just as if thousands of people weren't fighting to get away from the very places we hoped to reach.

There were two business men in our coupe going to France, an elderly Irish lady, an intransigent Unionist, with black goggles and umbrella, hoping to get through to her invalid brother in Diest, and a bright, sweet-faced little Eng-lishwoman, in nurse's dark-blue uniform and bonnet, bound for Antwerp, where her sister's convent had been turned into a hospital. She told about her little east-coast town as we crossed the sunny Channel; we trailed together into the great empty station at Ostend and, after an hour or two, found a few cars getting away, so to speak, of their own accord.

The low checker-board Belgian fields drifted quickly past;

then Bruges, with a wounded soldier leaning on the shoulders of two companions; then Ghent. There was a great crowd about the station—men thrown out of work, men in flat cloth caps smoking pipes—the town just recovering from the panic of that afternoon. Flags had been hauled down—the American consul was even asked if he didn't think it would be safer to take down his flag—some of the civic guards, fearing they would be shot on sight if the Germans saw them in uniform, tore off their coats and threw them in the canal. Others threw in cartridges, thousands of gallons of gasoline were poured on the ground, and everybody watched the church tower for the red flag which would signal that firing was about to begin. *Le Bien Public* of Ghent, however, protested stoutly because its mail edition had been refused at the station:

It is not alone on the field of battle that one must be brave. For us civilians real courage consists in doing our ordinary duty up to the last. In Limburg postmen made their rounds while Prussians inundated the region, and peasants went right along with their sowing while down the road troops were falling back from the firing-line.

Let us think of our sons sleeping forever down there in the trenches of Haelen and Tirlemont and Aerschot; of those brave artillerymen who, for twenty days, have been waiting in the forts at Liege the help so many times promised from the allies; of our lancers charging into mitrailleuse-fire as if they were in a tournament; let us remember that our heroic little infantrymen, crouched behind a hedge or in a trench, keeping up their fire for ten hours running until their ammunition was exhausted, and forced at last to retire, wounded and worn out, without a chief to take orders from, have had no other thought than that of finding some burgomaster or commissioner of police, in order not to be taken for deserters. Let us think a little of all these brave men and be worthy of them.

There were no music-halls in Belgium and there were posters on the blank walls, even of little villages, reminding bands and hurdy-gurdy players and the proprietors of dance-halls that this was no time for unnecessary noise. There were no soldiers going gaily off to war; the Belgians were coming back from war. They had been asked to hold out for three days, and they had held for three weeks. All their little country was a battle-field, and Belgium open to the invader.

It was too late to get to Brussels, but there was still a train to Antwerp. At Puers soldiers were digging trenches and stringing approaches with barbed wire. The dikes had been opened and part of the country flooded. Farther on we passed the Antwerp forts, then comely suburbs where houses had been torn down and acres of trees and shrubs—precious, as may be imagined, to a people who line their country roads with elms and lindens like avenues in parks, and build monuments to benevolent-looking old horticulturists—chopped down and burned. And go, presently, into the old city itself, dull-flaming with the scarlet, gold, and black, of the Belgian flag, and with something that seemed to radiate from the life itself of this hearty, happy people, after all their centuries of trade and war, and good food, and good art—like their own Rubenses and Van Dycks.

There was no business, not a ship moving in the Scheldt. All who worked at all were helping prepare for the possible siege; those who didn't crowded the sidewalk cafes, listening to tales from the front, guessing by the aid of maps whither, across the silent, screened southwest, the German avalanche was spreading.

"Treason," "betrayal," "savagery," were on everybody's lips. For Antwerp, you might say, had been "half German"; many of its rich and influential men were of German origin, although they had lived in Belgium for years. And now the Belgians felt they had lived there as spies, and the seizure of Belgium was an act long and carefully planned. One was told of the finding of rifles in German cellars, marked "Preserves," of German consuls authorized to give prizes for the most complete inventories of their neighbourhoods turned in by amateur spies.

Speaking to one man about the Rubens "Descent from the Cross" still hanging in the cathedral, I suggested that such a place was safe from bombardment. He looked up at the lace-like old tower, whose chimes, jangling down through leaping shafts and jets of Gothic stone, have so long been Antwerp's voice. "They wouldn't stop a minute," he said.

All eastern Belgium was cut off. Brussels, to which people run over for dinner and the theatre, might have been in China. Meanwhile Antwerp seemed safe for the time and I returned to Ghent, got a train next day as far south as Deynze, where the owner of a two-wheeled Belgian cart was induced to take me another thirty kilometres on down to Courtrai. It was rumoured that there had been a battle at Courtrai—it was, at any rate, close to the border and the German right wing and in the general line of their advance.

We rattled along the hard highroad, paved with Belgian blocks, with a well-pounded dirt path at the side for bicycles, between almost uninterrupted rows of low houses and tiny fields in which men and women both were working. Other carts like ours passed by, occasional heavy wagons drawn by one of the handsome Belgian draft-horses, and now and then a small loaded cart, owner perched on top, zipping along behind a jolly Belgian work dog—pulling as if his soul depended on it and apparently having the time of his life. Every one was busy, not a foot of ground wasted; a more incongruous place into which to force the waste and lawlessness of war it would be hard to imagine.

Past an old chateau, with its lake and pheasant-preserve; along the River Lys, with its miles of flax, soaked in this peculiarly potent water, now drying in countless little cones, like the tents of some vast Lilliputian army, and so at last into Courtrai.

It was like hundreds of other quaint old towns along the French and Flemish border, not yet raked by war, but motionless, with workmen idle, young men gone to the front, and nothing for people to do but exchange rumours and wait for the clash to come. I strolled round the old square and through some of the winding streets. One window was filled with tricolour sashes carrying the phrase: "Long live our dear Belgium! May God preserve her!"

On blank walls was this proclamation in parallel columns of French and Flemish:

VILLE DE COURTRAI AVIS IMPORTANT A LA POPULATION COURTRAISIENNE	STAD KORTRIJK BELANGRIJK BERICHT AAN DE KORTRIJKSCHE BEVOLKING

I am about to make an appeal to your reason and your sentiments of humanity.

If, in the course of the unjust war which we are now enduring, it happens that French or Belgian troops bring German prisoners to our city, I beseech you to maintain your calm and dignity. These prisoners, wounded or not, I shall take under my protection, became I say that they are not really to blame for acts which they have been ordered to do under threat of cruel punishment.

Yes, I say I shall take them under my protection because my heart bleeds to think that they, too, have left behind those dear to them—an aged father, an old mother, a wife, children, sisters, or sweethearts whom separation has plunged into deepest anguish. Do not forget when you see these prisoners passing by, I beg of you, and permit yourself to shout at and insult them. Keep, on the contrary, the respectful silence appropriate to thinking men. Fellow citizens, if, in these grave and painful circumstances, you will listen to my advice, if you will recall that it is now thirty years that I have been your burgomaster and during all that time of hard work I have never asked a favour of you, I feel sure that you will obey my request and, on your side, you may be sure that my gratitude will not be wanting.

A. Reynaekt

Burgomaster.

Although war had not touched Courtrai as yet, the rumour of it, more terrifying often than the thing itself, had swept through all Flanders. Along the level highways leading into Courtrai trooped whole families carrying babies and what few household things they could fling together in blankets. Covered wagons overflowed with men, women, and children. The speed with which rumour spread was incredible. In one village a group of half-drunken men, who insisted on jeering the Germans were put at the head of a column and compelled to march several miles before they were released. The word at once ran the length of dozens of highroads that the Germans "were taking with them every one between fifteen and fifty." I heard the same warning repeated on several of the roads about Courtrai by men and women, panting, red-faced, stumbling blindly on from they knew not what. Later, I met the same people, straggling back to their villages, good-naturedly accepting the jibes of those who had stayed behind.

A linen manufacturer who lived in the village of Deerlyck, not far from Courtrai, where German scouts had been reported, kindly asked me to come out and spend the night. For several miles we drove through the densely populated countryside, past rows of houses whose occupants all seemed to know him.

Women ran out to stop him and rattled away in Flemish; there were excited knots of people every few steps, and the heads kept turning this way and that, as if we were all likely to be shot any minute. We drove into the courtyard of the solid old Flemish house—a house in which he and his father before him had lived, with tiny rooms full of old paintings, garden, stable, and hothouse packed close in the saving Belgian fashion, and all as spick and span and shining as if built yesterday—and then into the street again. It was interesting to watch this square little man roll sturdily along, throwing out his stout arms impatiently and flinging at the nervous villagers—who treated him almost as a sort of feudal lord—guttural Flemish commands to keep cool and not make fools of themselves.

15

All at once, coming out of nowhere, a wave of panic swept down the street like a squall across a still pond.

"Bing—Bang!" went wooden shutters over windows, the stout housewives flinging the bars home and gathering up their children. Doors slammed, windows closed—it was like something in a play—and almost as soon as it takes to tell it there was not a head, not a sound; the low houses were one blank wall, and we stood in the street alone.

Just such scenes as this people must have known in the days when Europe was a general battle-ground—when the French or the Spanish came into Flanders; just such villages, just such housewives slamming shutters close—you can see them now in old Flemish pictures.

Slowly doors and windows opened, heads poked out. The little street filled, the knots of people gathered again. We walked up and down, the linen merchant flinging out his arms and his reassurances more and more vigorously. Half an hour passed, and then, all at once, it came again. And this time it was real. The Germans were coming!

Down the straight, paved highway, a mile or so away, at the farther end of an avenue of elms which framed them like a tunnel, was a band of horsemen. They were coming at an easy trot, half a dozen in single file on either side of the road. We could see their lances, held rakishly upstanding across the saddle, then the tail of the near horse whisking to and fro. One, crossing over, was outlined against the sky, and those who could see whispered: "One is standing sidewise!" as if this were somehow important. Tears rolled down the cheeks of the women huddled inside the door before which we stood.

Coming nearer and nearer up that long tunnel of trees, like one of those unescapable things seen in dreams, the little grey spot of moving figures grew to strange proportions—"the Germans!"—front of that frightful avalanche. A few hundred yards away they pulled down to a walk, and slowly, peering sharply out from under their helmets, entered the silent street. Another moment and the leader was alongside, and we found ourselves looking up at a boy, not more than twenty he seemed, with blue eyes and a clean-cut, gentle face. He passed without a look or word, but behind him a young officer, soldier-like and smart in the Prussian fashion, with a half-opened map in his hand, asked the way to a near-by village. He took the linen merchant's direction without pausing and the horses swung down the side street. "Do you speak English?" he called back, as if, in happier times, we might have been friends, and, without waiting for an answer, trotted on into the growing dusk.

They were but one of hundreds of such squads of light cavalry—uhlans for the most part—ranging all over western Belgium as far as Ostend, a dozen or so men in hostile country, prepared to be cut to pieces if they found the enemy they were looking for, or to be caught from ambush at any time by some squad of civic guards. But as one watched them disappear down their long road to France they grew into something more than that. And in the twilight of the quiet countryside these stern shapes that rode on without turning, lances upstanding from tired shoulders, became strange, grotesque, pathetic—again the Germans, legions of the War Lord, come too late into a world which must crush them at last, Knights of the Frightful Adventure, riding to their death.

CHAPTER 2

Paris at Bay

The Calais and Boulogne routes were already closed. Dieppe and Havre might at any moment follow. You must go now, people said in London, if you want to get there at all.

And yet the boat was crowded as it left Folkestone. In bright afternoon sunshine we hurried over the Channel, empty of any sign of war, unless war showed in its very emptiness. Next to me sat a young Frenchman, different from those we had met before hurrying home to fight. Good-looking, tall, and rather languid in manner, he spoke English with an English accent, and you would have taken him for an Englishman. A big canvas bag full of golf-clubs leaned against the wall behind him, and he had been trying to play golf at one of the east-coast seaside places in England. But one couldn't play in a time like this, and the young man sighed and waved his hands rather desperately—one couldn't settle down to anything. So he was going home. To fight?—I suggested. Possibly, he said—the army had refused him several years ago—maybe they would take him now. Very politely, in his quiet manner, he asked me down to tea. When he stood by the rail watching the tawny French cliffs draw nearer, one noticed a certain weary droop to his shoulders, in contrast to his well-tanned, rather athletic-looking, face—born a little tired, perhaps, like the young nobleman in Bernstein's "Whirlwind." His baggage was addressed to a Norman chateau.

On the other side was a pink-cheeked boy of seventeen, all French, though he spoke English and divided his time between writing post-cards to the boys he had been visiting in England and reading General von Bernhardi. "The first chapter, 'The Right to Make War,'" he said, "I understand that—yes! But the second chapter—'The Duty to Make War'"—he laughed and shook his head.

"No—no—no!" He was the son of an insurance agent who was already at the front, and, although under age, he hoped to enlist. We drew nearer Dieppe—tall French houses leaning inward with tricolours in the windows, a quay with the baggy red breeches of French soldiers showing here and there—just such a scene as they paint on theatre curtains at home. A smoky tug whistled uproariously, there was a patter of wooden shoes as children clattered along the stone jetty, and from all over the crowd that had come down to greet us came brave shouts of "Eep-eep Hoorah! Eep-eep Hoorah!"

No news, or at least no reliable news. A lot of wounded had been brought in, business was stopped, the great beach deserted; some thought the Germans would be in Dieppe in a day or two. Our train was supposed to start as soon as the boat arrived and reach Paris before ten that night. It was after dark before we got away and another day before we crawled into St. Lazare.

There was a wild rush for places as soon as the gates opened; one took what one could, and nine of us, including three little children, were glad enough to crowd into a third-class compartment. Two ladies, with the three little children, were hurrying away from the battle that their husbands thought was going to be fought near Dieppe within a day or two. From Paris they hoped to get to the south of France. Over and over again the husbands said good-by, then the guards whistled for the last time.

"Albaire!". . . and a boy of about six went to the door of the compartment to receive his father's embrace. "Don't let the Germans get you!" cried the father, with a great air of gayety, and kissed the boy again and again. He returned to his corner, rubbed his fists into his eyes, and the tears rolled out under them. Then the two little girls—twins, it seemed, about four years old, in little mushroom hats—took their turns, and they put their fists into their eyes and cried, and then the two mothers began to cry, and the men, dabbing their eyes and puffing vigorously at their cigars, cried good-by over and over, and so at last we moved out of the station.

The long train crept, stopped, backed, crept on again. Through the open windows one caught glimpses of rows of poplar-trees and the countryside lying cool and white in the moonlight. Then came stations with sentries, stray soldiers hunting for a place to squeeze in, and now and then empty troop-trains jolted by, smelling of horses. In the confusion at Dieppe we had had no time to get anything to eat, and several hours went by before, at a station lunchroom, already supposed to be closed, I got part of a loaf of bread. One of the young mothers brought out a bit of chocolate, the other a bottle of wine, and so we had supper—a *souper de luxe*, as one of them laughed—all, by this time, old friends.

Eleven o'clock—midnight—the gas, intended for a short journey, grew dimmer and dimmer, presently flickered out. We were in darkness—all the train was in darkness—we were alone in France, wrapped in war and moonlight, half real beings who had been adventuring together, not for hours, but for years. The dim figure on the left sighed, tried one position and another uneasily, and suddenly said that if it would not derange monsieur too much, she would try to sleep on his shoulder. It would not derange monsieur in the least. On the contrary. . .

"You must make yourself at home in France," laughed the mother of the two little girls. But the other was even more polite.

"*Nous sommes en Amerique!*" she murmured. The train jolted slowly on. An hour or two after midnight it stopped and a strange figure in turban and white robe peered in. "*Complet! Complet!*" cried the lady with the little girls. But the figure kept staring in, and, turning, chattered to others like him.

There was a crowd of them, men from France's African colonies, from Algeria or Morocco, who had been working in the French mines and were now going back to take the places of trained soldiers—the daredevil "Turcos"—sent north to fight the Germans.

They did not get into our compartment, but into the one next to it, and as there was no place to sit down, stood in patient Arab fashion, and after a time gradually edged into ours, where they squatted on the floor. They talked broken French or Italian or their native speech and now and then broke into snatches of a wild sort of song. In Paris girls ran into the street and threw their arms about the brave "Marocs" as they marched by, but the lady with the little girls felt that they were a trifle smelly, and, fishing out a bottle of scent, she wet a handkerchief with it and passed it round.

The young Frenchman lit a match—three-twenty. The little boy, rousing from his corner, suddenly announced, apropos of nothing, that the Germans ought to be dropped into kettles of boiling water; at once came the voice of one of the little girls, sound asleep apparently before this, warning him that he must not talk like that or the Germans might hear and shoot them. We jolted on, backed, and suddenly one became aware that the grey light was not that of the moon. The lady at my left sat upright. "The day comes!" she said briskly. It grew lighter. We passed sentries, rifles stacked on station platforms, woods—the forest of St. Germain. These woods were misty blue in the cool autumn morning, there were bivouac fires, coffee-pots on the coals, and standing beside these fires soldiers in kepis and red trousers and heavy blue coats with the flaps pinned back. Just such soldiers and scenes you have seen in the war pictures of Detaille and De Neuville. Bridges, more houses, the rectangular grass-covered faces of forts at last; just as Paris was getting up for breakfast, into St. Lazare station, heaped with trunks and boiling with people, Parisians, belated American tourists, refugees from northeast villages, going somewhere, anywhere, to get away. It was September 2.

There were miles of closed shops with placards on the shutters: "Proprietor and personnel have been called to the colours"; no buses or trams, the few 'cabs piled with the luggage of those trying to get away, almost no way to traverse the splendid distances but to walk. Papers could not be cried aloud on the streets, and the only news was the official communiqué and a word about some Serbian or Russian victory in some un-pronounceable region of the East.

"France is a history, a life, an idea which has taken its place in the world, and the bit of earth from which that history, that life, that thought, has radiated, we cannot sacrifice without sealing the stone of the tomb over ourselves and our children and the generations to follow us." Thus George Clemenceau was writing in *L'Homme Libre*, and people knew that this was true. And yet in that ghastly silence of Paris, broken only by the constant flight of military automobiles, screaming through the streets on missions nobody understood, those left behind did not even know where the enemy was, where the defenders were, or what was being done to save Paris. And it gradually, and not unnaturally, seemed to the more nervous that nothing had been done—the forts were paper, the government faithless, revolution imminent—one heard the wildest things.

Late that afternoon I walked down from the Madeleine toward the river. It was the "hour of the aperitif"—there were still enough people to fill cafe tables—and since Sunday it had been the hour of the German aeroplane. It had come that afternoon, dropped a few bombs—*quelques ordures*—and sailed away to return next day at the same hour. "You have remarked," explained one of the papers, "that people who are without wit always repeat their jokes." And just as I came into the Place de la Concorde, "Mr. Taube" came up out of the north.

You must imagine that vast open space, with the bridge and river and Invalides behind it, and beyond the light tracery of the Eiffel Tower, covered with little specks of people, all looking upward. Back along the boulevards, on roofs on both

22

banks, all Paris, in fact, was similarly staring—*Le nezen l'air.* And straight overhead, so far up that even the murmur of the motor was unheard, no more than a bird, indeed, against the pale sky, "Mr. Taube," circling indolently about, picking his moment, plotting our death.

I thought of the shudder of outraged horror that ran over Antwerp when the first Zeppelin came. It seemed the last unnecessary blow to a heroic people who had already stood so much. Very different was "Mr. Taube's" reception here. He might have been a holiday balloon or some particularly fancy piece of fireworks. Everywhere people were staring upward, looking through their closed fists, through opera-glasses. Out of the arcades of the Hotel de Crillon one man in a bath-robe and another in a suit of purple underclothes came running, to gaze calmly into the zenith until the "von" had gone.

As the little speck drew straight overhead, these human specks scattered over the Place de la Concorde suddenly realized that they were in the line of fire, and scattered just as people run from a sudden shower. This was the most interesting thing—these helpless little humans scrambling away like ants or beetles to shelter, and that tiny insolent bird sailing slowly far overhead. This was a bit of the modern war one reads about—it was a picture from some fanciful story of Mr. H. G. Wells. They scattered for the arcades, and some, quaintly enough, ran under the trees in the near-by Champs-Elysées. There was a *"Bang!"* at which everybody shouted "There!" but it was not a bomb, only part of the absurd fusillade that now began. They were firing from the Eiffel Tower, whence they might possibly have hit something, and from roofs with ordinary guns and revolvers which could not possibly have hit anything at all. In the grey haze that hung over Paris the next morning, I wandered through empty streets and finally, with some vague notion of looking out, up the hill of Montmartre. All Paris lay below, mysterious in the mist, with that strange, poignant beauty of something trembling on the verge. One could follow the line of the Seine and see the dome of the

Invalides, but nothing beyond. I went down a little way from the summit and, still on the hill, turned into the Rue des Abbesses, crowded with vegetable carts and thrifty housewives. The grey air was filled with their bargaining, with the smell of vegetables and fruit, and there, in front of two men playing violins, a girl in black, with a white handkerchief loosely knotted about her throat, was singing of the little Alsatian boy, shot by the Prussians because he cried "Vive la France!" and threatened them with his wooden gun.

True or not, it was one of those things that get believed. Verses were written about it and pictures made of it all over Paris—presently it would be history. And this girl, true child of the asphalt, was flinging it at them, holding the hearts of these broad-faced mothers in the hollow of her hand. She would sing one verse, pause, and sell copies of the song, then put a hand to her hoarse throat and sing again. The music was not sold with the song, and it was rather difficult—a mournful sort of recitative with sudden shifts into marching rhythm—and so the people sang the words over and over with her until they had almost learned the tune. You can imagine how a Frenchman—he was a young fellow, who lived in a rear tenement over on the other side of Montmartre—would write that song. The little boy, who was going to "free his brothers back there in Alsace" when he grew up, playing soldier—*Joyeux, il murmurait: Je suis petit, en somme, Mais viendra bien le jour, ou je serai un homme, Ardeat! Vaillanti . . .*—the Prussians—*monstres odieux*—smashing into the village, the cry *"Maman! Maman!"*—and after each verse a pause, and slowly and lower down, with the crowd joining in, *"Petit—enfant"* ("Little boy, close your big blue eyes, for the bandits are hideous and cruel, and they will kill you if they read your brave thoughts") *"ferme tes grands yeux bleus."*

The violins mixed with the voices of the market-women, crying their artichokes and haricots, and above them rang—*"Ardent! Vaillant!. . ."* Audit might have been the voice of Paris itself, lying down there in her mist, Paris of lost Alsace and

24

hopeless *revanche*, of ardour and charm crushed once, as they might be again, as the voice of that pale girl in black, with her air of coming from lights and cigarette smoke, and of these simple mothers rose above the noise of the street, half dirge, half battle-cry, while out beyond somewhere the little soldiers in red breeches were fighting, and the fate of France hung in the balance, that morning.

CHAPTER 3

After the Marne

At the end of the village the road climbed again from the ravine and emerged on open fields. A wall of timber, dark and impenetrable as the woods round an old chateau, rose at the farther end of these fields—the road cutting through it like a tunnel—and on the brow of the ravine, commanding the road and the little plain, was a line of trenches. Here evidently they had fought.

We walked on down the road. Below the northern horizon, where they were fighting now along the Aisne, rolled the sullen thunder of artillery, as it had been rolling since daylight. And the autumn wind, cold with the week of equinoctial rain, puffing out of thickets and across ravines, brought, every now and then, the horrible odour of death.

Ahead, to the right, one caught the glint of a French infantry's red trousers. A man was lying there, face downward, on the field. Then across the open space appeared another—and another—they were scattered all over that field, bright as the red poppies which were growing in the stubble and as still. They were in various positions. One lay on his back, with one knee raised like a man day-dreaming and looking up at the sky. Another was stretched stiff, with both hands clinched over his chest. One lay in the ditch close beside us, his head jammed into the muddy bank just as he had dived there in falling; another gripped a cup in one hand and a spoon in the other, as if, perhaps, he might have tried to feed himself in the long hours after the battle rolled on and left them there.

All these were French, but just at the edge of the thick timber was a heap—one could scarcely say of Germans, so utterly did the grey, sodden faces and sodden, grey uniforms merge into anonymity. A squad of French soldiers appeared at a turn in the road. Two officers rode beside them, and they were just moving off across the fields carrying shovels instead of rifles. Looking after them, beyond the belt of timber, one could see other parties like theirs on the distant slopes to the left, and here and there smoke. Two more French soldiers appeared pushing a wheelbarrow filled with cast-off arms. With the boyish good nature which never seems to desert these little men in red and blue, they stopped and offered us a few clips of German cartridges. They were burying their own men, they said, burning the Germans. The dead had been lying here for nearly a fortnight now while the battle line rolled northward, clear across France.

We turned back toward Crepy, passing again through the shattered village of Betz. For three days it had been the centre of a battle, the two forces lying outside it and shelling each other across the town. The main street, now full of French soldiers, was in ruins, the church on the edge of the ravine smashed and gaping, and a few peasant women stood about, arms folded patiently, telling each other over and over again what they had seen.

Past fields, where the wheat still waited to be stacked and thrashed, past the carcasses of horses sprawled stiff-legged in the ditch or in the stubble, we tramped on to Crepy-en-Valois. The country was empty, scoured by the flood that had swept across it, rolled back again, and now was thundering, foot by foot, farther and farther below the horizon to the north. The little hotel across from the railroad station in Crepy had kept open through it all. It was the typical Hotel de la Gare of these little old towns—a bar and coffee-room down-stairs, where the proprietor and his wife and daughters served their fleeting guests, a few chambers up-stairs, where one slept between heavy homespun sheets and under a feather bed. They were used to change, and the mere coming of armies could not be permitted to derange them.

Within a fortnight that little coffee-room of theirs had been crowded with English soldiers in retreat; then with Germans—stern, on edge, sure of being in Paris in a few days; then with the same Germans falling back, a trifle dismayed but in good order, and then the pursuing French. And now they were serving the men from the troop-trains that kept pouring up toward the Aisne, or those of the wounded who could hobble over from the hospital trains that as steadily kept pouring down.

Sometimes they coined money, and, again, when the locomotive unexpectedly whistled, saw a roomful of noisy men go galloping away, leaving a laugh and a few *sous* behind. Madame would come in from the kitchen, raise her arms and sigh something about closing their doors, but, after all, they knew they should keep right on giving as long as they had anything to give. One of their daughters, a strapping, light-hearted colt of a girl, told us some of the things they had seen as she paused in the hall after preparing our rooms. Her sister stood beside her, and together they declaimed in an inimitable sort of recitative.

How the English soldiers had come in, all laughing, and the young officers so handsome; but the German soldiers were all like this—and the young woman gave a quick gesture as of one taking nose and mouth in her hand and pulling it stiffly down a bit. The French officers and their men were like fathers and sons, but the Germans had a discipline you would not believe—she had seen one officer strike a man with his whip, she said, because he was not marching fast enough, and another, when a soldier had come too near, had kicked him. And they all thought surely they were going into Paris— "Two days more," they had laughed as they drank down-stairs, "Paris, and then—*kaput!*"

You can imagine that grey horde rolling through the streets—narrow, cobblestoned streets, with steep-roofed stone houses and queer little courts, and the air over all of having been lived in for generations on generations. There is the remnant in Crepy of one of the houses that used to belong to the Dukes of Valois, and at the end of one winding street you find yourself unexpectedly looking through a grilled iron gateway into the ordered stateliness of an old-time chateau. On the outward side the walls of the chateau garden drop a sheer thirty or forty feet to the edge of the ravine. What a place to wait for an approaching enemy, one thinks, walking underneath; and the Germans evidently thought so too, for from this part of town they carefully kept away. They burned one house, that of a dressmaker so unfortunate as to live next door to a shop in which arms were sold, they pillaged the houses whose owners had run away, and they ordered the town to pay them one hundred thousand francs, but those townspeople who had the fortitude to stay behind were not molested. The enemy were even polite, one woman told us—"*Pas peur!*" said the officer who visited her house, taking off his hat. On the gate of another house was scrawled in German script, "Sick Woman—keep away!" and as we passed the open windows, sure enough there was the pale young mother lying propped up in bed just as she had been when the Germans came.

On another door we read, also in German script, "Good people—they give everything!" and on several were orders to leave those within alone. And there was a curious and touching irony in that phrase: "*Gute Leute—Schoenen!*" chalked in stiff script by those now fighting for their lives to the north of us and likely never to see their fatherland again.

Crepy-en-Valois, more fortunate than some of the towns, whose mayors were dismissed for revealing "a lamentable absence of sang-froid," had a mayor who stuck to his post. He was there when three-fourths of the village had fled and, getting up from a sick-bed to receive the German commander, he saw that the latter's orders were carried out, and signed the order for the town's ransom while his daughter held smelling-salts under his nose.

Whether the mayor of the old town of Senlis, a few miles west of Crepy, was in any way tactless is scarcely of importance now, in so far as it concerns him for he and the other hostages were shot, and, however little good it may have done anybody, he at least gave France his life. It is said that his order to the townspeople to turn in their arms was not completely obeyed. It was also said—and this several people of Senlis told us—that a few Senegalese, lagging behind as the French left, fired on the Germans as they approached, and that it was possible that one or two excited civilians had joined in.

Granting that civilians did fire after hostages had been given, there remains the question of reprisal. It was the German commander's idea that Senlis should be taught a lesson, and this consisted of shooting the mayor and the hostages, and sacking and burning the main street—a half mile, perhaps—from end to end. The idea was carried out with thoroughness, and men ran along from house to house feeding the flames with petroleum and even burning a handsome new country house which stood apart at one end.

A nice-looking, elderly gentleman whom we met in front of the ruined Hotel du Nord said that the Germans came there and, finding champagne in the cellar after the *maitre d'hotel* had told them there wasn't any, set fire to the hotel, and, as I recall it, shot him. How true such stories are I cannot say, but there was no doubt that Senlis had been punished. At least half of the old city on the banks of the wistful Nonette—it is a much larger place than Crepy, with a cathedral of some consequence—was smashed as utterly as it might have been by a cyclone or an earthquake. The systematic manner in which this was done was suggested by the fact that, in the long street running parallel to the one picked for destruction, nearly every door still carried its chalked order to *"Schoenen."* One house spared was that of a town fireman. "I've got five little children," he told the German soldiers. "They're one, two, three, four, five years old, and I'm expecting another." And they went on.

These were common sights and sounds of that gracious country north of Paris—deserted, perhaps demolished, villages; the silent countryside, with dead horses, bits of broken shell, smashed bicycles or artillery wagons along the road; and the tainted autumn wind. Along the level French roads, under their arches of elms or poplars, covered carts on tall wheels, drawn by two big farm horses harnessed one behind another, and loaded with women, children, and household goods, were beginning to move northward as they had moved south three weeks before. Trains, similarly packed, were creeping up to within ear-shot of the constant cannonading, and it was on one of these trains that we had come.

In Paris, recovered now from the dismay of three weeks before, keen French imaginations were daily turning the war into terms of heroism and sacrifice and military glory. Even editors and play-writers fighting at the front were able to send back impressions now and then, and these, stripped by the censorship of names and dates, became almost as impersonal as pages torn from fiction. Sitting comfortably at some cafe table, reading the papers with morning coffee, one saw the dawn coming up over the Oise and Aisne, heard the French "seventy-fives" and the heavy German siege-guns resume their roar; saw again, for the hundredth time, some hitherto unheard-of little man flinging away his life in one brief burst of glory. And these thrills, repeated over and over again, without sight or sound of the concrete facts, in that strange, still city whose usual life had stopped, produced at last a curious sense of unreality. Meaux became as far away as Waterloo, and one read words that had been spoken yesterday exactly as one reads that the old guard dies but never surrenders.

A man could leave the Café de la Paix and in two hours be under fire, where killing was as matter of fact as driving tacks. And in between these two zones—the zone where war was at once a highly organized business and a splendid, terrible game, and that in which its disjointed, horrible surfaces were being turned into abstractions, into ideas, poetry, rhetoric—was this middle ground through which we were now tramping, where one saw only its silence and ruin and desolation.

We returned to Crepy. All that night the trains went clanking through the station, pouring more men—Frenchmen, Englishmen—into the sodden trenches along the Aisne. For a week it had rained, cold shower following cold shower. In Paris shivering concierges closed their doors in the middle of the day in mournful attempts to keep warm—autumn's quick sequel to the almost torrid heat in which the armies had fought across this same country a fortnight before. It was into trenches half filled with water that the new men were going—Frenchmen trundling over to the bar in big overcoats, with their air of good little boy, to go galloping back with a bottle of red wine and a long loaf of bread; Englishmen, noisy, laughing, trying to talk French with their fingers and wanting a nip of brandy or hot water for their tea.

There were Highlanders among them, men with necks like towers and straight, flat backs and a swing of the shoulders—like band music going past. One watched them stride back to their cars with a sort of pang. What grotesque irony that men like these, who in times when war was man's normal business might have fought their way through, must now, with all the diseased and hopeless bodies encumbering the earth, be cut off by a mere wad of unthinking lead!

All that night it rained, and, through the rain and dark, trains kept pouring on up into the terrible north. Once I heard cattle lowing as their cars clanked past, and again, in the gloomy clairvoyance of night, saw the faces on the field at Betz, beaten on by the rain that had beaten them for days. And just before a feeble daylight returned again, the steady rumble of artillery.

After noon there was a break in the clouds, and we started on foot for Villers-Cotterets, some fifteen kilometres away. The hard macadam road was no more than dampened, and ambulances and motor-trucks went scooting by as on a city street. Occasionally there was an abandoned trench, once a broken caisson, and the wreck of an aeroplane, but the wheat was harvested and stacked. Beyond Vaumoise the country grew more hilly, and the caves and quarries, which the Germans were making such effective use of along the Aisne, began to appear.

And all this time the cannon were thundering—so close that it seemed each hilltop would bring them into view, and as the detonation puffed across the landscape, one even fancied one could feel the concussion in one's ear. Up from a field ahead of us an aeroplane rose and, in a wide spiral, went climbing up the sky, now almost cleared, and presently disappeared in the north. Then, after satisfying a sentry that our papers were correct—such things could be done in those first days—we got into Villers-Cotterets. Instead of deserted houses we found that nearly every house was quartering soldiers. There were infantrymen, dragoons, flyers, Senegalese, Algerians in white turbans and burnooses on their desert horses, and everywhere officers. We had stumbled into a headquarters!

With somewhat the sensation of walking a tight rope, we sought the mayor to ask for permission to stay in town—finally to ask for safe-conducts to Soissons. The charming old gentleman, undisturbed by war's alarms, politely made them out.

Presently in a hotel full of officers we came on three civilians calmly eating dinner. They had arrived by train, although there were no trains for civilians; they were now dining at a long table set for officers from which we had a moment before been turned away; and we were rescued by a mysterious being at the head of the table—a dark, bald, bright-eyed, smiling, sanguine gentleman, who might have been an impresario or a press agent, and continually had the air of saying, as from time to time he actually said: "*Ssst!* Leave it all to me!"

He was an American, he said, but spoke vernacular French. The other two civilians were a London chartered accountant and a Canadian volunteer—a young Oxford man—waiting for his regiment. Across the table, a big French dragoon, just in from the firing-line, his horsetail helmet on the chair beside him, was also dining. This man was as different from the little infantry-men we had so often seen as the air of that town was different from deserted Paris. Just as he was, he might have stepped—or ridden, rather—from some cavalry charge by Meissonier or Détaille; a splendid fellow—head to spurs, all soldier.

After weeks of newspaper rhetoric and windy civilian par-tisanship, it was like water in the desert to listen to him—straight talk from a professional fighting man, modest, level-headed, and, like most fighting men, as contrasted with those who stay at home and write about fighting, ready to give a brave enemy his due. The German retirement was not at all a rout. When an army is in flight it leaves baggage and equip-ment behind, guns in the mud. The Germans had left very little; they were falling back in good order. Their soldiers were good fighters, especially when well led. They might lack the individual initiative of Frenchmen, the nervous energy with which Frenchmen would keep on fighting after mere bone and muscle had had enough, but they had plenty of courage. Their officers—the dragoon paused. Yesterday, he said, they had run into a troop of cavalry. The German officer ordered his men to charge, and instead they wavered and started to fall back. He turned on them. *"Schweinhunde!"* he shouted after them, and, flinging his horse about, charged alone, straight at the French lances.

"Kill him?" asked the man at the head of the table.

The dragoon nodded. "It was a pity. Joli garçon he was"—he ran a hand round a weather-beaten cheek as if to suggest the other's well-made face—"monocle in his eye—and he never let go of it until it fell off—a lance through his heart."

As we talked two secret-service-men entered, demanded our papers, examined them, and directed us to call at the Maine for them next morning at eight o'clock. Now, indeed, we were walking a tight rope. Following the genius who had got us our suppers, we emerged into the dark street, walked down it a few doors, entered a courtyard full of cavalry hors-es, where men in spurred boots were clanking up and down stairs. He thrust a heavy key into a lock, opened a door and ushered us into an empty and elegantly furnished house.

Here was a sombre dining-room with decanters and glasses, bedrooms with satin down quilts spread over the foot of the bed, and adjoining one of them a dressing-room with pomades and perfumes and rows of boots just as its owner had left it. Who he might be, why we should be here, how our mysterious, conductor—who knew no one in Villers-Cotteret and had but landed there himself that night—had arranged this occupation, was beyond finding out. At the moment, with military motor-trucks rumbling past outside, soldiers coming and going in the court and tramping about in the room overhead—an extension of the adjoining house—one scarcely thought of trying to find out. One merely accepted it, enchained by that uplifted finger and "Leave it to me!" For a time we talked under the dining-room light, with doors bolted and wooden shutters on street and courtyard closed, as if we were conspirators in Russian melodrama, and then we slept.

The Germans were evidently much nearer than Paris had supposed, and we should not have been greatly surprised to find them in the streets next morning. It was an Algerian horseman, however, muffled up in his dingy white and looking rather chilly, who was riding past the window as I first looked out.

We went to the Mairie—not the grandfatherly old mayor this time, but a sharp-eyed special commissioner of police.

"After all," said he, when we had put our case, "you want to get as near the front as possible."

True, I answered, we did.

"Well," he said, with a gesture at once final and wholly French, "you are already farther than that. You are inside the lines." He crossed out the safe-conduct and on the laissez-passer wrote: "Good for immediate return to Paris," and carefully set down the date. Half an hour later we were well on the road to Crepy, with the thunder which had drawn us hither rolling fainter and fainter in the north.

CHAPTER 4

The Fall of Antwerp

The storm which was to burst over Antwerp the following night was gathering fast when we arrived on Tuesday morning. Army motor-trucks loaded with dismantled aeroplanes, and the less essential impedimenta screamed through the streets bound away from, not toward, the front. The Queen, that afternoon, was seen in the Hotel St. Antoine receiving the good-bys of various friends. Consuls suddenly locked their doors and fled. And the cannon rumbling along the eastern horizon as they had rumbled, nearer and nearer, for a fortnight, were now beyond the outer line of forts and within striking distance of the town. That night, an hour or two after midnight, in my hotel by the water-front, I awoke to the steady clatter of hoofs on cobblestones and the rumble of wheels. I went to the window, on the narrow side street, black as all streets had been in Antwerp since the night that the Zeppelin threw its first bombs, and looked out. It was a moonlight night, clear and cold, and there along the Quai St. Michael, at the end of the street, was an army in retreat. They were Belgians, battered and worn out with their unbroken weeks of hopeless fighting; cavalrymen on their tired horses, artillerymen, heads sunk on their chests, drowsing on their lurching caissons; the patient little foot-soldiers, rifles slung across their shoulders, scuffling along in their heavy overcoats.

In the dark shadow of the tall old houses a few people came out and stood there watching silently, and, as one felt, in a sort of despair. All night long men were marching by—and in London they were still reading that it was but a "demonstration" the Germans were engaged in—down the quay and across the pontoon bridge—the only way over the Scheldt—over to the Tete-de-Flandres and the road to Ghent. They were strung along the street next morning, boots mud-covered, mud-stained, entrenching shovels hanging to their belts, faces unshaven for weeks, just as they had come from the trenches; yet still patient and cheerful, with that unshakable Flemish good cheer. Perhaps, after all, it was not a retreat; they might be swinging round to the south and St. Nicholas to attack the German flank...

But before they had crossed, another army, a civilian army, flowed down on and over the quay. For a week people had been leaving Antwerp, now the general flight began. From villages to the east and southeast, from the city itself, people came pouring down. In wagons drawn by huge Belgian draft-horses, in carts pulled by the captivating Belgian work dogs, panting mightily and digging their paws into the slippery cobbles; on foot, leading little children and carrying babies and dolls and canaries and great bundles of clothes and household things wrapped in sheets, they surged toward that one narrow bridge and the crowded ferry-boats. I saw one old woman, grey-haired and tanned like an Indian squaw with work in the fields, yet with a fine, well-made face, pushing a groaning wheelbarrow. A strap went from the handles over her shoulders, and, stopping now and then to ask the news, she would slip off this harness, gossip for a time, then push on again. That afternoon under my window there was a tall wagon, a sort of hay wagon, in which there were twenty-two little tow-headed children, none more than eight or ten and several almost babies in arms. By the side of the wagon a man, evidently father of some of them, stood buttering the end of a huge round loaf of bread and cutting off slice after slice, which the older children broke and distributed to the little ones. Two cows were tied to the back of the wagon and the man's wife squatted there milking them. All along the quay and in the streets leading into it were people like this—harmless, helpless, hard-working people, going they knew not where. The entrance to the bridge was soon choked. One went away and returned an hour later and found the same people waiting almost in the same spot, and, with that wonderful calm and patience of theirs, feeding their children or giving a little of their precious hay to the horses, quietly waiting their turn while the cannon which had driven them from their homes kept on thundering behind them.

That afternoon I walked up-town through the shuttered, silent streets—silent but for that incessant rumbling in the southeast and the occasional honking flight of some military automobile—to two of the hospitals. In one, a British hospital on the Boulevard Leopold, the doctor in charge was absent for the moment, and there was no one to answer my offer of occasional help if an outsider could be of use. As I sat waiting a tall, brisk Englishwoman, in nurse's uniform, came up and asked what I wanted. I told her.

"Oh," she said, and in her crisp, English voice, without further ado, "will you help me with a leg?"

She led the way into her ward, and there we contrived between us to bandage and slip a board and pillow under a fractured thigh. Between whispers of "Courage! Courage!" to the Belgian soldier, she said that she was the wife of a British general and had two sons in the army, and a third—"Poor boy!" she murmured, more to him than to me—on one of the ships in the North Sea. I arranged to come back next morning to help with the lifting, and went on to another hospital in the Rue Nerviens, to find that little English lady who crossed with me in the Ostend boat in August on the way to her sister's hospital in Antwerp.

Here in the quiet wards she had been working while the Germans swept down on Paris and were rolled back again, and while the little nation which she and her sister loved so well was being clubbed to its knees.

Louvain, Liege, Malines, Namur—chapters in all the long,

pitiless story were lying there in the narrow iron beds. There were men with faces chewed by shrapnel, men burned in the explosion of the powder magazine at Fort Waelhem, when the attack on Antwerp began—dragged out from the underground passage in which the garrison had sought momentary refuge and where most of them were killed, burned, and blackened. One strong, good-looking young fellow, able to eat and live apparently, was shot through the temples and blind in both eyes. It was the hour for carrying those well enough to stand it out into the court and giving them their afternoon's airing and smoke. One had lost an arm, another, a whimsical young Belgian, had only the stump of a left leg. When we started to lift him back into his bed, he said he had a better way than that. So he put his arms round my neck and showed me how to take him by the back and the well leg.

"*Bon!*" he said, and again "*Bon!*" when I let him down, and then, reaching out and patting me on the back, "*Bon!*" he smiled again.

That night, behind drawn curtains which admitted no light to the street, we dined peacefully and well, and, except for this unwonted seclusion, just outside which were the black streets and still the endless procession of carts and wagons and shivering people, one might have forgotten, in that cheerfully lighted room, that we were not in times of peace. We even loitered over a grate fire before going to bed, and talked in drowsy and almost indifferent fashion of whether it was absolutely sure that the Germans were trying to take the town.

It was almost exactly midnight that I found myself listening, half awake, to the familiar sound of distant cannon. One had come to think of it, almost, as nothing but a sound; and to listen with a detached and not unpleasant interest as a man tucked comfortably in bed follows a roll of thunder to its end or listens to the fall of rain.

It struck me suddenly that there was something new about this sound; I sat up in bed to listen, and at that instant a far-off, sullen "*Boom!*" was followed by a crash as if lightning had struck a house a little way down the street. As I hurried to the window there came another far-off detonation, a curious wailing whistle swept across the sky, and over behind the roofs to the left there was another crash.

One after another they came, at intervals of half a minute, or screaming on each other's heels as if racing to their goal. And then the crash or, if farther away, muffled explosion as another roof toppled in or cornice dropped off, as a house made of canvas drops to pieces in a play.

The effect of those unearthly wails, suddenly singing in across country in the dead of night from six—eight—ten miles away—Heaven knows where—was, as the Germans intended it to be, tremendous. It is not easy to describe nor to be imagined by those who had not lived in that threatened city—the last Belgian stronghold—and felt that vast, unseen power rolling nearer and nearer. And now, all at once, it was here, materialized, demoniacal, a flying death, swooping across the dark into your very room.

It was like one of those dreams in which you cannot stir from your tracks, and meanwhile *"Boom. . .Tzee-ee-ee-ee!"*—is this one meant for you?

Already there was a patter of feet in the dark, and people with white bundles on their backs went stumbling by toward the river and the bridge. Motors came honking down from the inner streets, and the quay, which had begun to clear by this time, was again jammed. I threw on some clothes, hurried to the street. A rank smell of kerosene hung in the air; presently a petrol shell burst to the southward, lighting up the sky for an instant like the flare from a blast-furnace, and a few moments later there showed over the roofs the flames of the first fire.

Although we could hear the wail of shells flying across their wide parabola both into the town and out from the first ring of forts, few burst in our part of the city that night, and we walked up as far as the cathedral without seeing anything but black and silent streets. Every one in the hotel was up and dressed by this time. Some were for leaving at once; one family, piloted by the comfortable Belgian servants—far cooler than any one else—went to the cellar, some gathered about the grate in the writing-room to watch the night out; the rest of us went back to bed.

There wasn't much sleep for any one that night. The bombardment kept on until morning, lulled slightly, as if the enemy might be taking breakfast, then it continued into the, next day. And now the city—a busy city of nearly four hundred thousand people—emptied itself in earnest. Citizens and soldiers, field-guns, motor-trucks, wheelbarrows, dog-carts, hay-ricks, baby-carriages, droves of people on foot, all flowing down to the Scheldt, the ferries, and the bridge. They poured into coal barges, filling the yawning black holes as Africans used to fill slave-ships, into launches and tugs, and along the roads leading down the river and south-westward toward Ostend.

One thought with a shudder of what would happen if the Germans dropped a few of their shells into that helpless mob, and it is only fair to remember that they did not, although retreating Belgian soldiers were a part of it, and one of the German aeroplanes, a mere speck against the blue, was looking calmly down overhead. Nor did they touch the cathedral, and their agreement not to shell any of the buildings previously pointed out on a map delivered to them through the American Legation seemed to be observed.

Down through that mass of fugitives pushed a London motor-bus ambulance with several wounded British soldiers, one of them sitting upright, supporting with his right hand a left arm, the biceps, bound in a blood-soaked tourniquet, half torn away. They had come in from the trenches, where their comrades were now waiting, with their helpless little rifles, for an enemy, miles away, who lay back at his ease and pounded them with his big guns. I asked them how things were going, and they said not very well. They could only wait until the German aeroplanes had given the range and the trenches became too hot, then fall back, dig themselves in, and play the same game over again.

Following them was a hospital-service motor-car, driven by a Belgian soldier and in charge of a young British officer. It was his present duty to motor from trench to trench across the zone of fire, with the London bus trailing behind, and pick up wounded. It wasn't a particularly pleasant job, he said, jerking his head toward the distant firing, and frankly he wasn't keen about it. We talked for some time, every one talked to every one else in Antwerp that morning, and when he started out again I asked him to give me a lift to the edge of town.

Quickly we raced through the Place de Meir and the deserted streets of the politer part of Antwerp, where, the night before, most of the shells had fallen. We went crackling over broken glass, past gaping cornices and holes in the pavement, five feet across and three feet deep, and once passed a house quietly burning away with none to so much as watch the fire. The city wall, along which are the first line of forts, drew near, then the tunnel passing under it, and we went through without pausing and on down the road to Malines. We were beyond the town now, bowling rapidly out into the flat Belgian country, and, clinging there to the running-board with the October wind blowing quite through a thin flannel suit, it suddenly came over me that things had moved very fast in the last five minutes, and that all at once, in some unexpected fashion, all that elaborate barrier of *laissez-passers, sauf-conduits,* and so on, had been swept aside, and, quite as if it were the most ordinary thing in the world, I was spinning out to that almost mythical "front."

Front, indeed! It was two fronts. There was an explosion just behind us, a hideous noise overhead, as if the whole zenith had somehow been ripped across like a tightly stretched piece of silk, and a shell from the Belgian fort under which we had just passed went hurtling down long aisles of air—farther—farther—to end in a faint detonation miles away.

Out of sight in front of us, there was an answering thud, and—*Tzee-ee-ee-er-r-r-ong!*—a German shell had gone over us and burst behind the Belgian fort. Under this gigantic antiphony the motor-car raced along, curiously small and irrelevant on that empty country road.

We passed great holes freshly made, neatly blown out of the macadam, then a dead horse. There were plenty of dead horses along the roads in France, but they had been so for days. This one's blood was not yet dry, and the shell that had torn the great rip in its chest must have struck here this morning.

We turned into the avenue of trees leading up to an empty chateau, a field-hospital until a few hours before. Mattresses and bandages littered the deserted room, and an electric chandelier was still burning. The young officer pointed to some trenches in the garden. "I had those dug to put the wounded in in case we had to hold the place," he said. "It was getting pretty hot."

There was nothing here now, however, and, followed by the London bus with its obedient enlisted men doing duty as ambulance orderlies, we motored a mile or so farther on to the nearest trench. It was in an orchard beside a brick farmhouse with a vista in front of barbed-wire entanglement and a carefully cleaned firing field stretching out to a village and trees about half a mile away. They had looked very interesting and difficult, those barbed-wire mazes and suburbs, ruthlessly swept of trees and houses, when I had seen the Belgians preparing for the siege six weeks before, and they were to be of about as much practical use now as pictures on a wall.

There are, it will be recalled, three lines of forts about Antwerp—the inner one, corresponding to the city's wall; a middle one a few miles farther out, where the British now were; and the outer line, which the enemy had already passed. Their artillery was hidden far over behind the horizon trees, and the British marines and naval-reserve men who manned these trenches could only wait there, rifle in hand, for an enemy that would not come, while a captive balloon a mile or two away to the eastward and an aeroplane sailing far overhead gave the ranges, and they waited for the shrapnel to burst. The trenches were hasty affairs, narrow and shoulder-deep, very like trenches for gas or water pipes, and reasonably safe except when a shell burst directly overhead. One had struck that morning just on the inner rim of the trench, blown out one of those crater-like holes, and discharged all its shrapnel backward across the trench and into one of the heavy timbers supporting a bombproof roof. A raincoat hanging to a nail in this timber was literally shot to shreds. "That's where I was standing," said the young lieutenant in command, pointing with a dry smile to a spot not more than a yard from where the shell had burst.

Half a dozen young fellows, crouched there in the bombproof, looked out at us and grinned. They were brand-new soldiers, some of them, boys from the London streets who had answered the thrilling posters and signs, "Your King and Country Need You," and been sent on this ill-fated expedition for their first sight of war. The London papers are talking about it as I am writing this—how this handful of nine thousand men, part of them recruits who scarcely knew one end of a rifle from another, were flung across the Channel on Sunday night and rushed up to the front to be shot at and rushed back again. I did not know this then, but wondered if this was what they had dreamed of—squatting helplessly in a ditch until another order came to retire—when they swung through the London streets singing *"It's a long, long way to Tipperary"* two months before.

Yet not one of the youngest and the greenest showed the least nervousness as they waited there in that melancholy little orchard under the incessant scream of shells. That unshakable British coolness, part sheer pluck, part a sort of lack of imagination, perhaps, or at least of "nerves," left them as calm and casual as if they were but drilling on the turf of Hyde Park. And with it persisted that almost equally unshakable sense of class, that touching confidence in one's superiors—the young clerk's or mechanic's inborn conviction that whatever that smart, clean-cut, imperturbable young officer does and says must inevitably be right—at least, that if he is cool and serene you must, if the skies fall, be cool and serene too.

We met one young fellow as we walked through an empty lateral leading to a bomb-proof prepared for wounded, and the ambulance officer asked him sharply how things had been going that morning.

"Oh, very well, sir," he said with the most respectful good humour, though a shell bursting just then a stone's throw beyond the orchard made both of us duck our heads. "A bit hot, sir, about nine o'clock, but only one man hurt. They do seem to know just where we are, sir; but wait till their infantry comes up—we'll clean them out right enough, sir."

And, if he had been ordered to stay there and hold the trench alone, one could imagine him saying, in that same tone of deference and chipper good humour, "Yes, sir; thank you, sir," and staying, too, till the cows came home.

We motored down the line to another trench—this one along a road with fields in front and, about a couple of hundred yards behind, a clump of trees which masked a Belgian battery. The officer here, a tall, upstanding, gravely handsome young man, with a deep, strong, slightly humorous voice, and the air of one both born to and used to command—the best type of navy man—came over to meet us, rather glad, it seemed, to see some one. The ambulance officer had just started to speak when there was a roar from the clump of trees, at the same instant an explosion directly overhead, and an ugly chunk of iron—a bit of broken casing from a shrapnel shell—plunged at our very feet. The shell had been wrongly timed and exploded prematurely.

"I say!" the lieutenant called out to a Belgian officer standing not far away, "can't you telephone over to your people to stop that? That's the third time we've been nearly hit by their shrapnel this morning. After all"—he turned to us with the air of apologizing somewhat for his display of irritation—"it's quite annoying enough here without that, you know."

It was, indeed, annoying—very. The trenches were not under fire in the sense that the enemy were making a persistent effort to clear them out, but they were in the zone of fire, their range was known, and there was no telling, when that distant boom thudded across the fields, whether that particular shell might be intended for them or for somebody's house in town.

We could see in the distance their captive balloon, and there were a couple of scouts, the officer said, in a tower in the village, not much more than half a mile away. He pointed to the spot across the barbed wire. "We've been trying to get them for the last half-hour."

We left them engaged in this interesting distraction, the little rifle-snaps in all that mighty thundering seeming only to accent the loneliness and helplessness of their position, and spun on down the transverse road, toward another trench. The progress of the motor seemed slow and disappointing. Not that the spot a quarter of a mile off was at all less likely to be hit, yet one felt conscious of a growing desire to be somewhere else. And, though I took off my hat to keep it from blowing off, I found that every time a shell went over I promptly put it on again, indicating, one suspected, a decline in what the military experts call morale.

As we bowled down the road toward a group of brick houses on the left, a shell passed not more than fifty yards in front of us and through the side of one of these houses as easily as a circus rider pops through a tissue-paper hoop. Almost at the same instant another exploded—where, I haven't the least idea, except that the dust from it hit us in the face. The motor rolled smoothly along meanwhile, and the Belgian soldier driving it stared as imperturbably ahead of him as if he were back at Antwerp on the seat of his taxicab.

You get used to shells in time, it seems, and, deciding that you either are or are not going to be hit, dismiss responsibility and leave it all to fate. I must admit that in my brief experience I was not able to arrive at this restful state. We reached at last the city gate through which we had left Antwerp, and the motor came to a stop just at the inner edge of the passage under the fort, and I said good-by to the young Englishman ere he started back for the trenches again.

"Well," he called after me as I started across the open space between the gate and the houses, a stone's throw away, "you've had an experience anyway."

I was just about to answer that undoubtedly I had when—*Tzee-ee-ee-er-r*—a shell just cleared the ramparts over our heads and disappeared in the side of a house directly in front of us with a roar and a geyser of dust. Neither the motor nor a guest's duty now detained me, and, waving him good-by, I turned at right angles and made with true civilian speed for the shelter of a side street.

The shells all appeared to be coming from a southeast direction, and in the lee of houses on the south side of the street one was reasonably protected. Keeping close to the house-fronts and dodging—rather absurdly, no doubt—into doorways when that wailing whistle came up from behind, I went zigzagging through the deserted city toward the hotel on the other side of town.

It was such a progress as one might make in some fantastic nightmare—as the hero of some eerie piece of fiction about the Last Man in the World. Street after street, with doors locked, shutters closed, sandbags, mattresses, or little heaps of earth piled over cellar windows; streets in which the only sound was that of one's own feet, where the loneliness was made more lonely by some forgotten dog cringing against the closed door and barking nervously as one hurried past.

Here, where most of the shells had fallen the preceding night, nearly all the houses were empty. Yet occasionally one caught sight of faces peering up from basement windows or of some stubborn householder standing in his southern doorway staring into space. Once I passed a woman bound away from, instead of toward, the river with her big bundle; and once an open carriage with a family in it driving, with peculiarly Flemish composure, toward the quay, and as I hurried past the park, along the Avenue Van Dyck—where fresh craters made by exploding shells had been dug in the turf—the swans, still floating on the little lake, placidly dipped their white necks under water as if it were a quiet morning in May.

47

Now and then, as the shell's wail swung over its long parabola, there came with the detonation, across the roofs, the rumble of falling masonry. Once I passed a house quietly burning, and on the pavement were lopped-off trees. The impartiality with which those far-off gunners distributed their attentions was disconcerting. Peering down one of the up-and-down streets before crossing it, as if a shell were an automobile which you might see and dodge, you would shoot across and, turning into a cosy little side street, think to yourself that here at least they had not come, and then promptly see, squarely in front, another of those craters blown down through the Belgian blocks.

Presently I found myself under the trees of the Boulevard Leopold, not far from the British hospital, and recalled that it was about time that promise was made good. It was time indeed, and help with lifting they needed very literally. The order had just come to leave the building, bringing the wounded and such equipment as they could pack into half a dozen motor-buses and retire—just where, I did not hear—in the direction of Ghent. As I entered the *porte-cochère* two poor wrecks of war were being led out by their nurses—more men burned in the powder explosion at Waelhem, their seared faces and hands covered with oil and cotton just as they had been lifted from bed.

The phrase "whistle of shells" had taken on a new reality since midnight. Now one was to learn something of the meaning of those equally familiar words, "they succeeded in saving their wounded, although under heavy fire."

None of the wounded could walk, none dress himself; most of them in ordinary times would have lain where they were for weeks. There were fractured legs not yet set, men with faces half shot away, men half out of their heads, and all these had to be dressed somehow, covered up, crowded into or on top of the buses, and started off through a city under bombardment toward open country which might already be occupied by the enemy.

Bundles of uniforms, mud-stained, blood-stained, just as they had come from the trenches, were dumped out of the storeroom and distributed, hit or miss.

British "Tommies" went out as Belgians, Belgians in British khaki; the man whose broken leg I had lifted the day before we simply bundled in his bed blankets and set up in the corner of a bus. One healthy-looking Belgian boy, on whom I was trying to pull a pair of British trousers, seemed to have nothing at all the matter with him, until it presently appeared that he was speechless and paralyzed in both left arm and left leg. And while we were working, an English soldier, shot through the jaw and throat, sat on the edge of his bed, shaking with a hideous, rattling cough.

The hospital was in a handsome stone building, in ordinary times a club, perhaps, or a school; a wide, stone stairway led up the centre, and above it was a glass skylight. This central well would have been a charming place for a shell to drop into, and one did drop not more than fifty feet or so away, in or close to the rear court. A few yards down the avenue another shell hit a cornice and sent a ton or so of masonry crashing down on the sidewalk. Under conditions like these the nurses kept running up and down that staircase during the endless hour or two in which the wounded were being dressed and carried on stretchers to the street. They stood by the buses making their men comfortable, and when the first buses were filled they sat in the open street on top of them, patiently waiting, as calm and smiling as circus queens on their gilt chariots. The behavior of the men in the trenches was cool enough, but they at least were fighting men and but taking the chance of war. These were civilian volunteers, they had not even trenches to shelter them, and it took a rather unforeseen and difficult sort of courage to leave that fairly safe masonry building and sit smiling and helpful on top of a motor-bus during a wait of half an hour or so, any second of which might be one's last. There was an American nurse there, a tall, radiant girl, whom they called, and rightly, "Morning Glory," who had been introduced to me the day before because we both belonged to that curious foreign race of Americans. What her name was I haven't the least idea, and if we were to meet to-morrow, doubtless we should have to be carefully presented over again, but I remember calling out to her, "Good-by, American girl!" as we passed in the hall during the last minute or two, and she said good-by, and suddenly reached out and put her hand on my shoulder and added, "Good luck!" or "God bless you!" or something like that. And these seemed at the moment quite the usual things to do and say. The doctor in charge and the general's wife apologized for running away, as they called it, and the last I saw of the latter was as she waved back to me from the top of a bus, with just that look of concern over the desperate ride they were beginning which a slightly preoccupied hostess casts over a dinner-table about which are seated a number of oddly assorted guests.

The strange procession got away safely at last, and safely, too, so I was told later, across the river; but where they finally spent the night I never heard. I hurried down the street and into the Rue Nerviens. It must have been about four o'clock by that time. The bright October morning had changed to a chill and dismal afternoon, and up the western sky in the direction of the river a vast curtain of greasy, black smoke was rolling. The petrol-tanks along the Scheldt had been set afire. It looked at the moment as if the whole city might be going, but there was no time then to think of possibilities, and I slipped down the lee side of the street to the door with the Red Cross flag. The front of the hospital was shut tight. It took several pulls at the bell to bring any one, and inside I found a Belgian family who had left their own house for the thicker ceilings of the hospital, and the nuns back in the wards with their nervous men. Their servants had left that morning, the three or four sisters in charge had had to do all the cooking and housework as well as look after their patients, and now they were keeping calm and smiling, to subdue as best they could the fears of the Belgian wounded, who were ready to jump out of bed, whatever their condition, rather than fall into the hands of the enemy. Each had no doubt that if he were not murdered outright he would be taken to Germany and forced to fight in the east against the Russians. Several, who knew very well what was going on outside, had been found by the nurses that morning out of bed and all ready to take to the street.

Lest they should hear that their comrades in the Boulevard Leopold had been moved, the lay sister—the English lady— and I withdrew to the operating-room, closed the door, and in that curious retreat talked over the situation. No orders had come to leave; in fact, they had been told to stay. They did have a man now in the shape of the Belgian gentleman, and from the same source an able-bodied servant, but how long these would stay, where food was to be found in that desolate city, when the bombardment would cease, and what the Germans would do with them—well, it was not a pleasant situation for a handful of women. But it was not of themselves she was thinking, but of their wounded and of Belgium, and of what both had suffered already and of what might yet be in store. It was of that this frail little sister talked that hopeless afternoon, while the smoke in the west spread farther up the sky, and she would now and then pause in the middle of a syllable while a shell sang overhead, then take it up again.

Meanwhile the light was going, and before it became quite dark and my hotel deserted, perhaps, as the rest of Antwerp, it seemed best to be getting across town. I could not believe that the Germans could treat such a place and people with anything but consideration and told the little nurse so. She came to the edge of the glass-covered court, laughingly saying I had best run across it, and wondering where we, who had met twice now under such curious circumstances, would meet again. Then she turned back to the ward—to wait with that roomful of more or less panicky men for the tramp of German soldiers and the knock on the door which meant that they were prisoners.

Hurrying across town, I passed, not far from the Hotel St. Antoine, a blazing four-story building. The cathedral was not touched, and indeed, in spite of the noise and terror, the material damage was comparatively slight. Soldiers were clearing the quay and setting a guard directly in front of our hotel—one of the few places in Antwerp that night where one could get so much as a crust of bread—and behind drawn curtains we made what cheer we could. There were two American photographers and a correspondent who had spent the night before in the cellar of a house, the upper story of which had been wrecked by a shell; a British intelligence officer, with the most bewildering way of hopping back and forth between a brown civilian suit and a spick-and-span new uniform; and several Belgian families hoping to get a boat down-stream in the morning.

We sat round the great fire in the hall, above which the architect, building for happier times, had had the bad grace to place a skylight, and discussed the time and means of getting away. The intelligence officer, not wishing to be made a prisoner, was for getting a boat of some sort at the first crack of dawn, and the photographers, who had had the roof blown off over their heads, heartily agreed with him. I did not like to leave without at least a glimpse of those spiked helmets nor to desert my friends in the Rue Nerviens, and yet there was the likelihood, if one remained, of being marooned indefinitely in the midst of the conquering army.

Meanwhile the flight of shells continued, a dozen or more fires could be seen from the upper windows of the hotel, and billows of red flame from the burning petrol-tanks rolled up the southern sky. It had been what might be called a rather full day, and the wail of approaching projectiles began to get on one's nerves. One started at the slamming of a door, took every dull thump for a distant explosion; and when we finally turned in I carried the mattress from my room, which faced the south, over to the other side of the building, and laid it on the floor beside another man's bed. Before a shell could reach me it would have to traverse at least three partitions and possibly him as well.

After midnight the bombardment quieted, but shells continued to visit us from time to time all night. All night the Belgians were retreating across the pontoon bridge, and once—it must have been about two or three o'clock—I heard a sound which meant that all was over. It was the crisp tramp—different from the Belgian shuffle—of British soldiers, and up from the street came an English voice, "Best foot forward, boys!" and a little farther on: "Look alive, men; they've just picked up our range!"

I went to the window and watched them tramp by—the same men we had seen that morning. The petrol fire was still flaming across the south, a steamer of some sort was burning at her wharf beside the bridge—Napoleon's veterans retreating from Moscow could scarcely have left behind a more complete picture of war than did those young recruits. Morning came dragging up out of that dreadful night, smoky, damp, and chill. It was almost a London fog that lay over the abandoned town. I had just packed up and was walking through one of the upper halls when there was a crash that shook the whole building, the sound of falling glass, and out in the river a geyser of water shot up, timbers and boards flew from the bridge, and there were dozens of smaller splashes as if from a shower of shot. I thought that the hotel was hit at last and that the Germans, having let civilians escape over the bridge, were turning everything loose, determined to make an end of the business. It was, as a matter of fact, the Belgians blowing up the bridge to cover their retreat. In any case it seemed useless to stay longer, and within an hour, on a tug jammed with the last refugees, we were starting down-stream.

Behind us, up the river, a vast curtain of lead-coloured smoke from the petrol-tanks had climbed up the sky and spread out mushroomwise, as smoke and ashes sometimes spread out from a volcano. This smoke, merging with the fog and the smoke from the Antwerp fires, seemed to cover the whole sky. And under that sullen mantle the dark flames of the petrol still glowed; to the right, as we looked back, was the blazing skeleton of the ship, and on the left Antwerp itself, the rich, old, beautiful, comfortable city, all but hidden, and now and then sending forth the boom of an exploding shell like a groan.

A large empty German steamer, the *Gneisenau*, marooned here since the war, came swinging slowly out into the river, pushed by two or three nervous little tugs—to be sunk there, apparently, in midstream. From the pontoon bridge, which stubbornly refused to yield, came explosion after explosion, and up and down the river fires sprang up, and there were other explosions, as the crushed Belgians, in a sort of rage of devastation, became their own destroyers.

By following the adventures of one individual I have en-deavoured to suggest what the bombardment of a modern city was like—what you might expect if an invading army came to-morrow to New York or Chicago or San Francisco. I have only coasted along the edges of Belgium's tragedy, and the rest of the story, of which we were a part for the next two days—the flight of those hundreds of thousands of homeless people—is something that can scarcely be told—you must follow it out in imagination into its countless uprooted, dis-organized lives. You must imagine old people struggling along over miles and miles of country roads; young girls, under bur-dens a man might not care to bear, tramping until they had to carry their shoes in their hands and go barefoot to rest their unaccustomed feet. You must imagine the pathetic ef-forts of hundreds of people to keep clean by washing in way-side streams or ditches; imagine babies going without milk because there was no milk to be had; families shivering in damp hedgerows or against haystacks where darkness over-took them; and you must imagine this not on one road, but on every road, for mile after mile over a whole countryside. What was to become of these people when their little sup-ply of food was exhausted? Where could they go? Even if back to their homes, it would be but to lift their hats to their conquerors, never knowing but that the next week or month would sweep the tide of war back over them again.

Never in modern times, not in our generation at least, had Europe seen anything like that flight—nothing so strange, so overwhelming, so pitiful. And when I say pitiful, you must not think of hysterical women, desperate, trampling men, tears and screams. In all those miles one saw neither complaining nor protestation—at times one might almost have thought it some vast, eccentric picnic. No, it was their orderliness, their thrift and kindness, their unmistakable usefulness, which made the waste and irony of it all so colossal and hideous. Each family had its big, round loaves of bread and its pile of hay for the horses, the bags of pears and potatoes; the children had their little dolls, and you would see some tired mother with her big bundle under one arm and some fluffy little puppy in the other. You could not associate them with forty-centimetre shells or burned churches and libraries or anything but quiet homes and peaceable, helpful lives. You could not be swept along by that endless stream of exiles and retain at the end of the day any particular enthusiasm for the red glory of war. And when we crossed the Dutch border that afternoon and came on a village street full of Belgian soldiers cut off and forced to cross the line, to be interned here, presumably until the war was over, one could not mourn very deeply their lost chances of martial glory as they unslung their rifles and turned them over to the good-natured Dutch guard. They had held back that avalanche long enough, these Belgians, and one felt as one would to see lost children get home again or some one dragged from under the wheels.

CHAPTER 5

Paris Again—and Bordeaux

These notes began in a London fog and ended in the south of France. I had hoped, on reaching Calais, to work in toward the fighting along the Yser, but, finding it impossible, decided to turn about and travel away from the front instead of toward it—down to see Bordeaux while it was still the temporary capital, and to see what life might be like in the French provincial towns in war time.

It was not, so the young woman at the hotel desk in London said, what you would call a fog, because she could still see the porter at the street-door—yet day after day the same rain, smoky mist, and unbroken gloom.

One breakfasted and tramped the streets by lamplight, as if there were no such thing as sun—-recalled vaguely a world in which it used to be—woods with the leaves turning, New York on a bright autumn morning, enchanted tropical dawns.

Through this viscous envelope—a sort of fungi thrown off by it—newspapers kept appearing—slaughter and more slaughter, hatred, the hunt for spies, more hysterical and shrill. One looked for fairness almost as for the sun, and, merely by blackguarding long enough men who could not answer back and, after all, were flinging their lives away bravely over there in France, one ended by giving them the very qualities they were denied.

They faded out as one picture on a stereopticon screen fades into another—even as one read "Huns" for the thousandth time the Huns turned into kindly burghers smoking pipes and singing songs. In the same way the England of tradition—Shakespeare, Dickens, Meredith, jolly old rumbling London, rides 'cross country, rows on the river—faded into this nightmare of hate and smoky lamplight. The psychology was very simple, but too much, it seems, for censors and even editors. And, unfortunately, at a time like this not the lighthearted, sportsmanlike fighting men at the front, nor sober people left behind in homes, but newspapers are likely to be an outsider's most constant companions.

A sort of spiritual asphyxiation overtook one at last, in which the mere stony Briticism of the London hotel seemed to have a part. If you awoke again into that taste of soft-coal smoke, went down to another of those staggering lamp-lit breakfasts. But why staggering? "Can you not take coffee and rolls in London as well as in some Paris café?" It would seem so, yet it cannot be done. The mere sight and sound—or lack of sound—of that warm, softly carpeted breakfast-room, moving like some gloomy, inevitable mechanism as it has moved for countless years, attacks the already weakened will like an opiate. At the first bewildering "'Q?" from that steely-fronted maid the ritual overpowers you and you bow before porridge, kippers, bacon and eggs, stewed fruit, marmalade, toast, more toast, more marmalade, as helpless as the rabbit before the proverbial boa—except that in this case the rabbit swallows its own asphyxiator.

Another breakfast like this, another day of rain and fog, another "Q?"—it was in some such state of mind as this that I packed up one night and took the early train for Folkestone.

Folkestone, Friday

Sunshine at last—a delicious autumn afternoon—clean air, quiet, and the sea. Far below the cliff walk, trawlers crawling slowly in; along the horizon a streak of smoke from some patrolling destroyer or battleship. And all along this cliff walk, Belgians—strolling with their children, sitting on the benches, looking out to sea. Just beyond that hazy white wall to

57

the east—the cliffs of France—the fight for Calais is being fought—they can almost hear the cannon.

In the stillness, as they drift by, you catch bits of their talk:

"It was two o'clock in the morning when we left Antwerp."

"And imagine—it was not three metres from our doorstep that the shell burst."

"We walked forty kilometres that night and in the morning—"

On the balcony of some one's summer-house, now turned into a hospital, four Belgian soldiers, one with his head bandaged, are playing cards—jolly, blond youngsters, caps rakishly tipped over one ear, slamming the cards down as if that were the only thing in the world. In the garden others taking the sunshine, some with their wheel-chairs pushed through the shrubbery close to the high iron fence, to be petted by nurse-maids and children as if they were animals in a sort of zoo.

The Belgians strolling by on the cliff walk smile at this quaint picture, for sun and space and quiet seem to have wiped out their terror—that passed through is as far away as that now hidden in the east. Is it merely quiet and sun? Perhaps it is the look of a "nice little people" who know that now they have a history. "Refugees," to be sure, yet one can fancy them looking back some day from their tight little villages, canals, and beet-fields, on afternoons like this, as on the days of their great adventure—when they could sit in the sun above the sea at Folkestone and look across the Channel to the haze under which their sons and husbands and brothers and King were fighting for the last corner of their country.

Calais, Saturday

Belgian officers, parks of Belgian military automobiles; up-country a little way the Germans going down in tens of thousands to win their "gate to England"—yet we came across on the Channel boat last evening as usual and had little trouble finding a room. There were tons of Red Cross supplies on board—cotton, chloroform, peroxide; Belgian soldiers patched up and going back to fight; and various volunteer nurses, including two handsome young Englishwomen of the very modern aviatrix type—coming over to drive motor-cycle ambulances—and so smartly gotten up in boots and khaki that a little way off you might have taken them for British officers. At the wharf were other nurses, some of whom I had last seen that Thursday afternoon in Antwerp as they and their wounded rolled away in London buses from the hospital in the Boulevard Leopold.

This morning, strolling round the town, I ran into a couple of English correspondents. There were yet several hours before they need address themselves to the arduous task of describing fighting they had not seen, and they talked, with a good humour one sometimes misses in their correspondence, of German collectivism and similar things. One had spent a good deal of time in Germany.

"They're the only people who have solved the problem of industrial cities without slums—you must say that for them. Of course, in those model towns of theirs, you've got to brush your teeth at six minutes past eight and sleep on your left side if the police say so—they're astonishing people for doing what they're told.

"One day in Dresden I walked across a bit of grass the public weren't supposed to cross. An old gentleman fairly roared the instant he saw me. He was ready to explode at the mere suggestion that any one could think of disobeying a rule made for all of them. '*Das kann man nicht thun! Es ist verboten!*'"

The other quoted the answer of an English factory-owner to some of his employees who did not want to enlist. "They've done a lot for working men over there," the man said. "Accident-insurance, old-age pensions, and all that— what do we want to fight the Kaiser for? We'd just about as soon be under Billy as George." And X———said to them: "If you were under Kaiser Billy, you'd enlist right enough, there's no doubt of that!"

He sat in the corner of our compartment coming down from Calais this afternoon, an old Algerian soldier, homeward bound, with a big, round loaf of bread and a military pass. He had a blue robe, bright-red, soft boots, a white turban wound with a sort of scarf of brown cord and baggy corduroy underneath, concealing various mysterious pockets.

"Paris? To-night?" he grunted in his queer French. The big Frenchman next him, who had served in Africa in his youth and understood the dialect, shook his head. "To-morrow morning!" he said. He laid his head on his hand to suggest a man sleeping, and held up three fingers. "Three days—Marseilles!" The old *goumier's* dark eyes blazed curiously, and he opened and shut his mouth in a dry yawn—like a tiger yawning.

Wounded? No—he pointed to his eyes, which were bloodshot, patted his forehead to suggest that it was throbbing, rubbed his legs, and scowled. "Rheumatism!" said the Frenchman. The Algerian pressed his palms together six times, then held up two fingers. "He's sixty-two years old!" said the Frenchman, and the old warrior obligingly opened his jaws and pointed to two or three lone brown fangs to prove it. They talked for a moment in the vernacular, and the Frenchman explained again, "Volunteer!" and then, "Scout!"

The old Arab made the motion of sighting along a rifle, then of brushing something over, and tapped himself on the chest.

"Deux!" he said. "Two Germans—me!" Evidently he was going back to the desert satisfied.

Train after train passed us, northward bound, some from Boulogne, some from the trenches north of Paris evidently, bringing artillery caked with mud—all packed with British soldiers leaning from doors of their cattle-cars, hats pushed back, pipes in their faces, singing and joking. At the end of each train, in passenger-coaches, their officers—tall, slim-legged young Olympians in leather puttees and short tan greatcoats, with their air of elegant amateurs embarking on some rather superior sort of sport.

The same cars filled with French soldiers equally brave, efficient, light-hearted would be as different as Corneille and Shakespeare, as Dickens and Dumas—and in the same ways!

An Englishman had been telling me in a London club a few nights before of the "extraordinary detachment" of Tommy Atkins.

"Take almost any of those little French soldiers—they've got a pretty good idea what the war is about—at any rate, they've got a sentiment about it perfectly clear and conscious, and they'll go to their death shouting for *la patrie*. Now, Tommy Atkins isn't the least like that. He doesn't fight—and you know how he does fight—for patriotism or glory, at least not in the same conscious way. He'd fight just as well against another of his own regiments—if you know what I mean. He's just—well, look at the soldiers' letters. The Germans are sentimental—they are all martyrs. The Frenchmen are all heroes. But Tommy Atkins—well, he's just playing football!"

The idea this Englishman was trying to express was put in another way by a British sailor at the time of the sinking of the *Aboukir*, *Cressy*, and *Rogue*.

Imagine, for a moment, that scene—the three great ships going over like stricken whales, men slipping down their slimy flanks into the sea, boats overturned and smashed, in the thick of it the wet nose of the German submarine coming up for a look round, and then, out of that hideous welter, the voice of a sailor, the unalterable Briton in the face of all this modern science and sea magic, grabbing an anchor or whatever it was he saw first, and bellowing:

"Smash the blighter's head!"

There are phrases like these which could only have been said by the people who say them; they are like windows suddenly opening down cycles of racial history and difference.

At a Regent Street moving-picture show a few evenings ago two young Frenchwomen sat behind us, girls driven off the Paris boulevards by the same impartial force which has driven grubbing peasant women from the Belgian beet-fields. One spoke a little English, and as the pictures changed she translated for her companion.

There were pictures of the silk industry in Japan—moths emerging from cocoons, the breeding process, the hatching of the eggs, the life history of these anonymous little specks magnified until for the moment they almost had a sort of personality. And one murmured: *"Comme c'est drole, la nature!"*

SUNDAY

It was dusk when we reached Boulogne last night—frosty dusk, with the distant moan of a fog-horn, and under the mist hilly streets busy with soldiers and bright with lights. It made one think of a college town at home on the eve of the great game, so keen and happy seemed all these fit young men—officers swinging by with their walking-sticks, soldiers spinning yarns in smoky cafes—for the great game of war.

The hotels were full of wounded or officers—to Boulogne comes the steady procession of British transports—but an amiable porter led me to a little side street and a place kept by a retired English merchant-marine officer who had married a Frenchwoman. Paintings, such as sailor-artists make, of the ships he had served in were on the walls, a photograph of himself and his mates taken in the sunshine of some tropical port; and with its cheerful hot stove, the place combined the air of a French cafe with the cosiness of an English inn.

Very comfortable, indeed, I leaned over one of the tables that ran along the wall, while two British soldiers alongside gossiped and sipped their beer, and ran over the columns of *La Boulonnaise*. Here, too, war seemed a jolly man's game, and I came to "Military Court Sitting at Boulogne," and beneath it the following:

Seventh, eighth, and ninth cases. Thefts by German prisoners of war. The accused are Antoine Michels, twenty-five years, native of Treves, Twenty-seventh German Chasseurs, made prisoner at Lens. Henriede Falk, twenty-seven years, native of Landenheissen (Grand Duchy of Hesse), Fourth Regiment Dragoons, made prisoner at Lille. Max Benninghoven, twenty-two years, Seventh German Chasseurs, made prisoner at Bailleul.

The three had in their possession at the moment of their capture: Michels, two pairs of earrings, a steel watch, two medals representing the town of Arras, and a cigar-holder; Falk, a woman's watch and chain in addition to his own; Benninghoven, a pocketbook, a pack of cards, and money that did not belong to him.

All were subjected to a severe examination and condemned: Michels, to five years in prison and a fine of five hundred francs; Falk, to twenty years at forced labour . . .

And these few words of newspaper type, which nobody else seemed to be noticing, somehow—as if one had stubbed one's toe—disturbed the picture. They did not fit in with the rakish grey motor-car, labelled "Australia," I saw after dinner, nor the young infantryman I ran across on a street corner who had been in the fighting ever since Mons and was but down "for a rest" before jumping in again, nor the busy streets and buzzing cafes. But across them, for some reason, all evening, one couldn't help seeing Henriede Falk, twenty-seven years old, of Landenheissen, starting down toward Paris last August, singing *"Deutschland uber Alles!"* and wondering what he might be thinking about the great game of war fifteen years from now.

While I was taking coffee this morning my mariner-host walked up and down the cafe, delivering himself on the subject of mines in the North Sea. The Germans began it, now the English must take it up; but as for him, speaking as one who had followed the sea, it was poor business. Why couldn't people knock each other out in a stand-up fight like men in a ring, instead of strewing the open road with explosives?

Walking about town after breakfast, I ran into a young man whom I had last seen in a white linen uniform, waiting patiently on the orderlies' bench of the American Ambulance at Neuilly. The ambulance is as hard to get into as an exclusive club, for the woods are full these days of volunteers who, leading rather decorative lives in times of peace, have been shaken awake by the war into helping out overtaxed embassies, making beds in hospitals, doing whatever comes along with a childlike delight in the novelty of work. This young man wore a Red Cross button now and paused long enough to impart the following—characteristic of the things we non-combatants hear daily, and which, authentic or not, help to "make life interesting":

1. An English general just down from the front had told him that four thousand soldiers had been sent out as a burial party after the fighting along the Yser, and had buried, by actual count, thirty-nine thousand Germans.

2. In a temporary hospital near the front some fifty German and Indian wounded were put in the same ward. In the night the Indians got up and cut the Germans' throats.

I climbed up through narrow, cobblestoned streets to the higher part of the town. It was pleasant up here in the frosty morning—old houses, archways, and courts, and the bells tolling people to church.

Up the long hill, as I went down, came three hearses in black and silver, after the French fashion, with drivers in black coats and black-and-silver cocked hats. People stopped as they passed, a woman crossed herself, men took off their hats—farther up the hill a French sentry suddenly straightened and presented arms.

The three caskets were draped in flags—not the tricolour, but the Union Jack. No mourners followed them, and as the ancient vehicles climbed over the brow of the hill the people kept looking, feeling, perhaps, that something was lacking, wondering who the strangers might be who had given their lives to France.

Monday

Paris again—a grey Paris, with bare tree-trunks, dead leaves on the sidewalk, and in the air the chill of approaching winter. Across the grey distances one fancies now and then to have seen the first stray flakes of snow, and in some old street, between tall, grey houses leaning backward, sidewise, each after its fashion—as some girl, pale, with shawl wrapped about her shoulders, hurries past with a quick upcasting of dark eyes, one thinks of Mimi and the third act of *"La Boheme."*

Old sentiments, old songs and verses return in this strange, grey stillness—that spirit so gracious, delicate, penetrating, and personal, which has drawn so many through the years, becomes more moving and real. There is more animation in the streets now: shops are opening, cabs tooting down the Avenue de l'Opera the greater part of the night; but most of the house-fronts are still shuttered and still. Tourists, pleasure-seekers, and the banalities they bring are gone—every thought and energy is with the men fighting on that long line across the north. It is a Paris of the French—of a France united as never before, perhaps, purified by fire, ardent, resolute, defending her life and her precious inheritance.

Tuesday

A journalist actually protests in print against the big loaves of coarse bread, long as half a stick of cord-wood and almost as hard—remember the almost carnivorous joy with which a Frenchman devours bread!—to which the military government, at the beginning of the war, condemned Paris.

The explanation was that rolls and fancy bread took too much time and there were not enough bakers left to do the work—and inspectors see that the law is obeyed, whether amiable bakers think they have time or not. And people want light bread, curly rolls, *pain de fantaisie*. All very well for General Gallieni! says the journalist; he likes hard bread; but why must several million people go on cracking their teeth because of that idiosyncrasy?

The government is obdurate. If fancy bread were made, only the big bakers would have time to make it, little ones would be without clients, and that this highly centralized, paternal government cannot allow. Hard bread it is, then, for another while at least—"*C'est la guerre!*"

Thursday

We have a dining-car on our Bordeaux express to-day, the first since war was declared. To-morrow night sleeping-cars go back again—more significant than one might think who had not seen the France of a few months ago, when everything was turned over to the army and people sat up all night in day coaches to cover the usual three hours from Dieppe to Paris.

Down through the heart of France—Tours, Poitiers, Angouleme—past trim little French rivers, narrow, winding, still, and deep, with rows of poplars close to the water's edge, and still a certain air of coquetry, in spite of bare branches and fallen leaves—past brown fields across which teams of oxen, one sedate old farm horse in the lead, are drawing the furrow for next spring's wheat. It's the old men who are ploughing—except for those in uniform, there is scarce a young man in sight. And everywhere soldiers—wounded ones bound for southern France, reserves not yet sent up.

Vines begin to appear, low brown lines across stony fields; then, just after dark, across the Garonne and into Bordeaux, where the civil government obligingly fled when the enemy was rolling down on Paris in the first week of September.

Bordeaux, Monday

Bordeaux is a day's railroad ride from Paris—twelve hours away from the German cannon, which even now are only fifty miles north of the boulevards, twelve hours nearer Spain and Africa. And you feel both these things.

All about you is the wine country—the names of towns and villages round about read like a wine-card—and, as you are lunching in some little side-street restaurant, a table is moved away, a trap-door opens, and monsieur the proprietor looks on while the big casks of claret are rolled in from the street and lowered to the cellar and the old casks hauled up again. You are close to the wine country and close to the sea—to oysters and crabs and ships—and to the hot sun and more exuberant spirits of the Midi. The pretty, black-eyed Bordelaise—there are pretty girls in Bordeaux—often seems closer to Madrid than to Paris; even the Bordelais accent has a touch of the Mediterranean, and the crisp words of Paris are broken up and even an extra vowel added now and then, until they ripple like Spanish or Italian. *"Pe-tite- ma- dame-a!"* rattles some little newsboy, ingratiating himself with an indifferent lady of uncertain age; and the porter will bring your boots in no time-in *"une-a pe-tite-a mi-nute-a."*

The war is in everybody's mind, of course—no one in France thinks of anything else—but there is none of that silence and tenseness, that emotional tremor, one feels in Paris. The Germans will never come here, one feels, no matter what happens, and as you read the communiqués in *La Petite Gironde* and *La Liberté du Sud-Ouest* the war seems farther away, I feel pretty sure, than it does in front of the newspaper billboards in New York.

In fact, one of the first and abiding impressions of Bordeaux is that it is a great place for things to eat—oysters from Marennes, lobsters and langoustes, pears big as cantaloupes, pomegranates, mushrooms—the little ones and the big *cepes* of Bordeaux—yellow dates just up from Tunis. The fruiterers' shops not only make you hungry, but into some of them you may enter and find a quiet little room up-stairs, where the proprietor and his wife and daughter, in the genial French fashion, will serve you with a cosy little dinner with wine for three francs, in front of the family grate fire, and the privilege of ordering up anything you want from the shop-window below.

There are attractive little chocolate and pastry shops and cheerful semi-pension restaurants where whole families, including, in these days, minor politicians with axes to grind and occasional young women from the boulevards, all dine together in a warm bustle of talk, smoke, the gurgle of claret, and tear off chunks of hard French bread, while *madame* the proprietress, a handsome, dark-eyed, rather Spanish-looking Bordelaise, sails round, subduing the impatient, smiling at those who wish to be smiled at, and ordering her faithful waiters about like a drill-sergeant.

And then there is the *Chapon fin.* When you speak to some elderly gentleman with fastidious gastronomical tastes and an acquaintance with southern France of your intention of going to Bordeaux, he murmurs reminiscently: "Ah, yes! There is a restaurant there. . ." He means the *Chapon fin.* It was famous in '70 when the government came here before, and to-day when the young King of Spain motors over from Biarritz he dines there. Coming down on the train, I read in the *Revue des Deux Mondes* the recollections of a gentleman who was here in '70-'71 and is here again now. He was inclined to be sarcastic about the present *Chapon fin.* In his day one had good food and did not pay exorbitantly; now "one needs a quasi-official introduction to penetrate, and the stylish servants, guarding the door like impassable dragons, ask with a discreet air if monsieur has taken care to warn the management of his intention of taking lunch."

We penetrated without apparent difficulty—possibly owing to the exalted position of the two amiable young attaches who entertained me—and the food was very good. There were diplomats of all sorts to be seen, a *meridional* head waiter, and an interesting restaurant cat. One end of the room is an artificial grotto, and into and out of the canvas rocks this enormous cat kept creeping, thrusting his round face and blazing eyes out of unexpected holes in the manner of the true *carnivora*, as if he had been trained by the management as an entertainer. The head waiter would have lured an anchorite into temporary abandon. Toward the end of the evening we discussed the probable character of a certain dessert, suggesting some doubt of taking it. You might as well have doubted his honour. *"Mais, monsieur!"* He waved his arms. *"C'est deli-cieux!... C'est merveilleux!... C'est quelque chose"*—slowly, with thumb and first finger pressed together— *"de r-r-raf-fi-we!"*. . .

It is to this genial provincial city that the President and his ministers have come. They distributed themselves about town in various public and private buildings; the Senate chose one theatre for its future meeting-place and the Chamber of Deputies another. And from these places, sometimes the most incongruous—one hears, for instance, of M. Delcasse maintaining his dignity in a bedroom now used as the office for the minister of foreign affairs—the red tape is unwound which eventually sends the life-blood of the remotest province flowing up to its appointed place at the front.

There must be plenty of real work, for an army like that of France, stretching clear across the country from Switzerland to the Channel, could not live unless it had a smoothly running civil machine in the quiet country behind. Neither of the chambers is in session, and except that the main streets are busy—one is told that one hundred thousand extra people are in town—you might almost never know that anything out of the ordinary had occurred. Things must be very different, of course, from '71, when, beaten to her knees and threatened with revolution, France had to decide between surrendering Alsace and Lorraine and going on with the war.

The theatres are closed, but there are moving-picture shows, an occasional concert, and twice a week, under the auspices of one of the newspapers, a conference. I went to one of these, given by a French professor of English literature in the University of Bordeaux, on the timely subject: "Kipling and Greater England."

You can imagine the piquant interest of the scene—the polite matinee audience, the row of erudite Frenchmen sitting behind the speaker, the table, the shaded lamp, and the professor himself, a slender, dark gentleman with a fine, grave face, pointed black beard, and penetrating eyes—suggesting vaguely a *prestidigitateur*—trying, by sheer intelligence and delicate, critical skill, to bridge the gaps of race and instinctive thought and feeling and make his audience understand Kipling.

Said the reporter of one of the Bordeaux papers next day: "Through the Kipling evoked by M. Cestre we admired the English and those who fight, in the great winds of the North Sea, that combat rude and brave. We admired the faithful indigenes, gathering from all her dominions, to put their muscular arms at the service of the empire. . ."

It would, indeed, have been difficult to pay a more graceful compliment to the entente cordiale than to try to run the author of "Soldiers Three" and the "Barrack Room Ballads," and with him the nation behind him, into the smooth mould of a conference—that mixture, so curiously French, of clear thinking and graceful expression, of sensitive definition and personal charm, all blended into a whole so intellectually neat and modulated that an audience like this may take it with the same sense of being cheered, yet not inebriated, with which their allies across the Channel take their afternoon tea.

A Frenchman of a generation ago would scarcely have recognized the England pictured by the amiable Bordeaux professor, and I am not sure that in this entirely altruistic big brother of little nations the English would have recognized themselves. But, at any rate, polite flutters of applause punctuated the talk, and at the end M. Cestre asked his audience to rise as he paid his final tribute to the people now fighting the common battle with France. They all stood up and, smiling up at the left-hand proscenium-box, saluted the British ambassador, Sir Francis Bertie, with long and enthusiastic applause. A man in the gallery even ventured a *"Heep! heep!"* and every one drifted out very content, indeed.

In the foyer I saw one lady carefully spelling out with her lorgnette one of the words on the list posted there of the subjects for conferences.

"Ah!" she said, considerably reassured apparently, *"Keepling!"* But then she may have come in late.

70

The war has been hard on the main business of the neighbourhood, of course—Germany was the heaviest buyer of Bordeaux wine, Russia next, and not as much as usual is going to England. The vintage this year, like that of 70, is said to be good, however, and, though the young men have gone, and the wine-making was not as gay as usual, there were enough old men and women left to do the work. I visited one of the older wine houses—nearly two centuries old—and tramped through cellars which burrow on two levels under a whole city block. There were some two million bottles down there in the dark and dust.

There is something patriarchal and princely about such a house, almost unknown in our businesses at home—from the portraits of the founders, from the cask makers, at lunch-time, broiling their own fish over a huge fireplace and drawing wine from the common cask as they have done for generations; the stencils in the shipping-room—"Baltimore," "Bogotá," "Buenos Aires," "Chicago," "Calcutta," "Christiania," "Caracas"—from things like these to the personality and point of view of the men who have the business in charge.

"Now, wine," began the charming gentleman who showed us round, "is a living thing." And though you could see that he had showed many people about in his day—and was not unaware of what might interest them—that he was, in short, an advertiser of the most accomplished kind, yet one could also see that he liked his work and believed in it, and grew wine as an amateur grows fancy tulips and not as a mere salesman.

To be sure, he was inclined to slur over the importance of white wine, while champagne and its perfidious makers didn't interest him in the least; but of the red wine of Bordeaux, its lightness, bouquet, and general beneficence, and the delicate and affectionate care with which it was handled, one could have heard him talk all day. Now and then younger houses discovered things that were going to revolutionize the wine trade.

"Of course," he said, "we examine such things. We look in our books, where records of all our experiments are kept, and there we find that we tried that new thing in 1856—or 1756, perhaps."

Far underground we came on some of the huge *majorums*, big as nine ordinary bottles. "The King of Spain ran over to Bordeaux one day, and came to us and said: 'I've got two hours; what can you show me?' We said: 'We can show you our cellars.' 'Very well,' said he; 'go ahead.' When he came to the *majorums* he said: 'What on earth do you do with those?' 'They are used when there is a christening or a wedding or some great event, and when a king visits us we give him two.'"

So they sent the *majorums* to the young King, and the King sent back a polite note, just as if he were anybody else, and that is all of that story.

Most of the newspapers which followed the government to Bordeaux have returned to the capital, but that intransigent government-baiter, the venerable Georges Clemenceau, still continues his bombardment from close range. His paper was formerly *L'Homme Libre—The Free Man*—but on being suppressed this fall by the censor its octogenarian editor gaily changed its name to *The Chained Man—L'Homme Enchainé*— and continued fire.

The mayor of a Paris commune in '71, prime minister from 1906-9, the editor of various papers, and senator now, Clemenceau is properly feared; and he was offered, it is said, a place in the present government, but would accept no post but the highest. He preferred his role of political realist and critical privateer, a sort of Mr. Shaw of French politics, hitting a head wherever he sees one.

The imperfections of the French army sanitary service, the censorship, and the demoralization of the postal service since the war have been favourite targets recently. There has been much complaint of the difficulty of getting news from men at the front. M. Viviani, the premier, in an address at Reims, ventured to say that it was his duty to "organize, administer, and intensify the national defence." On this innocent phrase the eye of M. Clemenceau fell the other day, and he now flings off a characteristic three-and-a-half-column front-page salvo so adroitly combining the premier's remark with the actual, pitiful facts that the reader almost feels that "intensifying" the suffering of parents and friends of men fighting for their country is something in which the present government takes delight.

I wish there was space to quote the editorial. I may, at any rate, quote from one or two of the letters written to M. Clemenceau, to suggest a stay-at-home aspect of the war of which we do not hear much. This is from the mayor of Pont-en-Royans:

"Officially," he writes, "on September 29 I was asked to notify the family of the soldier Regnier of his death. In the midst of their cries and tears, the family showed me the last letter, received that very morning, and dated the 27th September, two days before. Now, the notice of his death was dated September 7, and I said to the father:

"'I would not give you too much hope; your son probably died the 27th, suddenly, perhaps, and the secretary charged with writing the letter I have received forgot a figure—instead of 27 he put 7. Meanwhile, as a doubt exists, I will do what I can to clear the matter up.'

"The Administrative Counsel replied to me: 'There has been no error. The notice of decease is dated September 27. If, then, the soldier wrote the 27th, he is not dead. We shall inform the ministry, and you, on your side, should write to the hospital where he is being treated.'

"I wrote to the chief doctor at Besancon. No response. I sent him a telegram with the reply prepaid. No response. I wrote him a third letter, this time a trifle sarcastic. I received finally a despatch: 'Regnier is not known at this hospital.'

"I still had the telegram in my hand when to my house came the sister of the dead soldier, in mourning, and beaming, and gave me a letter. 'It is my brother who has written us.' So there was no mistake. The dead man wrote on the 2nd October.

"'Very well,' said I to the family. 'Are you sufficiently reassured now?'

"Some days after I received from the Red Cross hospital at Besancon a letter giving me news of Regnier and explaining that there were several hospitals in the town, that they had only just received my letter, etc., etc.

"I did not think more of the matter until October 23, when I received a circular from the prefecture of Isere, asking me to advise the Regnier family that the soldier Regnier, wounded, was being treated at the hospital of Besancon.

"At last I thought the affair was closed, when, to-day, October 30, I received the enclosed despatch, sent by I know not whom, informing me that the soldier Regnier is unknown in the hospital of Besancon!

"Oh, my head, my head!"

You can imagine what this slashing old privateer would do with a letter like this. The censor will not permit him to make any comment. Very well—he wishes to make none. "You see, Mr. Viviani, it isn't one of those execrable parliamentarians who makes these complaints. It is a mayor, a humble mayor, officially designated by you to transmit to his people the striking results of your 'organization,' of your 'administration,' of your 'intensification' in the cruelly delicate matter of giving news to families. He supplies the picture, and you see in plain daylight your 'intensification' at work. What do you think of it? What can you say about it? Do you believe that because you have given to your censor the right—pardon me, the power—to make white spaces in the columns of newspapers that that is going to suppress the fact? Do you believe," etc., etc.

In the same editorial was a letter from a father whose two sons, on the firing-line, had received none of the family letters since the beginning of the war and wrote pathetically asking if their parents and little sister were ill, or how they had offended. A wife enclosed a letter from her husband, telling how he was suffering from the cold because of insufficient

74

clothing; a doctor wrote protesting because there was not a single bottle of anti-tetanic serum in his field-hospital.

We found M. Clemenceau in his lodgings late one afternoon—a leonine old gentleman bundled up in cap and overcoat before a little grate fire, while a secretary ran through the big heap of letters piled on the bed. In the corner of the room was a roll-top desk—the sanctum, evidently, of *The Chained Man*.

As M. Clemenceau was insistent that he should not be interviewed, I may not repeat the exceedingly lively talk on all sorts of people and things with which he regaled us once—and it didn't take long—he "got going."

One purely personal little bit of information may be passed on, however, in the hope that it may be as interesting to other practitioners of a laborious trade as it was to me.

We were talking of the facility with which he reeled off, day after day, columns of lively, finished prose, and I asked whether he wrote in longhand, dictated, or used a typewriter.

This question seemed to amuse and interest the old warhorse greatly. He went to his desk and brought back a sheet of paper, half of which was covered with a small, firm handwriting. It was his next day's broadside, not yet finished.

"There is nothing mysterious about it," he said. "I get up at half past three every morning. I am at that desk most of the day; I go to bed at nine o'clock. If I had to write a banal note, it might take time, but there are certain ideas which I have worked with all my life. I worked a good many years without expressing them; they are all in my head, and when I want them I've only got to take them out. I am eighty-three years old, and if I couldn't express myself by this time"—the old gentleman lifted his eyebrows, smiled whimsically, and, with a quick movement of shoulders and hands, concluded—"it would be a public calamity—*a malheur public!*"

I thought of the padded lives of some of our literary charlatans and editorial gold bricks at home, of the clever young artists ruined as painters by becoming popular illustrators, the young writers content to substitute overpaid banality and bathos for honest work, and I must confess that the sight of this indomitable old fighter, who had known great men and held high place in his day, and now at eighty-three got up before daylight to pound out in longhand his columns of vivid prose, stirred every drop of what you might call one's intellectual sporting blood. Of his opinions I know little, of the justice of his attacks less, and, to be quite frank, I suspect he is something of a trouble-maker. But as he stood there, bundled up in his overcoat and cap, in that chilly lodging-house room, witty, unsubdued, full of fight and of charm, he seemed to stand for that wonderful French spirit—for its ardour and penetration, its fusion of sense and sensibility, its tireless intelligence and unquenchable fire.

MONDAY

The consul of Cognac! It sounded like a musical comedy when we met on the steamer last August; not quite so odd when we bumped into each other in Bordeaux; and now it turns out to mean, in addition to being a young University of Virginia man, thoroughly acquainted with the people he has to deal with, living in a town where the towers of Francis I's castle still stand, rowing on a charming old river in the summer, and in these days hearing a charming old French gentleman, vice-consul, tell how he fought against the Prussians in '70. Cognac is a real place, it appears—an old town of twenty thousand people or so, and it is really where cognac comes from, all other brandies being, of course, as one will learn here, mere upstart *eaux-de-vie*. We went through some of the cellars to-day, as venerable and vast as the claret cellars in Bordeaux, although not quite as interesting, perhaps, because not so "alive." For wine is a living thing, as the man said in Bordeaux, and it must be ignobly boiled and destroyed before turning into a distilled spirit. To some this pale spiritual essence may possess a finer poetry—the cellars are more fragrant, at any rate.

All the young men had gone to the front—their wages continued as usual—and the work was carried on by women and old servitors, scarcely one of the latter under seventy. They were pointed out as examples of the beneficent effect of the true cognac—these old boys who had inhaled the slightly pungent fragrance of the cellars and bottling-rooms all their lives. You get this perfume all over Cognac. It comes wandering down old alleyways, out from under dark arches, people live literally in a fine mist of it. The very stones are turned black by the faint fumes.

There must be scores of towns south of Paris which look more or less like this—the young men gone or drilling in the neighbourhood, the schools turned into hospitals, the little old provincial hotels sheltering families fled from Paris. There are several such at our hotel, nice, comfortable people—you might think you were in some semi-summer-resort hotel at home—Ridgefield, Conn., for instance, in winter time.

The making of cognac occupies nearly every one, one way or another, and it has made the place next to the richest town of its size in France. They make the cognac, and they make the bottles for it in a glass factory on a hill overlooking the town—about as airy and pleasant a place for a factory as one could imagine. The molten glass is poured into moulds, the moulds closed—*psst!* a stream of compressed air turned in, the bottles blown, and there you are—a score or so of them turned out every minute. As we came out of the furnace-room into the chilly afternoon a regiment of reservists tramped in from a practise march in the country. Some were young fellows, wearing uniforms for the first time, apparently; some looked like convalescents drafted back into the army. They took one road and we another, and half an hour later swung down the main street of Cognac behind a chorus of shrilling bugles. All over France, south of Paris, they must be marching like this these frosty afternoons.

Coming up from Bordeaux the other night we missed the regular connection and had to spend the night at Saintes.

The tall, quizzical, rather grim old landlady of the neat little Hotel de la Gare—characteristic of that rugged France which tourists who only see a few streets in Paris know little about—was plainly puzzled. There we were, two able-bodied men, and P————, saying nothing about being consul, merely remarked that he lived in Cognac. "In Cognac!" the old woman repeated, looking from one to the other, and then added, as one putting an unanswerable question: "But you are not soldiers?"

We went out for a walk in the frosty air before turning in. There was scarce a soul in the streets, but at the other end of the town a handful of young fellows passed on the other side singing. They were boys of the 1915 class who had been called out and in a few days would be getting ready for war. In Paris you will see young fellows just like them, decorated with flags and feathers, driving round town in rattle-trap wagons like picnic parties returning on a summer night at home. Arm in arm and keeping step, these boys of Saintes were singing as they marched:

Il est rouge et noir et blanc,
Et fendu au derriere—d.
He's red, white, and black,
And split up the back!

They saw themselves, doubtless, marching down the streets of Berlin as now they were marching down the streets of Saintes—and they kept flinging back through the frosty dark:
"Il est rouge—et noir—et blanc—Et fendu—au derriere—d . . ."

CHAPTER 6

"The Great Days"

They were playing *"The Categorical Imperative"* that evening
at the Little Theatre in Unter den Linden. It is an old-fashioned comedy laid in the Vienna of 1815—two love-stories,
lightly and quaintly told, across which, through the chatter of
a little Viennese salon, we dimly see Napoleon return from
Elba and hear the thunder of Waterloo. A young cub of a
Saxon schoolmaster, full of simple-hearted enthusiasm and
philosophy, comes down to the Austrian capital, and, taken
up by a kindly, coquettish young countess, becomes the tutor
of her cousin, a girl as simple as he. The older woman with
her knowing charm, the younger with her freshness, present
a dualism more bewildering than any he has ever read about
in his philosophy books, and part of the fun consists in seeing
him fall in love with the younger in terms of pure reason, and
finally, when the motherly young countess has quietly got
him a professorship at Konigsberg, present to his delighted
Elise his "categorical imperative."

You can imagine that thoroughly German mixture of
sentiment and philosophy, the quaint references to a Prussia not yet, in its present sense, begun to exist; how to that
audience—nearly every one of whom had a son or husband or brother at the front—the century suddenly seemed
to close up and the Napoleonic days became part of their
own *"grosse Zeit."* You can imagine the young schoolmaster
and the frivolous older man going off to war, and the two
women consoling each other, and with what strange elo-

quence the words of that girl of 1815, watching them from the window, come down across the years:

"Why is it that from time to time men must go and kill each other? There it stands in the paper—two thousand more men—it writes itself so easily! But that every one of them has a wife or mother or sister or a—. . . And when they cry their eyes out that means that it is a victory, and when some brave young fellow has fallen, he is only one of the 'forces'—so and so many men—and nobody even knows his name. . ."

You must imagine them coming back from the war, and pale, benign, leaning on their canes as returning heroes do in plays, talk across the footlights to real young soldiers you have just seen limping in with real wounds—pink-cheeked boys with heads and feet bandaged and Iron Crosses on black-and-white ribbons tucked into their coats, home from East Prussia or the Aisne. Then between the acts you must imagine them pouring out to the refreshment-room for a look at each other and something to eat—will they never stop eating?—fathers and mothers and daughters with their *Butterbrod* and *Schinken* and big glasses of beer in the genial German fashion, beaming on the young heroes limping by or, with heads bandaged like schoolboys with mumps, grinning in spite of their scars.

And when they drift out into the street at last, softened and brought together by the play—the street with its lights and flags, officers in long, blue-grey overcoats and soldiers every-where, and a military automobile shooting by, perhaps, with its gay *"Ta-tee! Ta-td!"*—the extras are out with another Rus-sian army smashed and two more ships sunk in the Channel. The old newspaper woman at the Friedrichsstrasse corner is chanting it hoarsely, *"Zwei englische Dampfer gesunken!"*—and they read that "the sands have run, the prologue is spoken, the curtain risen on the tragedy of England's destiny."

Great days, indeed! Days of achievement, of utter sacrifice, and flinging all into the common cause. Round the corner from Unter den Linden, under the dark windows of the In-formation Bureau, you may see part of the price. It is still and deserted there, except for a lone woman with a shawl over her head, trying to read, by the light of the street-lamp, the casualty lists. You must imagine a building like the Post Office in New York, for instance, or the Auditorium Hotel in Chicago, with a band of white paper, like newspapers, spread out and pasted end to end, running along one side, round the corner, and down the other. Not inches, but yards, rods, two city blocks almost, of microscopic type; columns of names, arranged in the systematic German way—lightly wounded, badly wounded—*schwer verwundet—gefallen*. Some have died of wounds—*tot*—some dead in the enemy's country—in *Feindesland gefallen*. Rank on rank, blurring off into nothingness, endless files of type, pale as if the souls of the dead were crowding here.

One tried to think of the "Categorical Imperative" in a New York playhouse—of the desperate endeavour to make the young schoolmaster really look simple and boyish, and yet as if he might have heard of Kant, and of convincing the two ladies that they lost their sweet comfortableness by dressing like professional manikins; how the piece might succeed with luck, or if it could somehow be made fashionable; and how here, with all the unaffected and affectionate intelligence with which it was played—and watched—it was but part of the week's work.

And, in spite of the desperation of the time, you might have seen a dozen such audiences in Berlin, that night—and yet tourists generally speak of Berlin, compared with some of the German provincial cities, as a rather graceless, new sort of place, full of bad sculpture and Prussian arrogance. You might have seen them at the opera or symphony concerts, at Shakespeare, Strindberg, or the German classics we used to read in college, or standing in line at six o'clock, sandwiches in hand, so that they might sit through a performance of *Peer Gynt*, with the Grieg music, beginning at seven and lasting till after eleven. A wonderful night, with poetry and music and splendid scenes and acting, and a man's very soul developing before you all the time—sandwiches and beer and more music and poetry, until that tragedy of the egoist is no longer a play but a part of you, so many years of living, almost, added to one's life. Yes, it is all here, along with the forty-two-centimetre shells—good music and good beer and good love of both; simplicity, homely kindness, and *Gemutlichkeit*.

Mere talk about plays would not be much encouraged in Germany nowadays. In one of the Cologne papers the other day there were two imaginary letters—one signed "One Who Means Well," asking that there be a little relief from war poems, war articles, and the like; and the other signed "One Who Means Better," demanding if it were possible for any German to waste time in artistic hair-splitting when the Germanic peoples, in greater danger than in their entire history, stood with their back to the wall, facing and holding back the world. A Berlin dramatic critic, going through the motions of reviewing a new performance of *Hedda Gabler* the other morning, finally dismissed the matter as "Women's troubles— if anybody can be interested in that nowadays!" Yet a woman, asking at the same time that the "finer and sweeter voices of peaceful society" be not forgotten, concluded her letter with "East and west the cannon thunder, but in men's souls sound many bells, and it is not necessary that they should always and forever be drowned out."

I mention the theatre only as an easy illustration of that many-sided vitality one feels at once on entering Germany, that development of all a people's capabilities, material and spiritual, which is summed up, I suppose, in that hapless word *Kultur*.

You may not like German learning or German art, and consider the one pedantic and the other heavy and uninspired. A Frenchman wrote very feelingly the other day, in the *Revue des Deux Mondes*, about a return to the old French culture, an escape from what he described as the German habit of accumulating mere facts to something that, in addition to feeding the brain, nourished the taste as well—carried with it, so to speak, a certain spiritual fragrance.

You may be of this persuasion. The thing one cannot escape, however, in Germany, whether one likes its manifestations or not, is the vitality, the moral and intellectual force, everywhere apparent, whether it be applied to smashing forts or staging a play. When a people can hold back England and France with one hand and the Russian avalanche with the other, and, cut off from overseas trade and living on rations almost, yet, to take but one of the first examples, maintain the art of the theatre at a level which makes that of New York or London in the most spacious time of peace seem crude and infantile, one is confronted with a fact which a reporter in his travels must record—a force which, as the saying goes, "must be reckoned with."

So far as the special business of keeping the war going is concerned, this vitality, after seven months of fighting, in spite of those lists in Dorotheenstrasse, seems ample. Here in Berlin, which is an all day's express journey from either front, you see thousands of fit young men marching through the streets, singing and whistling; you are told of millions ready and waiting to go. Every one seems confident that Germany will win—indeed, with a unity and resolution which could scarcely be more complete if they were defending their last foot of territory, determined that Germany must win.

When I was in London in the autumn a man who had made a flying trip to Berlin said that the German capital made him think of a man with his feet on the table smoking a cigar and pretending to be unconcerned although he knew all the time in his heart that he was doomed. I find little to suggest such a picture. The thing that at once impresses the stranger, along with the apparent reserve strength, is the moral earnestness behind that strength, the passionate conviction that they are fighting a defensive fight, that they are right. I shall not attempt to explain this here, but merely record it as a fact. Possibly all people in all great wars believe they are right—and that is why there are great wars.

Crossing the frontier from Rotterdam, I stopped for a day

or two at Cologne. The proprietor of the hotel, a typical, big, hearty German of the commercial class, such as you might expect to find running a brewery at home or a bank or coffee plantation in South America, came out of his office when he heard English spoken. There are no "loose Englishmen" in Germany nowadays.

"I suppose you are surprised to see the Dom, yes?" he laughed, pointing toward the cathedral towers in whose shadow we stood. And then—"What do you think about the war?" I asked him what he thought.

"Well," he said, and with the air of brushing aside what was taken for granted before considering more doubtful issues, "of course we win!"

He showed me a photograph of his son, just made an officer. "In a few weeks," he said, "maybe I volunteer myself." He was fifty-five years old, but thoroughly fit. He doubled up a big right arm and laughingly gripped it. "Like iron!" he boomed. "And there are five million men like me. Not men—soldiers!"

I found myself the other evening, after zigzagging all over Berlin with an address given me at a typewriter agency, in a little apartment on the outskirts of the town. The woman who lived there had been a stenographer in the city until the war cut off her business, and she was now supporting herself with the six marks (one dollar and fifty cents) weekly war benefit given by the municipality and by making soldiers' shirts for the War Department at fifty *pfennigs* (twelve and one-half cents) a shirt. She was glad to get typewriting, and without words on either side at once got to work. So we proceeded for a page or two until something was said about an Iron Cross stuck inside a soldier's coat.

"That is the Iron Cross of the second class," she interrupted; "they put that inside. The first class they wear outside," and, as if she could keep still no longer, she suddenly flung out, almost without a pause:

"My brother has the Iron Cross. I have seven brothers in

the army. Three are in the east and three are in the west, and one is in the hospital. He was shot three times in the leg—here—and here—and here. They hope to save his leg, but he will always be lame. He got the Iron Cross. He was at Dixmude. They marched up singing 'Deutschland ueber Alles.' They were all shot down. There were three hundred of them, and every one fell. They knew they must all be shot, but they marched on just the same, singing 'Deutschland ueber Alles.' They knew they were going against the English, and nothing could stop them."

Her brother would go back if he had to crawl back—if only she could go and not have to sit here and wait!

"I told you," she said, "when you first came in, that I was German. And I asked you if you were an American, because I know that dreadful things have been said in America about our Kaiser, and I will not have such things said to me. Our Kaiser did not want the war—he did everything he could to prevent the war—no ruler in the world ever did more for his people than our Kaiser has done, and there is not a man, woman, or child in Germany who would not fight for him." And this, you must remember, was from a woman whose support was cut off by the war and who was making a living by sewing shirts at twelve and a half cents a shirt.

I walked down the busy High Street that night in Cologne, and the bright shop-windows with their chocolates and fruit—apples from Canada and Hood River—crowded cafes, people overflowing sidewalks into the narrow streets somehow reminded me of the cheerful Bordeaux I tramped through in November. There are, indeed, many French suggestions in Cologne, and in the shops they still sometimes call an umbrella a parapluie.

An American who lives in Cologne told me that the decrease in the number of young men was noticeable, and that eleven sons of his friends had been killed. To a stranger the city looked normal, with the usual crowds. One did notice the people about the war bulletin-boards. They were not boys and street loungers, but grave-looking citizens and their wives and daughters, people who looked as if they might have sons or brothers at the front.

The express from Cologne to Berlin passed through Essen, where the Krupp guns are made, the coal and iron country of Westphalia, and the plains of the west. It is a country of large cities whose borders often almost touch, where some tall factory chimney is almost always on the horizon. All these chimneys were pouring out smoke; there is a reason, of course, why iron-works should be busy and manufacturing going on—if not as usual, at any rate going on.

The muddy plains between the factory towns were green with winter wheat, the crop which is to carry the country through another year. Meanwhile, one was told, the railroad rights of way would be planted, and land not needed for beets—for with no sugar going out Germany can produce more now than she needs—also be seeded to wheat.

Here in Berlin we are, it seems, being starved out, but in the complex web of a modern city it is rather hard to tell just what that means: In ordinary times, for instance, Germany imports thirty-five million dollars' worth of butter and eggs from Russia, which, of course, is not coming in now, yet butter seems to appear, and at a central place like the Victoria Cafe, at the corner of Unter den Linden and Friedrichsstrasse, two soft-boiled eggs cost fifty *pfennigs*, or twelve and a half cents, which is but two and a half cents more than they cost before the war, and that includes a morning paper and a window from which to see Berlin going by. Even were Berlin, in a journalistic sense, "starving," one presumes the cosmopolitans in the tea-rooms of the Kaiserhof or Adlon or Esplanade would still have their trays of fancy cakes to choose from and find no difficulty in getting plenty to eat at a—for them—not unreasonable price.

For weeks white bread has had to contain a certain amount of rye flour and rye bread a certain amount of potato—the so-called war bread—and, except in the better hotels, one was served, unless one ordered specially, with only two or three little wisps of this *Kriegsbrod*. For Frenchmen this would mean a real privation, but Germans eat so little bread, comparatively speaking, that one believes the average person scarcely noticed the difference. Every one must have his bread-card now, with coupons entitling him to so many grams a day—about four pounds a week—which the waiter or baker tears off when the customer gets his bread. Without these cards not so much as a crumb can be had for love or money. Yet with all this stiff and not unamusing red tape your morning coffee and bread and butter costs from thirty *pfennigs* (seven and one-half cents) in one of the Berlin "automats" to one *mark* fifty *pfennigs* (thirty-seven cents) in the quiet of the best hotels.

Meat is plentiful and cheap, particularly beef, and in any of the big, popular "beer restaurants," so common in Berlin, an ordinary steak for one person costs from thirty-five to fifty cents. Pork, the mainstay of the poorer people, is comparatively expensive, because hogs have been made into durable hard sausages for the army, and potatoes, also expensive, have been bought up in large quantities by the government, to be sold in the public markets to the poor, a few pounds to each person, at a moderate price. There are said to be eight hundred thousand prisoners now in Germany, and the not entirely frivolous suggestion has been made that the hordes of hungry Russians captured in the east are more dangerous now than they were with guns in their hands. Yet there are no visible signs of such poverty as one will see in certain parts of London or Chicago in times of peace, and a woman in charge of one of the soup-kitchens where people pinched by the war get one substantial meal a day at ten *pfennigs* told me there was no reason for any one in Berlin going hungry. Meanwhile, the scarcity of flour only adds fuel to the people's patriotism, and they are told everywhere on red placards that England never can starve them out if every German does his economical duty. Where so much thinking is done for the people, and done so efficiently, it is difficult not to feel that everything is somehow "arranged," and one finds it difficult to become acutely anxious while the hundreds of crowded cafes are running full blast until one o'clock every morning and the seal in the *Tiergarten* has the bottom of his tank covered with fresh fish he is too indolent to eat.

"Society," in its more visible, decorative sense, is as forgotten as it is in France, as it must be in such a time. There are no dances or formal parties; every one who is not going about his civil business has in one way or another "gone to the war." The gay young men are at the front, the idle young women knitting or nursing or helping the poor, and it is an adventure uncommon enough to be remembered to meet on the street a pretty young lady merely out to take the air, with hands in her muff and trotting in front of her the timorous dachshund, muzzled like a ravening tiger and looking at the world askance with his rueful eyes.

The apparent quietness and gravity is partially due to the lack of a "yellow" or, in the British or American sense of the word, popular press. There is none of that noisy hate continually dinned into one's ears in London by papers which, to be sure, represent neither the better-class English civilians nor the light-hearted fighting man at the front, yet which are entertainingly written, do contain the news, and get themselves read.

The German papers print comparatively little of what we call "news." They hide unpleasant truths and accent pleasant ones, and are working all the time to create a definite public opinion; but their partisanship is that of official proclamation rather than that of overworked and underpaid reporters striving to please their employers with all the desperation of servants working for a tip. The yelping after spies, the heaping of adjectives on every trifling achievement of British arms, the ill-timed talk of snatching the enemy's trade in a war theoretically fought for a high principle, all that journalistic vulgarity—which might be as characteristic of our own papers under similar circumstances—one is mercifully spared.

This taciturnity is astonishing toward the work of the men at the front. A few days ago flags were flung out all over Berlin at the news of Hindenburg's victory; military attaches were saying that there had been nothing like this since Napoleon; up and down the streets the newswomen were croaking: *"Sechsund-zwanzig tausend Russen gefangen... Hindenburg zahlt noch immer..."* ("Twenty-six thousand Russians captured ... and Hindenburg's still counting ..."). And all you could find in the papers was the General Staff report that "at one place the fighting has been very severe; up to the present we have made some twenty-six thousand prisoners," etc., and even this laconic sentence lost in the middle of the regular communiqué beginning: "Yesterday on the Belgian coast, after a period of inactivity..."

The picturesqueness and personalities of the war are left to the stage and the innumerable weeklies and humorous papers, yet even here there is little or no tendency to group achievements around individual commanders—it is "our army," not the man, although even German collectivism cannot keep Hindenburg's dependable old face off the post-cards nor regiments of young ladies from sending him letters and *Liebesgaben.*

In the theatre you see the *Feldgrau* heroes in dugouts in Flanders or in Galician trenches; see the audience weep when the German mother sends off her seven sons or the bearded father meets his youngest boy, *schwer verwundet*, on the battle-field; or cheer when the curtain goes down on noble blond giants in spiked helmets dangling miniature Frenchmen by the scruff of the neck and forcing craven Highlanders to bite the dust.

You may even see a submarine dive down into green water, see the torpedo slid into the tube, breech-block closed, and—"Now—for Kaiser and fatherland!"—by means of an image thrown on a screen from the periscope, see the English cruiser go up in a tower of water and founder.

In all this comment there is a very different feeling for each of the three allies. The Russians "don't count," so to speak. They are dangerous because of their numbers and must be flung back, but the feeling toward them is not unlike that toward a herd of stampeded range cattle.

Toward the French there is no bitterness either, rather a sort of pity and the wish to be thought well of. One is reminded now and then of the German captain quartered at Sedan, in Zola's *"Debacle,"* who, while conscious of the strength behind him, yet wanted his involuntary hosts to know that he, too, had been to Paris and knew how to be a *galant homme*. Men tell you "they've put up a mighty good fight, say!" or speaking of the young French sculptor allowed to go on with his work in the prison camp at Zossen, or the flower-beds in front of the French barracks there—"but, of course, the French are an artistic people. You can allow them liberties like that." Every now and then in the papers one runs across some anecdote from France in which the Frenchman is permitted to make the retort at the expense of the English.

Toward John Bull there is no mercy. He is shown naked, trying to hide himself with neutral flags; he is sprawled in his mill with a river of French blood flowing by from the battle-fields of France, while the cartoonist asks France if she cannot see that she is doing his grinding for him; he is hobnobbing cheek by jowl with cannibals and black men, and he is seriously discussed as a traitor to the Germanic peoples and the white race.

A German woman told me the other day that in her house it was the custom to fine everybody in the family ten *pfennigs* if they came down to breakfast without saying: *"Gott strafe die Englander!"* ("God punish the English!") In a recent *Ulk* there is a cartoon of a young mother holding up her baby to his proud father with the announcement that he has spoken his first words. "And what did he say?" *"Gott strafe England!"*

America is criticised for supplying the Allies with arms—shades of South American revolutions and the old *"Ypiranga"*!—while permitting itself, without sufficient protest, to be shut off from sending food to Germany. Yet, in spite of this and the extremely difficult situation created by the submarine blockade, the individual American is not embarrassed unless mistaken for an Englishman or unless he finds some super-sensitive patriot in a restaurant or theatre who objects even to hearing English.

At the frontier the honest customs inspector landed, first thing, on a copy of *Tartarin sur les Alpes*, which I had picked up at the railroad news-stand in the Hague.

"Franzosisch!" he declared, flapping over the pages. Next it was a bundle of letters of introduction, the top one of which happened to be in English. *"Englische Briefe!"* and forthwith he bellowed for help. A young officer sauntered out from the nearby office, saluted, and said, "Good morning!" glanced at *Tartarin* with a smile, and tossed it back into the bag, at letters and passport, said it must be very interesting to see both sides, and so, after a question or two, to the train for Koln.

On the way to Berlin from Koln, that rainy afternoon, I went into the dining-car toward five o'clock attired in a pepper-and-salt tweed suit and heavy tan boots, and, speaking German with evident pain, tactfully asked—everybody else drinking beer—for tea. The man across the way whispered to his companion and stared; a middle-aged man farther up the aisle stood stock-still and stared; a young woman at the other end of the car turned round and, gazing over the back of her chair, whispered aghast to her companion: *"Englaender!"*

Not particularly enlivened by the cup that cheers, I re-gained my compartment presently and glared out at the sodden landscape, with now and then a shot at the other occupant who had got on at Essen or one of the western stations and sat the day out without a word. One of those disagreeable Prussians evidently—until, actually needing to know, I broke the silence by asking which station we arrived at in Berlin. He answered with perfect good humour, and we began to talk. I mentioned the tea incident.

"Ignorant people!" he said, dismissing them with a wave of the hand. They ought to have seen my little flag—he had—

and, anyhow, a gentleman was a gentleman, and they were fighting England, not individual Englishmen. Then, reverting to my apologies for my German, he amiably shifted into French, and so we talked until reaching Berlin, when, hoping that I would get what I came for, he shook hands and wished me "Bon voyage!" So you never can tell.

The militarism which any man in the street-car at home can tell you all about, and which Cramb and Bernhardi make so interesting and understandable, is here on the spot not so easy to put one's finger on. Apparently nobody ever heard of Bernhardi, and you might talk with every man you meet for a fortnight without finding any one who could tell you—as any young girl who happens to sit next you at dinner can tell you at home—about the German belief in war as a great blessing, because it is the only way of asserting your own superior ideas over the other man's inferior ideas, and thus getting a world ahead.

People want to smash England, of course, because, as they explain, she brought on the war and is trying to starve them, and they roar with the applause when the lightning-change man at the *Wintergarten* impersonates Hindenburg, because Hindenburg is a grand old scout who is keeping those millions of slovenly Russians from overrunning our tidy, busy, well-ordered Germany. But Treitschke—who was he?

And then, of course, it is not always easy to put one's finger on just what people mean by militarism. Some have objected to militarism because they didn't like the manners of the German waiters at the Savoy, and some because—"Well, those people somehow rub you the wrong way!" It is not universal conscription, because many nations have that, nor the amount spent per capita on soldiers and ships, for we ourselves spend almost as much as the Germans, and the French even more.

One of our old-school cattlemen, used to shooting all the game, cutting all the timber, and using all the water he wanted to, would doubtless say, without seeing a soldier, that it was "their damned police!" No, when people think they are

92

talking about German militarism, they are quite as likely to be talking about the way German faces are made or about German collectivism—the uncanny ability Germans have for taking orders, for team-work, for turning every individual energy into the common end.

One may, however, run across a certain feeling toward war, quite local and unconscious, yet very different from the French love of *"gloire"* and the English keenness for war as a sort of superior fox-hunting or football. You are, let us say, watching one of the musical comedies which the war has inspired.

The curtain rises on a darkened stage, through whose blackness you presently discover, twinkling far below, as if you were looking down from an aeroplane, the lights of Paris, the silver thread of the Seine and its bridges. There is a faint whirring, and two faces emerge vaguely from the dark—the hero and heroine swinging along in a Taube. And as they fly they sing a wistful little waltz song, a sort of cradle song: *"Ich glau-u-be . . . Ich glau-u-be Da oben fliegt . . . 'ne Taube . . ."* They are thinking, so the song runs, that there is a Taube overhead; it has flown here out of its German nest, and let's hope it will not let anything fall on them. And, as they sing, the young man makes a motion with his hand, there is a sort of glow-worm flash, and a few seconds later, away down there among the Paris roofs a puff of red smoke and fire. The illusion is perfect, and the audience is enchanted—that ride through the velvet night, so still, so quaint, so roguish in its way, and the flash far below, that has flung some unsuspecting citizen on the cobblestones like a bundle of old rags.

And, whirring gently, the Taube sails on through the night: *'Ich glaube. . . Da oben fliegt Ich glaube. . . 'ne Taube'*

Again the glow-worm flash, and a moment later, over on the left bank, not far from the Luxembourg, apparently, another of those eloquent little puffs of fire. The crowd is as delighted as children would be with bursting soap-bubbles.

Or we are, let us say, at *"Woran Wir Denken"* ("What We're Thinking Of") with delightful music and such verses as we rarely enough hear in musical comedies at home. In the spot-light there is a square young man dressed in a metallic coat and conical helmet, so as to suggest the famous forty-two-centimetre shell—the shell which makes a hole like a cellar and smashed the Belgian forts as if an earthquake had struck them. And singing with him an exquisite, nun-like creature in a dove-coloured robe, typifying the Taube. They are singing to each other:

I am delicate and slender
And made for the salon. . .

And I am the biggest smasher
In all the present season. . .

High up above the clouds
I fly at heart's desire. . .

And I'm a child of Krupp's,
Whom nobody knew about. . .

I fly, trackless as a breath. . .
I slash on with smoke and roar. . .

They are in love with each other, you see, the Taube and the forty-two-centimetre shell, the "Brummer," or *"Grum-bler,"* as they call it in Germany—could anything be more piquant? You should hear them—the chaste, chic, nun-like Taube and the thick-chested old Brummer, singing that he is her dear old Grumbler and she his soft, swift Dove:

"Suesser, dicker Brummer . . . Du mein Taubchen, zart und flink . . ."

There is a sort of poetry about this—a new sort of poetry about a new sort of war. And it might possibly be proved that such poetry could only come from a people so bred to arms that they do not shrink, even in imagination, from the uses to which arms must be put—a people in love with war, having a mystical feeling for its instruments, such as their remote an-cestors had for their battle-axes and double-edged swords.

I shall not attempt to do this—heaven preserve Americans from being judged by their musical comedies!—and doubtless the children even of our most devoted advocates of universal peace have played with lead cannon and toy soldiers. I merely speak of it, this curious mixture of refinement and brutality, as something which, it struck me, we Americans—who always do everything exactly right—would not have thought of doing in just that way.

Many of the ways of this people are not our ways. You have heard, let us say, of the German parade step, sometimes laughed at as the "goose step" in England and at home. I was lunching the other day with an American military observer, and he spoke of the parade step and the effect it had on him.

"Did you ever see it?" he demanded. "Have you any idea of the moral effect of that step? You see those men marching by, every muscle in their bodies taut and tingling as steel wire, every eye on the Emperor, and when they bring those feet down—*bing! bang!*—the physical fitness it stands for, the unity, determination—why, it's the whole German idea—nothing can stop 'em!'"

"Did you ever see one of these soldiers salute?" Yes, I had seen hundreds of them, and I had been made extremely ill at ease one day in my hotel when a young officer with whom I had started, in the American fashion, comfortably to shake hands suddenly whacked his heels together like a couple of Indian clubs and, stiff as a ramrod, snapped his hand to his cap.

"Did you ever see them salute? They don't do it like a baggage porter—there's nothing servile about it. They square off and bring that hand to their heads and look that officer square in the eyes as if to say: 'Now, damn you, salute me!' And he gets his salute, too—like a man!"

You may not like this salute or you may not like the parade step, but you can be very sure of one thing—that it is not the militarism that pushes civilians off the sidewalk nor permits an officer to strike his subordinate—though these things have happened in Germany—that is holding back England and France and driving the Russian millions out of East Prussia. It is something bigger than that. Peasants and princes, these men are dying gladly, backed up by fitness, discipline, and a passionate unity such as the world has not often seen. This, and not the futile nurses' tales with which the American public permitted itself to be diverted during the early weeks of the war, is what strikes one in Germany. It is a fact, like the Germans being in Belgium, which you have got to face and think about, whether you like it or not. Berlin, February, 1915.

CHAPTER 7

Two German Prison Camps

Visiting a prison camp is somewhat like touching at an island in the night—one of those tropical islands, for instance, whose curious and crowded life shows for an instant as your steamer leaves the mail or takes on a load of deck-hands, and then fades away into a few twinkling lights and the sound of a bell across the water. You may get permission to see a prison camp, but may not stay there, and you are not expected, generally, to talk to the prisoners. You can but walk past those rows of eyes, with all their untold stories, much as you might go into a theatre in the midst of a performance, tramp through the audience and out again.

It is a strange experience and leaves one hoping that somebody—some German shut away in the south of France, one of those quick-eyed Frenchmen in the human zoo at Zossen—is keeping a diary. For while there have always been prison camps, have there ever been—at least, since Rome—such menageries as these! Behind the barbed-wire fence at Zossen—Zossen is one of the prisons near Berlin—there are some fifteen thousand men. The greater number are Frenchmen, droves of those long blue turned-back overcoats and red trousers, flowing sluggishly between the rows of low barracks, Frenchmen of every sort of training and temperament, swept here like dust by the war into common anonymity. I do not remember any picture of the war more curious, and, as it were, uncanny than the first sight of Zossen as our motor came lurching down the muddy road from Berlin—that huge, forgotten eddy, that slough of idle, aimless human beings against the grey March sky, milling slowly round and round in the mud.

But the French are only part of Zossen. There are Russians—shaggy peasants such as we see in cartoons or plays at home, and Mongol Russians with flat faces and almond eyes, who might pass for Chinamen. There are wild-eyed "Turcos" from the French African provinces, chattering untamed Arabs playing leap-frog in front of their German commandant as impudently as street boys back in their native bazaars. There are all the tribes and castes of British Indians—"I've got twenty different kinds of people in my Mohammedan camp," said the lieutenant who was showing me about—squat Gurkhas from the Himalayas, minus their famous knives—tall, black-bearded Sikhs, with the faces of princes. There are even a few lone Englishmen, though most of the British soldiers in this part of Germany are at Doberitz. Whether or not Zossen could be called a "show" camp, it seemed, at any rate, about as well managed as such a place could be. The prisoners were housed in new, clean, one-story barracks; well fed, so far as one could tell from their appearance and that of the kitchens and storerooms; they could write and be written to, and they were compelled to take exercise. The Roman Catholics had one chapel and the Greek Catholics another, and there was an effort to permit Indian prisoners to observe their rules of caste.

As we tramped through barracks where chilly Indians, Russians with broad, high cheek-bones, sensitive-looking Frenchmen with quick, liquid eyes, jumped to their feet and stiffened at attention as the commandant passed, a young officer, who had lived in England before the war and was now acting as interpreter, volunteered his guileless impressions. The Turcos were a bad lot—fighting, gambling, and stealing from each other—there was trouble with some of, them every day. The Russians were dirty, good-natured, and stupid.

The English—well, frankly, he was surprised at their lack of discipline and general unruliness—all except some of the

Indians, and those, he must say, were well-trained—fine fellows and good soldiers. One could surmise the workings of his mind as one thought of the average happy-go-lucky Tommy Atkins, and then came across one of those tall, straight, hawk-eyed Sikhs and saw him snap his heels together and his arms to his sides and stand there like a bronze statue.

It was a dreadful job getting the Frenchmen to take exercise—"they can't understand why any one should want to work, merely to keep himself fit!" Aside from this idiosyncrasy they were, of course, the pleasantest sort of people to get along with. We saw Frenchmen sorting mail in the post-office, painting signs for streets, making blankets out of pasted- together newspapers—everywhere they were treated as intelligent men to whom favours could be granted. And, of course, there was this difference between the French and English of the early weeks of the war—the French army is one of universal conscription like the German, and business men and farmers, writers, singers, and painters were lumped in together. There was one particularly good-looking young man, a medical officer, who flung up his head to attention as we came up.

"He helped us a lot—this man!" said the commandant, and laid his hand on the young man's shoulder. The Frenchman's eyes dilated a trifle and a smile flashed behind rather than across his face—one could not know whether it was gratitude or defiance.

A sculptor who had won a prize at Rome and several other artists had had a room set aside for them to work in. Some were making post-cards, some more ambitious drawings, and in the sculptor's studio was the head of the young doctor we had just seen and an unfinished plaster group for a camp monument. On the wall was a sign in Latin and French— "Unhappy the spirit which worries about the future," a facetious warning that any one who loafed there longer than three minutes was likely to be killed, and the following artistic creed from *La Fontaine:*

"Ne for fans point noire talent. Nous ne ferions rien avec grace. Ja-
mais un lourdaud quoiqu'il fosse, ne saurait passer pour gallant."

("Don't strain your talent or you'll do nothing grace-
fully. The boor won't pass for a gallant gentleman, no
matter what he does.")

The Germans, at different times in their history, have conquered the French and humbly looked up to and imitated
them. Generally speaking, they study and try to understand
the French, and their own intellectuality and idealism are
things French-men might be expected to like or, at any rate,
be interested in. Yet it is one of history's or geography's ironies
that the Frenchman goes on his way, neither knowing nor
wanting to know the blond beasts over the Rhine— *"Jamais
un lourdaud quoiqu'il fasse"*. . . the young sculptor must have
smiled when he tacked that verse on the wall of his prison!

Ruhleben is a race-track on the outskirts of Berlin, and
a detention camp for English civilians. This is quite another sort of menagerie. You can imagine the different kinds
of Englishmen who would be caught in Germany by the
storm—luxurious invalids taking the waters at Baden-Baden;
Gold Coast negro roustabouts from rusty British tramps at
Hamburg; agents, manufacturers, professors, librarians, officers
from Channel boats, students of music and philosophy.

All these luckless civilians—four thousand of them—had
been herded together in the stables, paddock, and stands of
the Ruhleben track. The place was not as suited for a prison
as the high land of Zossen, the stalls with their four bunks
were dismal enough, and the lofts overhead, with little light
and ventilation, still worse.

Some had suffered, semi-invalids, for instance, unable to
get along with the prison rations, but the interesting thing
about Ruhleben was not its discomfort, but the remarkable
fashion in which the prisoners had contrived to make the
best of a bad matter.

The musicians had their instruments sent in and organized an orchestra. The professors began to lecture and teach until now there was a sort of university, with some fifty different classes in the long room under the grand stand. And on the evening when we had the privilege of visiting Ruhleben it was to see a dramatic society present Bernard Shaw's *Androcles and the Lion.*

The play began at six o'clock, for the camp lights are out at nine, and it was in the dusk of another one of Berlin's rainy days, after slithering through the *Tiergarten* and past the endless concrete apartment-houses of Charlottenburg, that our taxicab swung to the right, lurched down the lane of mud, and stopped at the gate of Ruhleben. Inside was a sort of mild morass, overspread with Englishmen—professional-looking men with months-old beards, pink-cheeked young fellows as fresh as if they had just stepped off Piccadilly, men in faded knickerbockers and puttees, men in sailor blue and brass buttons, men with flat caps and cockney accent, one with a Thermos bottle, and crisp "Right you are!"—a good-natured, half-humorous, half-tragic cross-section of the London streets, drifting about here in the German mud.

There were still a few minutes before the play began, and we walked through some of the barracks with the commandant, a tall, bronzed officer of middle age, with gracious manners, one of those Olympian Germans who resemble their English cousins of the same class. Each barrack had its captain, and over these was a camp-captain—formerly an English merchant of Berlin—who went with us on our rounds.

The stables were crowded with bunks and men—like a cattle ship forecastle. One young man, fulfilling doubtless his English ritual of "dressing for dinner," was punctiliously shaving, although it was now practically dark; in another corner the devotee of some system of how to get strong and how to stay so, stripped to the skin, was slowly and with solemn precision raising and lowering a pair of light dumb-bells. Some saluted as private soldiers would; some bowed almost as to a friend, with a cheery *"Guten Abend, Herr Baron!"* There seemed, indeed, to be a very pleasant relation between this gentleman soldier and his gentlemen prisoners, and the camp-captain, lagging behind, told how one evening when they had sung "Elijah," the men had stood up and given three English cheers for the commandant, while his wife, who had come to hear the performance, stood beside him laughing and wiping her eyes.

As you get closer to war you more frequently run across such things. The fighting men kill ruthlessly, because that, they think, is the way to get their business over. But for the most part they kill without hate. For that, in its noisier and more acrid forms you must go back to the men who are not fighting, to the overdriven and under exercised journalists, sizzling and thundering in their swivel-chairs.

The dimly lit hall under the grand stand was already crowded as we were led to our seats on a rostrum facing the stage with the commandant and one of his officers. There was a red draw curtain, footlights made with candles and biscuit tins, and so strung on a wire that at a pull, between the acts, they could be turned on the spectators. A programme had been printed on the camp mimeograph, the camp orchestra was tuning up, and a special overture had been composed by a young gentleman with the beautiful name of Quentin Morvaren.

You will doubtless recall Mr. Shaw's comedy, and the characteristic "realistic" fun he has with his Romans and Christian martyrs, and the lion who, remembering the mild-mannered Androcles, who had once pulled a sliver from his foot, danced out of the arena with him instead of eating him. And you can imagine the peculiarly piquant eloquence given to the dialogue between Mr. Shaw's meek but witty Christians and their might-is-right Roman captors, spoken by British prisoners in the spring of 1915, in a German prison camp before a German commandant sitting up like a statue with his hands on his sword!

The Roman captain was a writer, the centurion a manufacturer, Androcles a teacher of some sort, the call-boy for the fights in the arena a cabin-boy from a British merchant ship, and the tender-hearted lion some genius from the "halls." Even after months of this sodden camp it was possible to find a youth to play Lavinia, with so pretty a face, such a velvet voice, such a pensive womanliness that the flat-capped, ribald young cockneys in the front row blushed with embarrassment. A professor of archaeology, or something, said that he had never seen more accurate reproductions of armour, though this was made but of gilded and silvered cardboard—in short, if Mr. Shaw's fun was ever better brought out by professional players, they must have been very good indeed.

It was an island within an island that night, there under the Ruhleben grand stand—English speech and Irish wit in that German sea. You should have seen the two young patricians drifting in, with the regulation drawl of the Piccadilly "nut"—"I say! He-ah's some Christians—let's chaff them!" The crowd was laughing, the commandant was laughing, the curtain closed in a whirl of applause, one had forgotten there was a war. The applause continued, the players straggled out, faltering back from the parts in which they had forgotten themselves into normal, self-conscious Englishmen. There was a moment's embarrassed pause, then the rattle of a sabre as the tall man in grey-blue rose to his feet.

"Danke Ihnen, meine Herren! Aeusserst nett!" he said briskly. ("Thanks, gentlemen! Very clever indeed!") He turned to us, nodded in stiff soldierly fashion. *"Sehr nett! Sehr nett!"* he said, and led the way out between a lane of Englishmen suddenly become prisoners again.

CHAPTER 8

In the German Trenches at La Bassée

We had come down from Berlin on-one of those excursions which the German General Staff arranges for the military observers and correspondents of neutral countries. You go out, a sort of zoo—our party included four or five Americans, a Greek, an Italian, a diminutive Spaniard, and a tall, preoccupied Swede—under the direction of some hapless officer of the General Staff. For a week, perhaps, you go hurtling through a closely articulated programme almost as personally helpless as a package in a pneumatic tube—night expresses, racing military motors, snap-shots at this and that, down a bewildering vista of long grey capes, heel clickings, stiff bows from the waist, and military salutes. You are under fire one minute, the next shooting through some captured palace or barracks or museum of antiques. At noon the guard is turned out in your honour; at four you are watching distant shell-fire from the Belgian dunes; at eleven, crawling under a down quilt in some French hotel, where the prices of food and wines are fixed by the local German commandant. Everything is done for you—more, of course, than one would wish—the gifted young captain-conductor speaks English one minute, French or Italian the next, gets you up in the morning, to bed at night, past countless sentries and thick-headed guards demanding an *Ausweis*, contrives never to cease looking as if he had stepped from a band-box, and presently pops you into your hotel in Berlin with the curious feeling of never having been away at all.

It isn't, of course, an ideal way of working—not like putting on a hat and strolling out to war, as one sometimes could do in the early weeks in Belgium and France. The front is a big and rather accidental place, however—you can scarcely touch it anywhere without bringing back something to help complete the civilian's puzzle picture of the war. Our moment came in the German trenches before La Bassée, when, with the English so near that you could have thrown a baseball into their trenches, both sides began to toss dynamite bombs at each other.

We had come across to Cologne on the regular night express, shifted to a military train, and so on through Aix, Louvain, Brussels, and by the next morning's train down to Lille. Armentieres was only eight miles away, Ypres fifteen, and a little way to the south Neuve Chapelle, where the English offensive had first succeeded, then been thrown back only a few days before.

Spring had come over night, the country was green, sparkling with canals and little streams, and the few Belgian peasants left were trying to put it in shape for summer. A few were ploughing with horses, others laboriously going over their fields, foot by foot, with a spade; once we passed half a dozen men dragging a harrow. Every tree in this country, where wood is grown like any other crop, was speckled with white spots where branches had been trimmed away, and below the timber was piled—heavy logs for lumber, smaller ones cut into firewood—the very twigs piled as carefully as so many stacks of celery.

So fresh and neat and clean-swept did it seem in that soft sunshine that one forgot how empty it was—so empty and repressed that one awoke startled to see three shaggy farm horses galloping off as the train rolled by, kicking up their heels as if they never had heard of war. It seemed frivolous, almost impertinent, and the *landsturm* officer, leaning in the open window beside me in the passageway, thinking perhaps of his own home across the Rhine, laughed and breathed a deep-chested *"Kolossal!"* We passed Enghien, Leuze, Tournai, all with that curious look of a run-down clock. On the outskirts of one town, half a dozen little children stopped spinning tops in the road to demand tribute from the train. They were pinched little children, with the worried, prematurely old faces of factory children, and they begged insistently, almost irritably, as if payment was long overdue. Good-natured soldiers tossed them chocolate and sausage and slices of buttered *Kriegsbrod*, which they took without thanks, still repeating in a curious jumble of German and French, *"Pfennig venir! Pfennig—Pfennig—Pfennig venir!"*

Two officers from division headquarters were waiting for us in the station at Lille—one, a tall, easy-going young fellow in black motor-gauntlets, who looked as if he might, a few years before, have rowed on some American college crew; the other, in the officers' grey-blue frock overcoat with fur collar, a softer type, with quick, dark eyes and smile, and the pleasant, slightly languid manners of a young legation secretary.

We had just time to glance at the broken windows in the station roof, the two or three smashed blocks around it, and be hurried to that most empty of places—a modern city hotel without any guests—when three grey military motor-cars, with the imperial double eagle in black on their sides, whirled up. The officers took the lead, our happy family distributed itself in the others, and with cut-outs drumming, a soldier beside each chauffeur blowing a warning, and an occasional gay *"Ta-ta ta-ta!"* on a silver horn, we whirled out into the open country.

We passed a church with a roof smashed by an aeroplane a few days before—and caught at the same time the first *"B-r-r-rurm!"* from the cannonading to the west—a supply-train, an overturned motor-van, and here and there packed ammunition wagons and guns. Presently, in the lee of a little brick farmhouse a short distance from the village of Aubers, we alighted, and, with warnings that it was better not to keep too close together, walked a little farther down the road. Not a man was in sight, nor a house, nor gun, not even a trench, yet we were, as a matter of fact, in the middle of a battle-field. From where we stood it was not more than a mile to the English trenches and only two miles to Neuve Chapelle; and even as we stood there, from behind us, from a battery we had passed without seeing, came a crash and then the long spinning roar of something milling down aisles of air, and a far-off detonation from the direction of Neuve Chapelle.

Tssee-ee-rr. . . Bong! over our heads from the British lines came an answering wail, and in the field, a quarter of a mile beyond us, there was a geyser of earth, and slowly floating away a greenish-yellow cloud of smoke. From all over the horizon came the wail and crash of shells—an "artillery duel," as the official reports call it, the sort of thing that goes on day after day.

Somebody wanted to walk on to the desolate village which raised its smashed walls a few hundred yards down the road. The tall young officer said that this might not be done—it would draw the enemy's fire, and as if to accent this advice there was a sudden Bang! and the corner of one of the houses we were looking at collapsed in a cloud of dust.

Under these wailing parabolas, swinging invisibly across from horizon to horizon, we withdrew behind the farmhouse for lunch—sandwiches, frankfurters kept hot in a fireless cooker, and red wine—when far overhead a double-decker English aeroplane suddenly sailed over us. It seemed to be about six thousand feet above us, so high that the sound of its motors was lost, and its speed seemed but a lazy, level drifting across the blue. Did it take those three motor-cars and those little dots for some reconnoitring division commander and his staff? Aeroplanes not only drop bombs, but signal to their friends; there was an uncomfortable amount of artillery scattered about the country, and we watched with peculiar interest the movements of this tiny hawk.

But already other guns, as hidden as those that might be threatening us, had come, as it were, to the rescue. A little ball of black smoke suddenly puffed out behind that sailing bird, and presently a sharp crack of a bursting shrapnel shell came down to our ears. Another puff of smoke, closer, one in front, above, below. They chased round him like swallows. In all the drab hideousness of modern warfare there is nothing so airy, so piquant, so pretty as this.

Our bird and his pursuers disappeared in the north; over the level country to the south floated a German observation balloon, and presently we rumbled over a canal and through the shattered village of La Bassée. La Bassée had been in the war despatches for months, and looked it. Its church, used as a range-finder, apparently, was a grey honeycomb from which each day a few shells took another bite. Roofs were torn off, streets strewn with broken glass and brick; yet it is in such houses and their cellars that soldiers fighting in the trenches in a neighbourhood like this come back for a rest, dismal little islands which mask the armies one does not see at the front.

The custom of billeting soldiers in houses—possible in territory so closely built up—adds to the vagueness of modern warfare. Americans associate armies with tents. When we mobilized ten thousand men at San Antonio, you were in a city of soldiers. Ten thousand men in this war disappear like water in sand. Some of them are in the trenches, some in villages like this, out of the zone of heavier fire, but within a few minutes' walk of their work, so to speak. Others are distributed farther back, over a zone perhaps ten miles deep, crisscrossed with telephone-wires, and so arranged with assembling stations, reserves, and sub-reserves that the whole is a closely knit organism all the way up to the front. There is continual movement in this body—the men in the trenches go back after forty-eight hours to the near-by village, after days or weeks of this service, back clear out of the zone of fire; fresh men come up to take their places, and so on. All you see as you whirl through is a sentry here, a soldier's head there at a second-story window, a company shuffling along a country road.

Women watched us from the doors of La Bassée—still going on living here, somehow, as human beings will on the volcano's very edge—and children were playing in the street. Husbands gone, food gone, the country swept bare—why did they not go, too? But where? Here, at any rate, there was a roof overhead—until a shell smashed it—and food soldiers were glad to share. There must be strange stories to tell of these little islands on the edge of the battle, where the soldiers who are going out to be killed, and the women whose husbands, perhaps, are going to help kill them, huddle together for a time, victims of a common storm.

We whirled past them down the road a bit, then walked up a gentle slope to the right. Over this low ridge, from the English trenches, rifle-bullets whistled above our heads. In the shelter of a brick farmhouse a dozen or so German soldiers were waiting, after trench service, to go back to La Bassée. They were smallish, mild-looking men, dusted with the yellow clay in which they had burrowed—clothes, boots, faces, and hands—-until they looked like millers.

"How are the English?" some one asked. "Do they know how to shoot?" A weary sort of hoot chorused out from the dust-covered men.

"*Gut genug!*" they said. The house was strewn with rusty cartridge clips and smashed brick. We waited while our chaperon brought the battalion commander—a mild-faced little man, more like a school-teacher than a soldier—and it was decided that, as the trenches were not under fire at the moment, we might go into them. He led the way into the communication trench—a straight-sided winding ditch, shoulder-deep, and just wide enough to walk in comfortably. Yellow clay was piled up overhead on either side, and there was a wooden sidewalk. The ditch twisted constantly as the trenches themselves do, so as not to be swept by enfilading fire, and after some hundreds of yards of this twisting, we came to the: first-line trench and the men's dugouts.

It was really a series of little caves, with walls of solid earth and roofs of timber and sand-bags, proof against almost anything but the plunging flight of heavy high-explosive shells. The floors of these caves were higher than the bottom of the trench, so that an ordinary rain would not flood them, and covered with straw. And they were full of men, asleep, working over this and that—from one came the smell of frying ham. The trench twisted snakelike in a general north and south direction, and was fitted every few feet with metal firing-shields, loopholed for rifles and machine guns. In each outer curve facing the enemy a firing platform, about waist-high, had been cut in the earth, with similar armoured port-holes.

The Germans had been holding this trench for three months, and its whole outer surface was frosted a sulphurous yellow from the smoke of exploded shells. Shrapnel-casings and rusted shell-noses were sticking everywhere in the clay, and each curve exposing a bit of surface to the enemy was honeycombed with bullet holes. In one or two places sand-bags, caves, and all had been torn out.

Except for an occasional far-off detonation and the more or less constant and, so to speak, absent-minded cracking of rifles, a mere keeping awake, apparently, and letting the men in the opposite trenches know you are awake, the afternoon was peaceful. Pink-cheeked youngsters in dusty *Feldgrau*, stiffened and clapped their hands to their sides as officers came in sight, heard English with an amazement not difficult to imagine, and doubtless were as anxious to talk to these strange beings from a world they'd said good-by to, as we were to talk to them.

At one of the salient angles, where a platform had been cut, we stopped to look through a periscope: one cannot show head or hand above the trench, of course, without drawing fire, and looks out of this curious shut-in world as men do in a submarine—just as the lady in the old-fashioned house across from us in New York sits at her front window and sees in a slanting mirror everything that happens between her and the Avenue. We had not been told just where we were going (in that shut-in ditch one had no idea), and there in the mirror, beyond some straggling barbed wire and perhaps seventy-five yards of ordinary grass, was another clay bank—the trenches of the enemy! Highlanders, Gurkhas, Heaven knows what—you could see nothing—but—over there was England!

So this was what these young soldiers had come to—here was the real thing. Drums beat, trumpets blare, the *Klingelspiel* jingles at the regiment's head, and with flowers in your helmet, and your wife or sweetheart shouldering your rifle as far as the station—and you should see these German women marching out with their men!—you go marching out to war. You look out of the windows of various railway trains, then they lead you through a ditch into another ditch, and there, across a stretch of mud which might be your own back yard, is a clay bank, which is your enemy. And one morning at dawn you climb over your ditch and run forward until you are cut down. And when you have, so to speak, been thrown in the stream for the others to cross over, and the trench is taken, and you are put out of the way under a few inches of French earth, then, perhaps, inasmuch as experience shows that it isn't worth while to try to keep a trench unless you have captured more than three hundred yards of it, the battalion retires and starts all over again.

We had walked on down the trenches, turned a bend where two trees had been blown up and flung across it, when there was a dull report near by, followed a moment later by a tremendous explosion out toward the enemy's trench. *"Unsere Minen!"* ("One of our bombs!") laughed a young soldier beside me, and a crackle of excitement ran along the trench. These bombs were cylinders, about the size of two baking-powder tins joined together, filled with dynamite and exploded by a fuse. They were thrown from a small mortar with a light charge of powder, just sufficient to toss them over into the opposite trench. The Germans knew what was coming, and they were laughing and watching in the direction of the English trenches.

"Vorsicht! Vorsicht!"

There was a dull report and at the same moment something shot up from the English trenches and, very clear against the western sky, came flopping over and over toward us like a bottle thrown over a barn.

"Vorsicht! Vorsicht!" It sailed over our heads behind the trench, there was an instant's silence, and then *"Whong!"* and a pile of dirt and black smoke was flung in the air. Again there was a dull report, and we sent a second back—this time behind their trench—and again— *"Vorsicht! Vorsicht!"*—they sent an answer back. Four times this was repeated. A quainter way of making war it would be hard to imagine. They might have been boys playing "anty-over" over the old house at home.

Bombs of this sort have little penetrating power. If thrown in the open they go off on the surface much like a gigantic firecracker. They are easy to dodge by daylight, when you can see them coming, but thrown at night as part of a general bombardment, including shrapnel and heavy explosive shells, or exploding directly in the trench, they must be decidedly unpleasant.

The bomb episode had divided us, two officers and myself waiting on one side of the bend in the trench toward which the bombs were thrown, the others going ahead. It was several minutes before I rejoined them, and I did not learn until we were outside that they had been taken to another periscope through which they saw a space covered with English dead. There were, perhaps, two hundred men in khaki lying there, they said, some hanging across the barbed-wire entanglements at the very foot of the German trench, just as they had been thrown back in the attack which had succeeded at Neuve Chapelle. Several Englishmen had got clear into the German trench before they were killed. Here was another example of the curious localness of this dug-in warfare, that one could pass within a yard or two of such a battle-field and not know even that it was there.

By another communication trench we returned to the little house. The sun was low by this time and the line of figures walking down the-road toward the automobiles in its full light. Perhaps the glasses of some British lookout picked us up—at any rate the whisper of bullets became uncomfortably frequent and near, and we had just got to the motors when— *Tssee—ee—rr. . . BONG!* a shell crashed into the church of La Bassée, only three hundred yards in front of us.

Before ours had started, another, flying on a lower trajectory, it seemed, shrieked over our heads and burst beside the road so close to the first motor that it threw mud into it. Apparently we were both observed and sought after, and as the range of these main highways, up and down which troops and munitions pass, is perfectly known, there was a rather uncomfortable few minutes ere we had whirled through La Bassée, with the women watching from their doors—no racing motors for them to run away in!—and down the tree-arched road to ordinary life again.

No, not exactly ordinary, though we ourselves went back to a comfortable hotel, for the big city of Lille, which had shown trolley-cars and a certain amount of animation earlier in the day, was now, at dusk, like a city of the dead. The chambermaid shrugged her shoulders with something about a *"punition"* and, when asked why they were punished, said that some French prisoners had been brought through Lille a week or two before, and "naturally, the people shouted *'Vive la France!'*"

So the military governor, as we observed next morning in a proclamation posted on the blank wall across the street, informing the inhabitants that they "apparently did not, as yet, understand the seriousness of the situation," ordered the city to pay a 'fine of five hundred thousand francs, and the citizens for two weeks to go within doors at sundown and not stir abroad before seven next morning. Another poster warned people that two English aviators had been obliged to come down within the city, that they were still at large, and that any one who hid them or helped them escape would be punished with death, in addition to which the commune would be punished, too.

It was through black and silent streets, therefore, that our troop was led from the hotel in which we were lodged to one in which we dined. Here everything was warm and light and cheerful enough. Boyish lieutenants, with close-clipped heads after the German fashion, were telling each other their adventures, and here and there were older officers, who looked as if war had worn them a bit, and they had come here to forget for a moment over a bottle of champagne and the talk of some old friend. The bread was black and hard, but the other food as usual in France, with wine plenty and cheap, and even some of the round-shelled, coppery oysters—captured somehow, in spite of blockades and bombardments—just up from Ostend. It was bedtime when we emerged into the black streets again, to discover, with something like surprise, a sky full of stars and a pale new moon.

The rest of that civilian tour was very civil, indeed—a sort of loop-the-loop of Belgium, with scarce a pause for breath. You can imagine _that cosmopolitan menagerie trooping next morning up the stone stairs of the castle of the Counts of Flanders in Ghent; at noon inspecting old lace in Bruges, and people coming home from church, the German guard changing, and the German band playing in the central square; at two o'clock lunching in one of the Ostend summer hotels, now full of German officers; at four pausing for a tantalizing moment in Middelkerk, while the German guns we were not allowed to see on the edge of the town were banging away at the British at Nieuport down the beach. Next day Brussels— out to Waterloo, in a cloud of dust—the Congo Museum— the King's palace at Laaken, an old servitor with a beard like the tall King Leopold's leading these vandals through it, and looking unutterable things—a word with the civil governor, here—a charming lunch at a barracks, there—in short, a wild flight behind the man with the precious *"Ausweis."*

We saw and sometimes met a good many German officers in a rather familiar way. Many of the younger men reminded one of our university men at home; several of the older men resembled their well-set-up English cousins. This seemed particularly true of the navy, which has acquired a type—lean, keen, firm-lipped young men, with a sense of humour—entirely different from the German often seen in cafes, with no back to his head, and a neck overflowing his collar. Particularly interesting were those who, called back 'into uniform from responsible positions in civil life, were attacking, as if building for all time, the appallingly difficult and delicate task of improvising a government for a complex modern state, and winning the tolerance, if not the co-operation, of a conquered people confident that their subjection was but for the day.

Our progress everywhere was down a continuous aisle of heel-clickings and salutes. Sometimes, when we had to pass through three rows of passport examiners between platform and gate, these formalities seemed rather excessive. In the grenadier barracks in Brussels we had been taken through sleeping-rooms, cool storerooms with their beer barrels and loops of sausages—"all made by the regiment"—and were just entering the kitchen when a giant of a man, seeing his superior officers, snapped stiff as a ramrod and, as it is every German subordinate's duty to do, bellowed out his *"Meldung"*—who and what the men in his room were, and that they were going to have meat and noodle soup for dinner.

No Frenchman, Englishman, or American could be taught, let alone achieve of his own free will, the utter self-forgetfulness with which this vast creature, every muscle tense, breathing like a race-horse, roared, or rather exploded:

"Herr Hauptmann! Mannschafts-Kuche-desten-Landwehr-Regiments! Belegt-mit-einem-Unter-offizier-und-zehn-Mann! Wir essen heute Suppe mit Nudeln und Fleisch! Zu Befehl!"

He had stepped down a century and a half from the grenadiers of the Great Frederic, and even our hosts may have smiled. It was different with the soldiers' salute, or the ordinary coming to attention, which we saw repeated scores of times a day. Whatever men might be doing, however awkward or inconvenient it might be, whether any one saw them or not, they stopped short at the sight of these long, grey-blue

115

coats and stiffened, chin up, eyes on their superior, hands at their sides. If they were talking, they became silent; if laughing, their faces smoothed out, and into their eyes came an expression which, when you have seen it repeated hundreds of times, you will not forget. It is a look of seriousness, self-forgetfulness, of almost religious devotion, not to the individual, but to the idea for which he stands. I saw a soldier half-dressed, through a barracks window under which we passed, sending after his officer, who did not even see him, that same look, the look of a man who has just volunteered to charge the enemy's trench, or who sees nothing absurd in saying the Germans fear God and nothing else in the world!

One seemed to see the soul of Germany, at least of this "great time," in these men's eyes. The Belgian soul we did not see much of, but there came glimpses of it now and then.

In Antwerp we stopped in a little café for a cup of chocolate. It was a raw, cheerless morning, with occasional snowflakes whipping by on the damp north wind, the streets were all but deserted, and in the room that used to be full of smoke and talk there were only empty tables, and you could see your breath.

A man was scrubbing behind the bar, and a pale girl in black came out from behind the cashier's counter to make our chocolate. It was good chocolate, as Antwerp chocolate is likely to be, and as we were getting ready to go out again I asked her how things were. She glanced around the room and answered that they used to have a good business here, but the good times were gone— *"les beaux jours sont partis."* Two others drifted over and asked questions about the bombardment. She answered politely enough, with the air of one to whom it was an old story now—she had left on the second day, when the building across the way was smashed, and walking, catching rides, stumbling along with the other thousands, had got into Holland. As to why the city fell so quickly—she pulled her shawl about her shoulders and murmured that there were things people did not know, if they did they did not talk about them.

And the Germans—how were they? They had no com-

plaints to make, the girl said; the Germans were well behaved— *"tres correct."* Possibly, then—it was our young Italian
who put the question—the Belgians would just as soon. . . I
did not catch the whole sentence, but all at once something
flashed behind that non-committal cafe proprietress's mask.
"Moi, je suis fiere d'etre Belge!" said the girl, and as she spoke
you could see the colour slowly burning through her pale
face and neck—she was proud to be a Belgian—they hoped,
that one could keep, and there would come a day, we could
be sure of that— *"un jour de revanche!"*

But business is business, and people who run cafes must, as
every one knows, not long indulge in the luxury of personal
feelings. The officers turned up their fur collars, and we but-
toned up our coats, and she was sitting behind the counter,
the usual little woman in black at the cafe desk, as we filed
out. Our captain paused as we passed, gave a stiff little bow
from the waist, touched his cap gallantly, and said: "Bon jour,
mademoiselle!" And the girl nodded politely, as café propri-
etresses should, and murmured, blank as the walls in the Antwerp streets: "Bon jour, monsieur!"

117

CHAPTER 9

The Road To Constantinople

RUMANIA AND BULGARIA

The express left Budapest in the evening, all night and all next day rolled eastward across the Hungarian plain, and toward dusk climbed up through the cool Carpathian pines and over the pass into Rumania.

Vienna and the waltzes they still were playing there, Berlin and its iron exaltation, slow-rumbling London—all the West and the war as we had thought of it for months was, so to speak, on the other side of the earth. We were on the edge of the East now, rolling down into the Balkans, into that tangle of races and revenges out of which the first spark of the war was flung.

Since coffee that morning the lonely train had offered nothing more nourishing than the endless Hungarian wheat-fields, with their rows of peasants, men and women, working comfortably together, and rows of ploughs creeping with almost incredible leisure behind black water-buffalo cattle; but as we rolled down into Predeal through the rain, there, at last, in the dim station lamps, glittered the brass letters and brown paint of the *Compagnie Internationale des Wagons Lits*—and something to eat.

The cars of this beneficent institution—survivors of a Europe that once seemed divided between tourists and hotel-keepers—out dash the most dashing war correspondents, insinuate themselves wherever civilians are found at all, and once aboard you carry your oasis with you as you do in a

Pullman through our own alkali and sage-brush. The steward (his culture is intensive, though it may not extend beyond the telegraph- poles, and includes the words for food in every dialect between Ostend and the Golden Horn) had just brought soup and a bottle of thin Hungarian claret, when the other three chairs at my table were taken by a Rumanian family returning from a holiday in Budapest—an urbane gentleman of middle age, a shy little daughter, and a dark-eyed wife, glittering with diamonds, who looked a little like Nazimova.

"*Monsieur* is a stranger?" said the Rumanian presently, speaking in French as Rumanians are likely to do, and we began to talk war. I asked—a question the papers had been asking for weeks—if Rumania would be drawn into it.

"Within ten days we shall be in," he said.

"And on which side?"

"Oh!" he smiled, "against Austria, of course!"

That was in April. When I came through Rumania three months later soldiers were training everywhere in the hot fields; Bucharest was full of officers, the papers and cafes still buzzing with war talk. Rumania was still going in, but since the recapture of Lemberg and the Russian retreat the time was not so sure—not, it seemed, "until after the harvest" at any rate.

I asked the Rumanian what he thought about Italy. "Italy began as a coquette. She will end"—he made the gesture of counting money into his hand—"she will end as a cocotte." He waved a forefinger in front of his face.

"*Elle n'est plus vierge!*" he said.

The wife demurred. Italy was poor and little, she must needs coquette. After all, *il faut vivre*—one must live.

Something was said of America and the feeling there, and the wife announced that she would like of all things to see America, but—she did not wish to go there with her husband. I suggested that she come with me—an endeavour to rise to the Rumanian mood which was received with tolerant urbanity by her husband, and by the lady who looked like Nazimova with very cheering expressions of assent.

"When you return from Constantinople," she flashed back as they left the table, "don't forget!"

These were the first Rumanians I had met. They were amiable, they spoke French—it almost seemed as if they had heard the tales that are usually told of their little capital, and were trying to play the appropriate introduction to Bucharest.

Here it is, this little nation, only a trifle larger than the State of Pennsylvania, a half-Latin island in an ocean of Magyars and Slavs. On the north is Russia, on the south the grave and stubborn Bulgars (Slav at any rate in speech), on the west Hungary, and here, between the Carpathians and the Black Sea, this Frenchified remnant of the empire of ancient Rome. Their speech when it is not French is full of Latin echoes, and a Rumanian, however mixed his blood, is as fond of thinking himself a lineal and literal descendant of the Roman colonists as a New Englander is of ancestors in the Mayflower. At the Alhambra in Bucharest next evening, after the cosmopolite artistes had done then-perfunctory turns and returned to their street clothes and the audience, to begin the more serious business of the evening, the movie man in the gallery threw on the screen—no, not some military hero nor the beautiful Queen whose photograph you will remember, but the head of the Roman Emperor Trajan! And the listless crowd, drowsing cynically in its tobacco smoke, broke into obedient applause, just as they would at home at the sight of the flag or a picture of the President.

Bucharest, like all the capitals of Spanish America, is another "little Paris," but the Rumanians, possibly because unhampered by sombre Spanish tradition or perhaps any traditions at all, succeed more completely in borrowing the vices and escaping the virtues of the great capital they are supposed to imitate. It would be more to the point to call Bucharest a little Buenos Aires. There is much the same showiness; a similar curious mixture of crudeness and luxury. But Buenos Aires is one of the world's great cities, and always just beyond the asphalt you can somehow feel the *pampa* and its endless cattle and wheat. The Rumanian capital is a town of some three hundred thousand people in a country you could lose in the Argentine, and there is nothing, comparatively speaking, to offset its light-mindedness, to suggest realities behind all this life of *patisserie*.

You should see the Calea Vittorei on one of these warm summer evenings between five and eight. It is a narrow strip of asphalt winding through the centre of the town, with a tree-shaded drive at one end, and the hotels, sidewalk cafes, and fashionable shops at the other, and up and down this narrow street, in motors, in open *victorias* driven by Russian coachmen in dark-blue velvet gowns reaching to their heels, all Bucharest crowds to gossip, flirt, and see.

Down the centre in the open carriages flows a stream of women—and many look like Nazimova—social distinctions so ironed out with enamel, paint, and powder that almost all might be café *chantant* singers or dressmakers' marionettes. Some cities have eagles on their crests, and some volcanoes. If you were going to design a postage-stamp for Bucharest, it struck me that the natural thing would be a woman in the corner of an open *victoria*—after seeing scores of them all alike, you feel as though you could do it in a minute: one slashing line for the hat, two coal-black holes, and a dash of carmine in a patch of marble white, and a pair of silk-covered ankles crossed and pointed in a way that seems Parisian enough after one has become used to the curious boxes in which women enclose their feet in Berlin. Coming up from Bulgaria, which is not unlike coming from Idaho or Montana; or from Turkey, where women as something to be seen of men in public do not exist; or even across from the simple plains of Hungary, these enamelled orchids flowing forever down the asphalt seem at the moment to sum up the place—they are Bucharest.

Officers in light blue, in mauve and maroon—mincing butterflies, who look as if an hour's march in the sun would send them to the hospital, ogle them from the sidewalk. Along with them are many young bloods out of uniform, barbered and powdered like chorus men made up for their work. You will see few young men in Europe with whom the notion of general conscription and the horrors of war can be associated with less regret.

Streams of more frugal nymphs, without *victorias* but with the same rakish air, push along with the sidewalk crowd, hats pinned like a wafer over one ear, coiffures drawn trimly up from powdered necks. Waiters scurry about; the café tables, crowded in these days with politicians, amateur diplomats, spies, ammunition agents, Heaven knows what, push out on the sidewalk. The people on the sidewalk are crowded into the street, motors honk, hoofs clatter, the air is filled with automobile smoke, the smoke carries the smell of cigarettes and coffee and women's perfumes—it is *"Bucharest joyeux!"*

Some French music-hall singer—when I came through it was Miss Nita-Jo—will tell you all about it at one of the open-air theatres in the evening. All about the people you bump into in this sunset promenade—

"Des gens d'la haute, des petits crevés, Des snobs, des sportsmans, des coquets, Les noctambules, les vieux noceurs, Les grandes cocottes— oui! tous en choeur. . ."—all about Capsa's, which, though but a little pastry shop and tea-room, is as seriously regarded in Bucharest as Delmonico's or the Blackstone, which is, of course, with dreadful seriousness (to see one of the gilded youths of Bucharest enter Capsa's at five-thirty, solemnly devour a large chocolate éclair, and as solemnly stalk out again, is an experience itself), and all about the politicians and the men who are running things. Everything is in miniature, you see, in a little nation like this, which, although only as large as one of our smaller States, has a King and court, diplomats, and army, and foreign policy. All in the family, so to speak, and the chanteuse will sing amusing verses about the prime minister as if she really knew what he was going to do, and, curiously enough—for things are sometimes very much in the family, indeed, in these little capitals—maybe she does know!

Of course the Calea Vittorei is not Rumania, though a good deal more so than Fifth Avenue is America; nor are the officers posing there those who would have much to do with directing the army if Rumania went to war. Ten minutes away from the city limits and you might be riding through the richest farming country in Wisconsin or Illinois: hour after hour of corn and wheat, orchards, hops, and vineyards, cultivated by peasants who, though most of them have no land and little education, at least look care-free, and dress themselves in exceedingly pleasing homespun linen, hand-embroidered clothes. Then higher land, and hills as thick with the towers of oil-wells as western Pennsylvania, and, just before you cross into Hungary, the cool pines of the Carpathians and the villas of Sinaia, the summer home of the court, the diplomats, and the people one does not see very often, perhaps, in the afternoon parade.

It is a pleasant and a rich little country. You can easily understand why its ruling class should love it, and, set apart from their Slav and Magyar neighbours by speech and temperament, want to gather all Rumanians under one flag and push that, too, into its place in the sun.

And this, of course, is Rumania's time—the time of all these little Balkan nations, which have been bullied and flattered in turn by the powers that need them now, and cut up and traded about like so much small change.

Rumania wants the province of Bessarabia on her eastern border, a strip of which Russia once took away; she wants the Austrian province of Bukowina and the Hungarian *banat* of Temesvar on the west, but most of all the pine forests and the people of Transylvania, just over the divide—you cross it coming from Budapest—largely Rumanian in speech and sympathy, though a province of Hungary. As the Rumanians figure it out, they once stood astride the Carpathians—"a cheval" ("on horseback"), as they say—and so, they feel, they must and should stand now.

We are a nation of fourteen million souls—six less than

Hungary, but a homogeneous state, solidly based. Our soil gives us minerals and fuel and almost suffices for our needs. Our people are one of the most prolific in the world and certainly not the least intelligent. We have behind us a continuity of national existence lacking in other nations in this quarter of the globe. In our modern epoch we have assimilated French culture with indisputable success, and have given in every field proof of a great faculty of adaptability and progress. We can become the most important second-class power in Europe the day after the war stops; in fifty years, when our population will have passed twenty-five millions, a great power. We shall be a nation content with our lot, and for that reason a factor for peace. A greater Rumania responds not only to our ideas but to the interests of Europe. The Magyars have had every chance, and they have lost. It is now our turn.

This is a characteristic editorial paragraph from *La Roumanie*, which is the voice of Mr. Take Ionesco, who, more than anybody else, is the voice of those who want war. Once in the government, but at the moment out of it, Mr. Ionesco keeps up a continuous bombardment of editorials and speeches, and with his vigour, verve, and facility reminds one a bit, though a younger man, of Clemenceau and his *L'Homme Enchaîné*. Rich, well-informed, daring, and clever, with a really fascinating gift of expression, he will talk to you in French, English (his wife is English), Rumanian—I don't know how many other languages—about anything you wish, always with the air of one who knows. We have no such adventurous statesmen, or statesmen-adventurers, at home—men who have all the wires of European diplomacy at their finger ends; look at people, including their own, in the aggregate, without any worry over the "folks at home"; know what they want much better than they do, and to get it for them are quite ready to send a few hundred thousand to their death.

Mr. Ionesco writes a long, double-leaded editorial every day, and very often he prints with it the speech, or speeches, he made the night before. In a time like this, he says, those of his way of thinking can't say too much; they must be "like the French Academicians, who never stop writing." Now and then, in the intervals of fanning the sparks of war, he takes his readers behind the scenes of European politics, of which he knows about as much, perhaps, as any one.

I arrived in Paris the 31st of December, 1912, in the evening. M. Poincaré received me the 1st of January, at half past eight o'clock in the morning—an absurd hour in Paris. But I had to go to London in the afternoon, and M. Poincaré to the Elysee at ten o'clock for the felicitations of the New Year. I asked M. Poincaré for the support of France in our difficulties with Bulgaria. M. Poincaré said. . . I said. . . and later events proved that I was right.

He is always sure of himself, like this—no doubts, no half-truths, everything clear and irresistible. I went to see Mr. Ionesco one evening in Bucharest—a porte-cochere opening into a big stone city house, an anteroom with a political secretary and several lieutenants, and presently a quiet, richly furnished library, and Mr. Ionesco himself, a polished gentleman of continental type, full of animation and sophisticated charm, bowing from behind a heavy library table.

The room, the man, the facile, syllogistic sentences in which it was established that Austria-Hungary was already moribund, that Germany could never win, that Rumania must go in with the Entente—it was like the first scene from some play of European society and politics: one of those smooth, hard, swiftly moving things the Parisian Bernstein might have written.

Across it I couldn't help seeing the Berlin I had just left, and people standing in line with their sandwiches at six o'clock to get into the opera or theatre—the live human beings behind that abstraction "Germany." And I said that it seemed unfortunate that two peoples with so many apparent grounds of contact as the Germans and French must so misunderstand each other. Their temperament and culture were different, to be sure, but they were both idealistic, sentimental people, to whom things of the mind and spirit were important.

It seemed particularly unfortunate that everything should be done to force them apart instead of bringing them together.

Mr. Ionesco listened with some impatience. Unfortunate, no doubt, but what do you wish? War itself is unfortunate—we must take the world as it is. No, they were with France and down with the Germans. France conquered meant the end of Rumania, subservience to Austria; France victorious, freedom, fresh air.

He gave me a copy of a speech in which he gladly admitted that he was a "responsible factor." People talked of going slow and sparing blood. Well, they might get something by sitting still, even become a great country, but they could never become a great nation. It was not territory and population they wanted, but the sword of Rumania to join in remaking the map of Europe. When the delegates gathered around the green table, they did not want the one from Rumania, as he was at the Congress of Berlin, only able to make visits to chancelleries. He must go in the same door with them, and say: "In proportion to my population, I have shed as much blood as you."

He had always regretted not having children, never so much as to-day; but if he had a dozen sons, and knew that all of them would fall in the war, he would not be cast down. Even if the territory they wished could be occupied by a simple act of gendarmerie—he would say no—they must enter Budapest itself (it is only twenty-four hours' railway journey from Bucharest!)—not till then would Austria admit Rumania's superiority. People accused him of working for himself. Who was Take Ionesco in comparison with the fate of a race? As for ambition, well, he had one, and only one—he wanted to see the Rumanian tricolour floating from Buda palace, and before he died to know the moment in which he could pass before his eyes the eighteen hundred years of Rumanian history from the arrival of Trajan at Severin to the entry of Ferdinand at Budapest, and cry: "Now, Lord, let thy servant go in peace, for mine eyes have seen the saving of my race!"

The Rumanian tricolour was no nearer Buda palace when

I returned several months later, but Mr. Ionesco was no less hot for war. Even if Germany won, he said, they still should go in, because they would at least keep their own and Germany's respect. "Go to war?"—the phrase was inexact. "We have been at war for eleven months, only others are firing at us, but we are not firing at them. We are in a war that will decide our existence, but the soldiers dying to defend our rights, instead of being our soldiers, are soldiers of the Allies. The Allies will win, but if any one thinks that, having won without us, they will have won for us, he must be mad. Their victory without us may preserve our material life, but it will never save our moral life nor that of future generations."

Mr. Ionesco and those who agree with him belong, it will be observed, with the romanticists—they are for the bright face of danger, great stakes, and, win or lose, putting all to the touch. Those who did not agree with them were men without souls, hagglers and traders, as if a nation could figure out the number of cannon-shots and prisoners, and go where the going's good! It made interesting reading as you sat at one of the café tables, with the crowd flowing by and the five-o'clock papers coming fresh from the press. The other side—and it included the King and most of the government, inasmuch as Rumania had not yet gone to war—had the more difficult task of making caution interesting. In their editorials and speeches Ionesco and his followers were jingoes trying to drive the nation to a Rumanian Sedan.

"A people is great, not only for its numbers of soldiers, but for its civilization, its artists, and intellectuals. A nation militarized is marked for eternal death, for a people lives by its thought and not by force." There was an amusing retort, the afternoon I returned to Bucharest, to one of the fire-eating retired generals, picturing the quaint old fellow as thinking that people were born only to die bravely, and knowing nothing of Rumania's rule as the "defender of Latinism" in the Balkans, "tooting the funereal flute and showing us the mountains—there is to be your tomb!"

There was a time, when the Russians were taking Prze-mysl, when Rumania's tide seemed to be at the flood—if ever it was going to be. That chance was lost, and Rumania found herself standing squarely in the track of the stream of ammunition which used to flow down from Düsseldorf to the Turks—when I was at the front with the Turks, practically all the ammunition boxes I saw, and there were hundreds of them, were marked *"Gut uber Rumanien"*—and, later, in Rus-sia's path to Bulgaria and Serbia.

One of these days a hot thrill might run down the Calea Vittorei, and all at once Capsa's and the other little booths in this miniature Vanity Fair would seem strange and far-away. But until that day one could fancy the romanticists and real-ists lambasting each other in the papers, the soldiers grind-ing away in their dusty camps, the pretty ladies rolling gaily down the sprinkled asphalt, and the chanteuse singing over the footlights:

"Que pense le Premier Ministre? On n'sait pas—"
("What thinks the Prime Minister? Nobody knows—")

"Is he for the Germans? Has he made a convention With perfidious Albion? Nobody knows. . ."

THE GATE TO CONSTANTINOPLE

Only the Danube separates Rumania from Bulgaria, yet the people—of the two capitals, at least—are as different as the French and Scotch. The train leaves Bucharest after break-fast; you are ferried over the river at Rustchuk at noon, and, after trailing over the shoulders of long, rolling plateaus, are up in the mountains in Sofia that evening. The change is al-most as sharp as that between Ostend and Folkestone.

You leave French, or the half-Latin Rumanian language, for a Slavic speech, and the Cyrillic, or Russian, alphabet; names ending in "sco" or "ano" (Ionesco, Filipesco, Bratiano) for names ending in "off" (Radoslavoff, Malinoff, Ghenadieff, Antinoff, and the like), and all the show and vivacity, the cafes and cocottes of Bucharest, for a clean little mountain capital as determined and serious as some new town out West.

It seemed, though of course such impressions are mostly chance, that the difference began at the border. In Rumania, at the Hungarian border, they took away my passport, which in times like these is like taking away one's clothes, and, though I assured the customs inspector that I was on my way to Constantinople, and in a hurry, it required four days' wait in Bucharest, and innumerable visits to the police before the paper was returned. Every one, apparently, on the train had the same experience—the Austrian drummers looked wise and muttered "baksheesh," and in Bucharest an evil-eyed hotel porter kept pulling me into corners, saying that this taking of passports was a regular "commerce," and that for five francs he would have it back again.

There is a popular legend that the clerks in Bucharest hotels are supposed to offer incoming guests all the choices of a Mohammedan paradise, and the occasional misogynist, who prefers a room to himself, is received with sympathy, and the wish politely expressed that monsieur will soon be himself again. My own experience was less ornate, but prices were absurdly high, the waiter's check frequently needed revision, and one had a vague but more or less continual sense of swimming among sharks.

These symptoms were absent in Bulgaria. The border officials seemed sensible men who would "listen to reason"; the porters, coachmen, waiters, and the like, crude rather than cleverly depraved, and the air of Sofia clear and clean, in more senses than one.

Modern Bulgaria is only a couple of generations old, and though all this part of the world has been invaded and re-invaded and fought over since the beginning of things, the little kingdom (it seems more like a republic) has the air of a new country.

The aristocracy had been wiped out before Bulgaria got her autonomy in 1878, and, unlike Rumania, where the greater portion of the land is in the hand of large proprietors, Bulgaria is a country of small farmers, of shepherds, peasants, each with his little piece of land. The men who now direct its fortunes are the sons and grandsons of very simple people. Possibly it is because we Americans are also a new people, with still some of the prejudices of pioneers, that we are likely to feel something in common with the people of this "peasant state." They seemed to me, at any rate, the most "American" of the Balkan peoples.

There is, of course, one concrete reason for this: Robert College and the American School for Girls (Constantinople College) at Constantinople. It was men educated at Robert College who became the leaders of modern Bulgaria. The only Bulgarian I had known before—I met him on the steamer—had gone from a little village near Sofia to Harvard. His married sister had learned English at the American School for Girls; her husband, a Macedonian Bulgar, had worked his way through Yale. The amiable old general, who was always in the library at the Sofia Club at tea time, ready to tell how the Dardanelles and Constantinople could be taken, had learned English at Robert College and had a son there; the photographer who developed my films also had a son there—and so on.

Snow-capped mountains rise just behind Sofia, and the brown hills thereabout, like the rolling plateaus along the shoulders of which the train crawls on the way down from Rumania, are speckled with sheep. Sometimes even in Sofia you will meet a shepherd patiently urging his little flock up a modern concrete sidewalk and stopping now and then for some passer-by to pick up a lamb, "heft" it, poke it, and feel its wool before deciding whether or not he should take it home for dinner.

These shepherds wear roomy, short box-coats of sheepskin, with the leather outside and the wool turned in, like a motor-coat; homespun breeches embroidered, very likely in blue, and laced from the knee down, and a sort of moccasin or laced soft shoe. They are as common in the streets of Sofia as are the over-barbered young snipes in the streets of Bucharest. On market days the main down-town street is filled with them—long-limbed, slow-moving old fellows, with eyes and foreheads wrinkled from years of squinting in the bright plateau sun, faces bronzed and weathered like an old farmhouse, shuffling down the pavement and into and out of shops with the slow, soft-footed gait of so many elk. And if you were designing a stamp for Bulgaria you might well put one of these hard-headed old countrymen on it, just as in the other capital you would put the girl in the *victoria* pattering down the asphalt.

Two newspaper correspondents of the more or less continuous string that were filing from one Bulgarian leader to another to find out what Bulgaria was going to do, amiably permitted me to trail about with them, and thus to see and talk a little with some of those who are steering Bulgaria's exceedingly delicate course—men whose grandfathers very likely wore those sheepskin coats with the wool turned in.

None had the peculiar verve and dash of Take Ionesco, but one or two were decidedly "smooth" in a grave, slightly heavy way, and all suggested stubbornness, intense patriotism, and a keen eye for the main chance.

There is little "society" or formal entertaining in Sofia, little display and little, apparently, of that state of mind which, in Bucharest, is suggested by the handsome, two-horse public carriages at a time when there are not enough horses and carriages to go round. One-horse carriages are impracticable, because the Rumanian, or at least the Bucareiio, thinks one horse beneath his dignity, while a trolley-car—although there are trolley-cars—is, of course, not to be thought of.

People on the streets and in the parks were "nice"-looking rather than smart, and the young officers from the military school, who were everywhere, as fine and soldier-like young men as I had seen anywhere in Europe. They and the common soldiers, with their fine shoulders and chests and wiry torsos, looked as though they were made for their work, and took to it like ducks to water.

The palace is on the central square—an unpretentious building in the trees, with a driveway leading up from two gates, at which stand two motionless sentries, each with one stiff feather in his cap. It is such an entrance as you might expect to find at any comfortable country place at home, and one day, when some student volunteers went by on a practise march, and cheered as they passed, I saw the King, with the Queen and one or two others, stroll down the drive and bow just as if he, too, were some comfortable country gentleman.

There is a music-hall in Sofia, but on the two nights I went to it there were scarce twenty in the audience. There are various beer gardens with music, and, of course, moving pictures, but it was interesting, in contrast with Bucharest to find the crowd going to the National Theatre to see Tolstoi's *"Living Corpse."* The stock company, moderately subsidized by the government, gives drama and opera on alternate nights. I barely got a seat for the Tolstoi play, and the doorkeeper said that the house was always sold out.

The Bulgarians, in short, are simple, and what the Rumanians would call *"serieux"*—you must abandon all notion of finding here anything like the little comic-opera kingdoms invented by some of our novelists. It was in Bulgaria, as I recall it, that Mr. Shaw put "Arms and the Man," and the fun lay, as you will remember, in the contrast between the outworn, feudal notions of the natives and the intense matter-of-factness of the modern Swiss professional soldier.

You will recall the doubts of the heroine's male relatives as to whether Bluntschli was good enough for her, their ingenuous attempts to impress him, by describing the style in which she was accustomed to live, and his unimpressed response that his father had so and so many table-cloths, so many horses, so many hundreds of plates, etc. Who was he, then—king of his country? Oh, no, indeed—he ran a hotel. Mr. Shaw's fun is all right of itself, but has about as much application to Bulgaria or Sofia as to Wyoming or Denver.

By one of those frequently fascinating chances of geography, this little nation, which has a territory about as big as Ohio, is set squarely in front of the main gate to Constantinople, and saw, in consequence, the powers which ruthlessly bullied it yesterday now almost at its feet.

Rumania stands in Russia's path, on the one hand, and, with its railway, in Germany's on the other; but Bulgaria does both, and, in addition, blocks the whole western frontier of Turkey and the only feasible chance to land an army from the Aegean.

After their disastrous attempt to run the Dardanelles in March, the English and French had been somewhat in the position of an army trying to capture Jacksonville, Florida, for instance, and instead of marching over from Georgia, compelled to go away down to Key West, and fight their way up through the Everglades. They had in front of them hills behind hills and an entrenched enemy whom they could not see generally and who could always see them. Behind them was only a strip of beach, the sea, and the more or less uncertain support of their ships. So narrow was their foothold that even if they had had more men, they could scarce find place to use them.

Could they but land in Bulgaria, they might cut off the Turks from Europe at once, accumulate at their leisure a sufficient force, and push down methodically from a proper base to the Chatalja line, fighting like men instead of amphibious ducks. The thing looks easy, and the twisted hills and hidden batteries of Gallipoli Peninsula were so heart-breaking a maze to fling good men into that you can well imagine the Allies used what pressure they could. But if it was important to them that the gate be opened—let alone that Bulgaria come in herself—it was just as important to the Germans and Austrians that it be closed. And who was to say that if Bulgaria threw in her lot with the Allies and attacked the Turks the Central Powers might not even start a grand offensive down through Serbia—and people talked of this in Sofia months before it actually began—connect up their lines all the way to Constantinople—and good-by to their little peasant state and her hard-won independence!

A little state must think of these things. She hasn't the men nor the staggering supply of ammunition lightly to go into a world war like this. And then the Bulgarians had had their fingers burned once—they were not looking for adventures.

You will remember the Balkan War of 1912-3, and how the Bulgars fought their way down almost to Constantinople and were everybody's heroes for a time. Then came the quarrel between the Balkan allies, and presently Bulgaria was fighting for her life—Serbia on the west, Greece on the south, Turkey on the east—and then, when she was quite helpless, the Rumanians coming down from the north to perform the coup de grace.

It was not a particularly sporting performance on the part of the Rumanians, nor could the turning over to them of the Bulgarian part of the province of Dobrudja greatly increase Bulgaria's trust in the powers which permitted it in the treaty of Bucharest.

"It's our own fault," an Englishman said to me, speaking somewhat sardonically of the failure of the Rumanians to go in with Italy in spite of having accepted a timely loan from England. "We put our money on the wrong horse! No, they'll keep on talking—they're the chaps who want to get something for nothing. Think of the treaty of Bucharest and the way we patted Rumania on the back—she was the gendarme of Europe then. 'Gendarme of Europe!'. . . I tell you that any army that would do what the Rumanians did to Bulgaria has something wrong with its guts!"

An army goes where it is ordered, of course, but it is true, nevertheless, that the Bulgarians are likely to think of their neighbours on the north as people who want to get something for nothing, and that they who had borne the brunt of the war with Turkey lost everything they had gained. The Turks, "driven from Europe," calmly moved back to Adri-

134

anople; Rumania took the whole of Dobrudja; Bulgarian Macedonia went to Serbia and Greece. However much Bulgaria may have been to blame for the break-up of the Balkan League—and she was stubborn and headstrong to say the least—there is no denying that the treaty of Bucharest did not give her a square deal. It was one of those treaties of peace (and you might think that the men who sit around the green table and make such treaties would learn it after a time) that are really treaties of war.

No, Bulgaria was not looking for adventures, nor accepting promises unless she had securities that they would be carried out. You could not talk to any intelligent Bulgarian five minutes without feeling the bitterness left by the treaty of Bucharest and the fixed idea that Bulgarian Macedonia must come under the flag again. But though this was true, and the army mobilized, and on a fine day every other man on the streets of Sofia an officer, the stubborn Bulgars were still sitting tight. If they got what they wanted without fighting for it, they were not anxious to throw away another generation of young men as they had thrown them away for nothing in the Balkan War.

By this negative policy—the pressure, that is to say, of not going to war—Bulgaria had induced Turkey, by the time I came through Sofia again three months later, to turn over enough territory on the east so that the Bulgars could own the railroad down to Dedeagatch and reach the Aegean without being obliged to go into Turkey and out again. It even seemed that Bulgaria might be able to keep her neutrality to the end. Her compromise with Turkey was not so odd as it seemed to many at first. She had fought the Turks, to be sure, but now got what she wanted, and when you come to think of it, it might well be more comfortable from the Bulgars' point of view to have the invalid Ottomans in Constantinople than the healthy and hungry Russians.

Both these small states, in their present hopes, fears, and, dangers, are an instructive spectacle to those who fancy that in the crowded arena of Europe a little nation can always do as it wants to, or that its neutrality is always the simple open-and-shut matter it looked to be, for instance, in the first weeks of August, 1914. We are likely, at home, to look on all this cold-blooded weighing of the chances of war with little patience, to think of all these "aspirations" as merely somebody else's land. Fear or envy of our neighbours, international hatred, is almost unknown with us. All that was left behind, three thousand miles away, and the green water in between permits us to indulge in the rare luxury of altruism. Yet these hatreds, these fears, and ambitions, inherited and carefully nourished, are just as real—particularly in little states like these—as the fact, odd and apparently unreasonable as it may be, that in a bit of country, which might be included in one of our larger States, one lot of people should speak French and think like Latins, and another speak Slavic and think another way, and that neither wants to be absorbed by the other any more than we want to be compelled to speak Spanish or be absorbed by the Mexicans.

The "aspirations" of both these little countries have realities behind them. It is a fact that one gets a whiff of French clarity and verve in Rumania, though it comes from a small minority educated in France, and the Rumanian people may be no more "Latin" than we are. And it is an interesting notion—though perhaps only a notion—that Rumania should be the outpost or rear-guard of Latinism in this part of the world; a bit of the restless West on the edge of the Orient.

For virility and earnestness like that of the Bulgars there is a place, not only in the Balkans, but everywhere. The qualities they have shown in their short life as an independent nation are those which deserve to be encouraged and preserved. And if it were true that this war were being fought to establish the right of little nations to live, one of the tasks it ought to accomplish, it seemed then, was to give the Bulgars back at least part of what was taken from them.

CHAPTER 10

The Adventure of the Fifty Hostages

Gallipoli lies by the Sea of Marmora, and looks out across it to the green hills of Asia, just where the blue Marmora narrows into the Dardanelles. It is one of those crowded little Turkish towns set on a blazing hillside—tangled streets, unpainted, grey, weather-warped frame houses, with overhanging latticed windows and roofs of red tiles; little walled-in gardens with dark cedars or cypresses and a few dusty roses; fountains with Turkish inscriptions, where the streets fork and women come to fill their water-jars—a dreamy, smelly, sun-drenched little town, drowsing on as it has drowsed for hundreds of years. Nothing ever happens in Gallipoli—I speak as if the war hadn't happened! The graceful Greek sloops, with their bellying sails and turned-up stems and sterns, come sailing in much as they must have come when the Persians, instead of the English and the French, were battering away at the Hellespont. The grave, long-nosed old Turks pull at their bubble pipes and sip their little cups of sweet, black coffee; the camel trains, dusty and tinkling, come winding down the narrow streets from the Thracian wheat country and go back with overseas merchandise done up in faded carpets and boxes of Standard Oil. The wind blows from the north, and it is cold, and the Marmora grey; it blows from the south, and all at once the world is warm and sea and sky are blue—so soft, so blue, so alive with lifting radiance that one does not wonder the Turk is content with a cup of coffee and a view.

Nothing ever happens in Gallipoli—then the war came, and everything happened at once. It was a still May morning, a Sunday morning, when the English and French sent some of their ships up into the Gulf of Saros, on the Aegean side of the peninsula, over behind Gallipoli. Eight or ten miles of rolling country shut away the Aegean, and made people feel safe enough. They might have been in the other wars which have touched Gallipoli, but a few miles of country were nothing at all to the guns of a modern battleship.

An observation-balloon looked up over the western horizon, there was a sudden thunder, and all at once the sky above Gallipoli rained screaming shells and death. You can imagine—at any rate remembering Antwerp, I could very well imagine—how that hurricane of fire, sweeping in without warning, from people knew not where, must have seemed like the end of the world. You can imagine the people—old men with turbans undone, veiled women, crying babies—tumbling out of the little bird-cage houses and down the narrow streets. Off went the minaret, as you would knock off an icicle, from the mosque on the hill. The mosque by the water-front went down in a cloud of dust, and up from the dust, from a petrol shell, shot a geyser of fire. Stones came rumbling down from the old square tower, which had stood since the days of Bayazid; the faded grey houses squashed like eggs. It was all over in an hour—some say even twenty, minutes—but that was long enough to empty Gallipoli, to kill some sixty or seventy people, and drive the rest into the caves under the cliffs by the water, or across the Marmora to Lapsaki.

Now, while the bombardment of Gallipoli may not appear from a merely human point of view, a particularly sporting performance, yet, as most of those killed were soldiers, as Gallipoli had been a staff head-quarters not long before and always has been a natural base for the defence of the Dardanelles, the attack was doubtless justified by the rules of war. It happens, however, that people who live in defenceless, bombarded towns are never interested in the rules of war. So a

138

new and particularly disturbing rumour went flying through the crowded streets of Constantinople.

It is a city of rumours, this beautiful, bewildering Baghdad of the West, where all the races of the world jostle each other in the narrow streets, and you never know how the man who brushes past you lives—let alone feels and thinks. The Constantinople trolley-cars are divided by a curtain, on one side of which sit the men, on the other the veiled women. When there are several women the conductor slides the curtain along, so that half the car is a harem; when there are none he slides it back, and there is no harem at all.

And life is like that. You are at once in a modern commercial city and an ancient Mohammedan capital, and never know when the one will fade out like a picture on a screen and leave you in the Orient, facing its mystery, its fatalism, its vengeance that comes in a night.

You can imagine what it must become, walled in with war and censorship, with the English and French banging away at the Dardanelles gate to the south, the Russian bear growling at the door of the Bosporus, so close that you can every now and then hear the rumble of cannon above the din of Constantinople—just as you might hear them in Madison Square if an enemy were bombarding the forts at Sandy Hook. You wake up one morning to hear that all the influential Armenians have been gathered up and shipped to the interior; you go down to the ordinary-looking hotel breakfast-room and the three Germans taking coffee in the corner stop talking at once; at lunch some one stoops to whisper to the man across the table, there is a moment's silence until the waiter has gone, and the man across the table mutters:"The G. V. says not to worry"—"G. V." meaning Grand Vizier. Tomorrow the Goeben is to be blown up, or there will be a revolution, or a massacre—heaven knows what! Into an atmosphere like this, with wounded pouring back in thousands from the Dardanelles, there came the news of the bombardment of Gallipoli. And with it went the rumour of reprisal—all the English and

French left behind in Constantinople, and there were a good many who had been permitted to go about their business more or less as usual, were to be collected, men, women, and children, taken down to the peninsula and distributed in the "unfortified" towns. The American ambassador would notify England and France through Washington, and if then the Allies chose to bombard, theirs was the risk.

The American ambassador, Mr. Morgenthau, set about to see what could be done. Presently the word went round that the women might stay behind, but the men, high and low, must go. They came flocking to the embassy, already besought for weeks by French Sisters of Mercy and Armenians in distress, some begging for a chance to escape, some ready to go anywhere as their share of the war. The Turks were finally induced to include only those between twenty and forty, and at the last moment this was cut to an even fifty—twenty-five British subjects, twenty-five French. The plan eliminated, naturally, the better-known remnants of the French and English colonies, and disappointed the chief of police, who had not unreasonably hoped, as he wistfully put it, "to have some notables." Of the fifty probably not more than a dozen had been born in England or France, the others being natives of Malta, Greece—the usual Levantines. Yet if these young bank clerks and tradesmen were not "important," according to newspaper standards, they were, presumably, important to themselves. They were very important, indeed, to the wives and mothers and sisters who fought up to the Galata sea wall that Thursday morning, weeping and wailing, and waving their wet handkerchiefs through the iron fence.

The hostages, one or two of whom had been called to their doors during the night and marched away without time to take anything with them, had been put aboard a police boat, about the size of a New York revenue cutter, and herded below in two little cabins, with ten fierce-looking Constantinople policemen, in grey astrakhan caps, to guard them. It was from the water-line port-holes of these cabins that they waved their farewells.

With them was a sturdy, bearded man in black knickerbockers and clerical hat, the rector of the Crimean Chapel in Constantinople—a Cambridge and Church of England man, and a one-time dweller in the wilds of Kurdistan, who, though not called, had volunteered to go. The first secretary of the American embassy, Mr. Hoffman Philip, an adventurous humanitarian, whose experience includes an English university, the Rough Riders, and service as American minister to Abyssinia, also volunteered, not, of course, as hostage, but as friendly assistant both to the Turkish authorities and to their prisoners.

To him was given the little deck-cabin, large enough for a man to stretch out on the seat which ran round it; here, also the clergyman volunteer was presently permitted, and here too, thanks to passports vouchsafed by the chief of police, the chroniclers of the expedition, Mr. Suydam of the Brooklyn Eagle, and myself.

The passports, mysterious scratches in Turkish, did not arrive until the last minute, and with them came the chief, the great Bedri Bey himself—a strong man and a mysterious one, pale, inscrutable, with dark, brooding eyes and velvety manners, calculated to envelop even a cup of coffee and a couple of boiled eggs in an air of sinister romance.

The chief regretted that the craft was not "a serious passenger boat," for we should probably have to spend the night aboard. Arrangements for the hostages and ourselves would be made at Gallipoli, though just what they would be it was difficult to say, as there were, he said, no hotels in the place and the houses were all destroyed.

With this cheerful prospect he bade us farewell, and all being ready, we waited two hours, and finally, just before noon, with deck-hands hanging life belts along the rail to be ready for possible English submarines, churned through the crowded shipping of the Golden Horn, round Stamboul, and out into the blue Marmora.

The difficulties of the next few days—for which most of the hostages, city-bred and used to the bake-shop round the corner, were unprepared—promptly presented themselves. Lunch-time came, but there was no lunch. There was not even bread. Philip and Suydam had tinned things, and the former some cake, which by tea-time that afternoon—so appallingly soon does the spoiled child of town get down to fundamentals—seemed an almost immoral luxury. But the luckless fifty, already unstrung by the worry of the last forty-eight hours, fed on salt sea air, and it was not until sundown that one of the British came to ask what should be done. Philip dug into his corned beef and what was left of the bread, and so we curled up for the night, the hostages and policemen below, the rest of us in the deck-house, rolled up in all the blankets we had, for one of the Black Sea winds was blowing down the Marmora and it was as cold as November.

The launch came up to Gallipoli wharf in the night and not long after daylight we were shaken out of our blankets to receive the call of the *mutessarif*, or local governor, a big, slow, saturnine man in semi-riding-clothes, with the red fez and a riding-whip in his hand, who spoke only Turkish and limited himself to few words of that. He was accompanied by a sort of secretary or political director—a plump little man, with glasses and a vague, slightly smiling, preoccupied manner, who acted as interpreter.

The governor and Philip were addressed as "Excellence," the secretary as *"Monsieur Le Directeur,"* and, considering that all concerned were only half awake, and we only half dressed, the interview, which included the exchange of cigarettes and many salutes, was extremely polite. We joined the *mutessarif* and his secretary in a stroll about the town.

It was deserted—closed shutters, empty houses and shops, not so much as the chance to buy a round, flat loaf of black bread—a shell of a town, with a few ravenous cats prowling about and forgotten chickens pecking the bare cobblestones. We saw the shell hole in the little Mohammedan cemetery, where four people, "come to visit the tombs of their fathers," had been killed, the smashed mosques, yawning house-fronts, and dangling rafters, and there came over one an indescribable irony as one listened, in this Eastern world of blazing sun, blue sky, and blue water, to the same grievances and indignations one had read in London editorials and heard in the beet-fields of Flanders months ago.

The *mutessarif* took us to a little white villa on the cliff by the sea, with a walled garden, flat black cedar, and a view of the Marmora, and we breakfasted on tea, bread and butter, and eggs. Meanwhile the hostages had been marched to an empty frame house on the beach, from the upper windows of which, while gendarmes guarded the street-door, they were gloomily peering when we returned to the launch. Philip, uneasy at the emptiness of the town and leisurely fashion in which things were likely to move, started for Lapsaki, across the Marmora, for food and blankets, and Suydam and I strolled about the town. We had gone but a few steps when we observed an aimless-looking individual in fez and civilian clothes following us. We tramped up-hill, twisted through several of the hot little alley-like streets—he followed like our shadow. We led him all over town, he toiling devotedly behind, and when we returned to the beach, he sat himself down on a wood-pile behind us, as might some dismal buzzard awaiting our demise.

He, or some of his fellow sleuths, stuck to us all that day. Once, for exercise, I walked briskly out to the edge of the town and back again. The shadow toddled after. I went up to the basin beside the ruined mosque, a sort of sea-water plaza for the town, and, taking a stool outside a little cafe, which had awakened since morning, took coffee. The shadow blandly took coffee also, which he consumed silently, as we had no common tongue, rose as I rose, and followed me back to the beach.

Out in the Marmora, which is but little wider here than the Hudson at Tappan Zee, transports crammed with soldiers went steaming slowly southward, a black destroyer on the lookout for submarines hugging their flanks and breaking trail ahead of them. Over the hills to the south, toward Maidos and the Dardanelles, rolled the distant thunder—the cannon the hapless fifty, looking out of their house on the beach, had been sent down to stop—and all about us, in the dazzling Turkish sunshine, were soldiers and supply-trains, landing, disembarking, pushing toward the front. Fine-looking men they were, too, these infantry-men, bronzed, well-built fellows, with heavy, high cheek-bones, longish noses, black moustaches, and dark eyes, who, whatever their qualities of initiative might be, looked to have no end of endurance and ability to stay put. Bullock-carts dragged by big, black buffalo cattle, carrying their heads far back, as if their big horns were too heavy for them, crowded the street leading to the quay, and camels, strung in groups of five, came swinging in, or kneeling in the dust, waved their long, bird-like necks, and lifted up a mournful bellow, as if protesting in a bored, Oriental way, at a fate which compelled them to bear burdens for the nagging race of men.

It was to an accompaniment of these howls that a young Turkish officer came over to find out who these strangers might be. We spoke of the hostages, and he at once said that it was an excellent idea. The English and French were very cruel—if now they chose to bombard. . . . . "If a man throws a penny into the sea," he said, "he loses the penny. It isn't the pocket-book that's hurt." I did not quite grasp this proverb, but remarked that after all they were civilians and had done nothing. "That is true," he said, "but the English and French have been very unjust to our civilians. They force us to another injustice—*c'est la guerre.*"

Toward the end of the afternoon the hostages, closely guarded, were marched up into the town and lodged in two empty houses—literally empty, for there was neither bed nor blanket, chair nor table—nothing but the four walls. A few had brought mattresses and blankets, but the greater number, city-bred young fellows, unused to looking after themselves out of doors, had only the clothes they stood in. The north wind held; directly the sun went down it was cold again, and, only half fed with the provisions Philip brought over from

Lapsaki, they spent a dismal night,' huddled on the bare floor, under their suitcases or whatever they could get to cover them, and expecting another bombardment at dawn.

We, on the contrary—that is to say, Philip and his two guests—were taken to a furnished house over-looking the Marmora—the house, as it presently appeared, from the pictures of Waterloo on the walls and the English novels in a bookcase up-stairs, lately occupied by the British consular agent. To his excellency a room to himself up-stairs, with a real bed, was given; the historians were made perhaps even more comfortable on mattresses on the dining-room floor. We were all sleepy enough to drop on them at once, but another diplomatic dinner had been planned, it appeared, and Turkish politeness can no more be hurried nor overcome than can that curious impassive resistance which a Turk can maintain against something he does not wish done. It was nine o'clock before we sat down with the *mutessarif*, his secretary, and the voluble journalist to a whole roast kid, a rather terrifying but exceedingly palatable dish, stuffed with nuts, rice, and currants, and accompanied by some of the wine of Lapsaki, rice pudding, and a huge bowl of raw eggs, which were eaten by cracking the shell, elevating one's head, and tossing them down like oysters.

The dinner was served by one Dimitri, a brawny, slow-moving Greek. Dimitri was dressed in a home-spun braided jacket and homespun Turkish trousers, shaped like baggy riding-breeches, and his complete impenetrability to new ideas was only equalled by the solemnity and touching willingness with which he received them. It was after he had served us in the ignoble capacity of dish-washer and burden-carrier for several days that we were informed one evening by the governor's secretary, in his vague way, that Dimitri was an "architect."

"*Architecte naturel,*" suggested the urbane Philip, and the governor's secretary assented. Slow Dimitri might be, but once he grasped an idea, no power could drag it from him. When one asked him where he learned to build houses of a certain style, he always replied that so they were built by

Pappadopoulos—Pappadopoulos being dead these twenty or thirty years. Dimitri, the secretary ventured, had been architect of the mosque on the water-front, and when he found that we were pleased with this idea, everything else in Gallipoli became Dimitri's. The lighthouse, the hospital, the three white houses by the quay—we had but to mention a building and he would promptly murmur, in his dreamy, half-quizzical way: *"Oui-i-i. . . c'est Dimitri!"*

Early next morning, just after we had discovered that under the cliff was water like liquid lapis lazuli and flat-topped rocks rising just above it on which you would not have been in the least surprised to find mermaids combing their hair, or sirens sitting, and that it was a simple matter to climb down and be mermen, the clergyman-volunteer arrived with reports of the first night. It had been dismal, there were one or two intransigent kickers, and the aesthetic young Frenchman who spent his idle time drawing pictures of fashion-plate young ladies, had become so unstrung that he had regularly "thrown a fit" and been unconscious for half an hour until they could massage him back to life again. Humour was quite gone out of them, and when the clergyman suggested that it was a compliment to be sent out to be shot at—flattering, at any rate, to the prowess of the Allies—a Frenchman emphatically denied it. "Pas du tout!" he exploded. While we talked there was a knock at the front door, and through the grating we saw the red fez and vaguely smiling visage of the *mutessarif's* secretary. It was the first of a series of visits, which, before we left Gallipoli, were renewed almost every hour, of dialogues deserving a better immortalization than can be given here.

You must imagine, on one side of the dining-room table, the plump little bey, with his fez and glasses, quick little salutes each time he took a match or cigarette; facing him the tall, urbane Philip, in ineffable flannels or riding-clothes—for the embassy secretary is one of those who believe that clothes should express rather than blot out the inner man. Cigarettes—coffee—assurances to his excellency that the house

146

is his, to *Monsieur Le Directeur* of our pleasure and profound consideration. Minutes pass, an hour—the bey knows no such thing as time, the other is as unhurried as he. The talk, in somewhat halting French, is of war, weather, French culture, marriage, those dreadful Russians, punctuated by delicate but persistently recurring references, on one side, to mattresses and food for the hostages, by the little bey's deep sighs and his *"Mais. . . que faire."*

That "But what can be done?" like the Mexican's "Who knows?" fell like a curtain on every pause, it was the bey's answer to all life's riddles—the plight of the hostages, the horrors of war, his own dream of being governor of a province close to Constantinople. One can hear him now through that cloud of cigarette smoke, *"Mais—"* with a pause and scarcely perceptible lifting of the shoulders— *"que faire. . ."*

We went across to Lapsaki again that day to get blankets and buy or order mattresses, and found it much what Gallipoli must have been a few days before—sunshine and soldiers, camels loaded with stretchers and Red Cross supplies, the hot little twisting streets, noisy with traders and refugees.

You can imagine the excitement over this mysterious stranger with an unlimited supply of gold lire and big silver *medjidies*, asking not what kind of blankets, but how many did they have, how long would it take them to make not one, but fifty mattresses! Greek traders, Jews from the Dardanelles, one or two hybrid youths in fez and American clothes, with recommendations from American Y. M. C. As—it was a great afternoon for Lapsaki!

A round-faced, jolly German nurse, dropped all alone in the little town by the chance of war, met us in the street, and later we went to her hospital. It had been started only a fortnight before, there were no beds, and the wounded lay on narrow mattresses on the floor. One man, whose face was a mere eyes and nose poking through patches of plaster, had been burned at Gallipoli. Another, up from the Dardanelles, had a hideous wound in his cheek, discharging constantly

147

into his mouth. In spite of it he took Philip's cigarette and smoked it. He was dead when we came back three days later. On another mattress was a poor little brown bundle, a boy of twelve or thirteen, hit in the spine and paralyzed by a fragment of shell at Gallipoli and now delirious. Philip later took him back to Constantinople, to the X-ray and care that might save his life.

It was sundown when we got back to the hostages with our spoils. The thing had begun to get on their nerves. The English said little, determined evidently to remain Britons to the last, but some of the Levantines let themselves go completely. A pale gentleman with a poetic beard, a barber by profession, was among the most eloquent. It was not a jail, it was a mad-house, he cried. Another declared that without bedding, doctor, or medicines, shut up here until the end of the war, probably, they must at least have food—that was a need "primordial!"

Another stood apart, whacking his chest and addressing the empty air, *"C'est moi, c'est moi, qui n'a pas d'argent!"*—it was he who had no money and nothing to cover him, and what did they want him to do? If he had come down to be shot at, well and good, but if he was to be frozen and starved by inches. . .

Philip smoothed them down as best he could and returned to invite the governor's secretary to stay for dinner, a repast for which Hassan, the embassy *khavass* who accompanied the expedition, had procured, as he put it, "some fresh eggies from a nice little man."

The bey, who, that morning, had leaned toward the French, now warmed to America. The French were enlightened, he said, but without morals, the English civilized but jealous; if he had any sons he would send them to America, the only place where young men were both civilized and properly *"serieux."* In the midst of these amiable speculations it was suggested that, in view of the difficulty of getting mattresses, the government might even requisition them. The suggestion drew a regretful sigh from the bey, for Turkey was a constitutional country, he said, the shops and houses were closed and their owners gone, and there was no way in which such a thing could be done.

In addition to Hassan's eggies, Philip's Man Friday, the incomparable Levy, had constructed some rice puddings, and it was in despair that he announced, just before they were to be served, that two had "gone by the cats"! We had, indeed, by this time attracted most of the cats in Gallipoli. They streaked through the rooms like chain lightning, and in the dead of night went galloping over the piano keyboard with sounds so blood-curdling that Suydam put his mattress on the sofa and his sleeping-bag on top of that, and, shutting himself in, defied them. The incomparable Levy was Italian by his birth and cheerfulness, Jewish on his father's side, Turkish by the fez he wore and a life spent in guiding strangers about Constantinople. He had the face of a dean of a diplomatic corps or one of those comfortable old gentlemen in spats who have become fixtures in some city club.

It was his employer's humour to befriend and defend him in private, but to his face assume, with the most delicate irony, that this marvel among men was always late, forgetful, rattle-brained, and credulous. And it was Levy's gift to play up to this assumption, to hang on his employer's words with breathless anxiety, to relax into a paternal smile when safe, and to support his omelettes and his delays with oaths and circumlocutions stranger even than the dishes themselves. They were odd enough, those dinners, sitting in our little oasis of light in that deserted town, not knowing what the next hour might bring.

Next day we again went to Lapsaki, and, although the entire industrial resources of the place had apparently been cornered in the meantime by a Dardanelles Jew, returned with several more mattresses and the promise of the remainder. We found the hostages more cheerful. With the relief money Philip had distributed the day before, and the food they had been able to buy, they had shaken themselves together, gifted cooks had turned up, they had made a baseball out of rags, painted humorous signs on the doorways of their rooms—they had actually begun to sing.

And now, with that curious subsequentness with which things sometimes happen in Turkey, the *mutesarif* discovered half a dozen mattresses himself, and announced that to-morrow there would be enough for all. Nay, more—the government would allow each hostage four *piastres* a day for food, a cook would be brought down from Constantinople and meals served in a restaurant, that they might be saved, as his secretary observed, from the unlovely *"odeurs de'cuisine."*

Then it was discovered that the men might stroll about town, provided they were in groups. They went to the beach and discussed the feasibility of swimming, they even demurred against the Constantinople cook as limiting their means of amusing themselves; the aesthetic young man recovered now, polished his shoes and put a lavender handkerchief in his breast pocket. The hostages were in a fair way to annex the deserted village, when a bombshell burst in the shape of a despatch from the American ambassador that permission had been obtained for all to come home.

The changing wind now swung full upon us. Scarcely had the message arrived ere the *mutessarifs* secretary followed it, lamenting that we must go. A peacock reposing majestically in the arms of a patient *hamal* appeared at the front door, a souvenir for "his excellency."

Appeared also, out of thin air, a neat little horse and phaeton, and a trooper perched on a high Turkish saddle, with a rifle slung rakishly across his back, and the bey himself, glasses, fez, and all, astride an Arab steed. We were to be taken for a drive. Toward the end of it we reached the flour-mill, the only modern edifice in this ancient town, and were ushered into the office to sit in a constrained circle, with the slightly ironical-looking young proprietor—accustomed, perhaps, to such visits—and his associates, while coffee and cigarettes were brought. The engineer, an Italian, welcomed us in French; the proprietor, who spoke nothing but Turkish, smiled inscrutably, and overhead, in several brass cages, canaries sang.

Philip, gazing upward, admired their song, whereat the bey at once announced that they were his. The American protested that, much as the gift delighted his taste and roused his gratitude, it was impossible to think of carrying a canary back to Constantinople.

"If you please. . ." insisted the imperturbable bey. "It is yours!" Scarcely had we returned, indeed, before another patient *hamal* knocked, lugging the hapless bird.

The hostages, not to be outdone, invited Philip, the bey, and ourselves to lunch. There was chicken soup and chicken, and salad and native wine, and, for the corner of the improvised table, where the guests were seated, the hospitable young men had actually procured several bottles of Gallipoli champagne. The barber with the poetic beard leaped to his feet, as fluent in welcoming us as he had been in protestations a few evenings before, while the aesthetic young man smiled pensively down at a long-stemmed fleur-de-lis which he slowly twirled in his fingers. The cashier of a Constantinople department store sang from "Tosca."

With him as leader they all sang—a song of the Pyrenees mountaineers, then a waltz from the cafes *chantants*: *"Bien gentiment l'on se balade. C'est la premiere promenade—"*

In another week we should have had a Gallipoli Glee Club.

And so ended the adventure of the fifty hostages, who went out to be shot at—the end of the comedy, which had its climax at the beginning. The next morning we were up at daylight, and after several hours' delay the *mutessarif* and his lieutenant came down to permit us to leave. There were cigarettes and salutes, the secretary scribbled in Turkish characters on his knee, the governor signed the permit, and we said good-by to Gallipoli. Next morning we again threaded the shipping in the Golden Horn.

The ten policemen who had looked so formidable a week before, expressed a wish for what was left of the tinned corned beef. And with *hackmen* yelling from the street and *caique* men shouting from the water, the fifty hostages were swallowed up in the sunshine and smells and clatter of Constantinople.

CHAPTER 11

With The Turks at the Dardanelles

The little side-wheeler—she had been built in Glasgow in 1892, and done duty as a Bosporus ferry-boat until the war began—was supposed to sail at four, but night shut down and she still lay at the wharf in Stamboul. We contrived to get some black bread, hard-boiled eggs, oranges, and halva from one of the little hole-in-the-wall shops near by, watched Pera and its ascending roofs turn to purple, and the purple to grey and black, until Constantinople was but a string of lights across Galata Bridge, and a lamp here and there on the hills. Then, toward midnight, with lights doused and life-belts strung along the rail—for English submarines were in the Marmora—we churned quietly round the corner of Stamboul and into the cool sea.

The side-wheeler was bound for the Dardanelles with provisions for the army—bread in bags, big hampers of green beans, and cigarettes—and among them we were admitted by grace of the minister of war, and papers covered with seals and Turkish characters, which neither of us could read. We tried to curl up on top of the beans (for the Marmora is cold at night, and the beans still held some of the warmth of the fields), but in the end took to blankets and the bare decks.

All night we went chunking southward—it is well over a hundred miles from Constantinople to the upper entrance to the straits—and shook ourselves out of our blankets and the cinders into another of those blue-and-gold mornings which belong to this part of the world. You must imagine it behind all this strange fighting at the Dardanelles—sunshine and blue water, a glare which makes the Westerner squint; moons that shine like those in the tropics. One cannot send a photograph of it home any more than I could photograph the view from my hotel window here on Pera Hill of Stamboul and the Golden Horn. You would have the silhouette, but you could not see the sunshine blazing on white mosques and minarets, the white mosques blazing against terra-cotta roofs and dusty green cedars and cypresses, the cypresses lifting dark and pensive shafts against the blue—all that splendid, exquisite radiance which bursts through one's window shutters every morning and makes it seem enough to look and a waste of time to try to think.

It is the air the gods and heroes used to breathe; they fought and played, indeed, over these very waters and wind-swept hills. Leander swam the Dardanelles (or Hellespont) close to where the *Irresistible* and *Bouvet* were sunk; the wind that blew in our faces that morning was the same that rippled the drapery of the Winged Victory. As we went chunking southward with our beans and cigarettes, we could see the snows of Olympus—the Mysian Olympus, at any rate, if not the one where Jove, the cloud-compelling, used to live, and white-armed Juno, and Pallas, Blue-Eyed Maid. If only our passports had taken us to Troy we could have looked down the plains of Ilium to the English and French ships, and Australian and French colonials fighting up the hillside across the bay. We got tea from the galley, and–with bread and halva (an insinuating combination of sugar and oil of sesame, which tastes of peanuts and is at once a candy and a sort of substitute for butter or meat) made out a breakfast.

A Turkish soldier, the only other occupant of the deck, surveyed these preparations impassively; then, taking off his boots, climbed on a settee and stood there in his big bare feet, with folded hands, facing, as he thought, toward Mecca. The boat was headed southwest, and he looked to starboard, so that he faced, as a matter of fact, nearly due west. He had knelt and touched his forehead twice to the bench, and was going on with the *Mussulman* prayer when the captain, a rather elegant young man who had served in the navy, murmured something as he passed. The soldier looked round thoughtfully; without embarrassment, surprise, or hurry stepped from the settee, pointed it toward the Asiatic shore, and, stepping up again, resumed his devotions.

Five times that day, as the faithful are commanded, he said his prayer—a sight that followed us everywhere that week. One evening after dusk, on another boat, a fireman came up from below, climbed on a settee, and began his prayer. Several passengers, who had not seen him in the dark, walked in front of him. He broke off, reviled them in true fire-room style, then with a wide gesture, as though sweeping the air clear ahead of him all the way to the holy city, began at the beginning again. Soldiers up in the Gallipoli hills, the captain on the bridge, a stevedore working on a lighter in the blaze of noon with the winch engines squealing round him—you turn round to find a man, busy the moment before, standing like a statue, hands folded in front of him, facing the east. Nothing stops him; no one seems to see him; he stands invisible in the visible world—in a world apart, 'indeed, to which the curious, self-conscious Westerner is not admitted, where, doubtless, he is no more than the dust which the other shakes from his feet before he is fit to address his God.

The Marmora narrowed, we passed Gallipoli on the European side, where the English and French hostages had had their curious adventure the week before, and on into the Dardanelles proper and the zone of war. It was some forty miles down this salt-water river (four miles wide at its widest, and between the forts of Chanak Kale and Kilid Bahr, near its lower end, a fraction over a mile) from the Marmora gateway to the Aegean. On the left were Lapsaki and the green hills of Asia, cultivated to their very tops; on the right Europe and the brown hills of the peninsula, now filled with guns and horses and men.

Over there, up that narrow strip of Europe, running down between the Dardanelles and the Aegean, the Allies had been trying for weeks to force their way to Constantinople. They had begun in February, you will recall, when they bombarded the forts at the outer entrance to the Dardanelles—Sedd ul Bahron the European side, at the tip of the peninsula, and Kum Kale, across the bay on the Asiatic shore. . . These forts occupy somewhat the relation to Constantinople that Sandy Hook does to New York, although much farther away—they face, that is to say, the open sea, and the guns of the fleet, heavier than those of the old forts, could stand off at a safe distance and demolish them.

When the ships pushed on up the strait toward Kilid Bahr and Chanak Kale—somewhat like trying to run the Narrows at New York—there was a different story. They were now within range of shore batteries and there were anchored mines and mines sent down on the tide. On March 18 the *Irresistible*, *Ocean*, and *Bouvet* were sunk, and it began to be apparent that the Dardanelles could not be forced without the help of a powerful land force. So in April landing parties were sent ashore: at Kum Kale and Sedd ul Bahr, at Kaba Tepe and Art Burnu, some twelve or fourteen miles farther north on the Aegean side of the peninsula, and at another point a few miles farther up. At Sedd ul Bahr and along the beach between Kaba Tepe and Art Bumu the Allies made their landing good, dug themselves in, and, reinforced by the fire of the ships, began a trench warfare not unlike that which has dragged on in the west.

The peninsula is but ten or twelve miles wide at its widest, and the Dardanelles side is within range of the fleet's great guns, firing clear overland from the Aegean. It was by this indirect fire that Maidos was destroyed and Gallipoli partly smashed and emptied of its people. There were places toward the end of the peninsula where Turkish infantrymen had to huddle in their trenches under fire of this sort coming from three directions. Whenever the invaders had it behind they were naturally at an advantage; whenever it ceased they were likely to be driven back. The Turks, on the other hand, had the advantage of numbers, of fighting on an "inside line," and of a country, one hill rising behind another, on the defence of which depended their existence as a nation in Europe.

Under these conditions the fighting had been going on for weeks, the English and French holding their ground at Sedd ul Bahr and Ari Burnu, but getting no nearer Constantinople. And as we went chunking down the strait that night and into Ak-Bash in the dark, two new forces were coming in. The next day a German submarine—come all the way round through the Mediterranean—was to sink the Triumph and the Majestic, while another American correspondent, who had intended to come with us but took the transport *Nagara* instead, saw the head of an English submarine poke through the Marmora. A blond young man in overalls and white jersey climbed out of the conning-tower. "Will you give us time to get off?" cried the American, the only one on board who could speak English.

"Yes," said the young man, "and be damned quick about it." Ten minutes later, from the boats into which they had tumbled, the passengers saw a cloud of yellow smoke, and the *Nagara* simply disintegrated and sank, and with her the heavy siege-gun she was taking to the Dardanelles.

Pleasantly unaware of what might as well have happened to the bread and beans, we drew up to a hill-side speckled with lights, a wharf, and a hospital boat smelling of *iodoform*, through a cabin window of which a doctor was peacefully eating dinner. Boxes and sacks were piled near the wharf, and from over behind the hills, with startling nearness, came the nervous Crack...crack...crack-crack-crack! of rifle and machine-gun fire.

We went to sleep to the tune of it, moved a few miles down the coast in the night, and crawled out into a world of dusty brown—brown hillsides and camels and soldiers and sacks of wheat piled on the flat, immersed in an amber dawn.

This was the destination of the side-wheeler, and by sunup we were loaded into a machine with a horse, several goats, three or four passengers, and four barefooted boatmen, who pushed us over the strait to Chanak Kale.

We were now at the narrowest part of the Dardanelles, behind us, on the European side, the old round tower of Kilid Bahr and Medjidie Fort, in front Fort Hamidie, and on the horizon to the south, where the strait opened into the sea, the tiny silhouettes of several of the Allies' ships. Chanak was smashed like the towns in west Belgium, and, but for the garrison and the Turkish and German commandants tucked away in the trees, all but deserted, except by flies and half-starved cats. These unhappy creatures, left behind in the flight, were everywhere, and in front of the bake shop they crowded in literal scores—gaunt, mangy, clawed and battered from constant fights. It was hot, there was little to eat, and after hours of wrangling it appeared that our precious scratches of Turkish took us to the Gallipoli instead of the Asiatic side.

The two were under different jurisdictions; though the fault was not ours, the local commandant had the right to ship us back to Constantinople, and after a sort of delirium of flies, cats, gendarmes, muggy heat, and debates, night descended to find us going to sleep in the middle of a vegetable farm, in a house lately inhabited by whirling dervishes, with two lynx-eyed police-men in grey lamb's-wool caps seated at the gate. By them we were marched next day to the wharf and suddenly there translated into the upper ether by the German admiral and his thoughtful aid, who, on their way to the headquarters of the land forces across the strait, whirled us over in style in a torpedo-boat.

We landed at the same place at which we had touched in the dark two nights before—busy and blazing now in the afternoon sun, with gangs of stevedores shuffling to and from the ships at the brand-new wharfs, Turkish officers galloping about on their thick-necked, bobtailed, fiery little stallions, and the dusty flat, half a mile across, perhaps, between its encircling hills, crowded with ox and horse carts, camel trains, and piles of ammunition-boxes and sacks of food.

The admiral and his aid were greeted by a smart young German officer with a monocle, and galloped off into the hills, while we fell into the hospitable hands of another German, a civilian volunteer in red fez and the blue and brass buttons of the merchant marine, cast here by the chance of war. He was a Hamburg-American captain, lately sailing between Buenos Aires and Hamburg, and before that on an Atlas Line boat between the Caribbean and New York. He talked English and seemed more than half American, indeed, and when he spoke of the old Chelsea Hotel, just across the street from the Y. M. C. A. gymnasium in which I had played hand-ball, we were almost back in Twenty-third Street. He took us up to his tent on the hill, overlooking the men and stores, and, he explained, reasonably safe from the aeroplanes which flew over several times a day. Over his cigarettes and tea and bottled beer we talked of war and the world.

It was the captain's delicate and arduous duty to impose his tight German habits of work and shipshapeness on camel drivers, stevedores, and officials used to the looser, more leisurely methods of the East.

He could not speak Turkish, was helpless without his interpreter, at best a civilian among soldiers—men have got Iron Crosses for easier jobs than that! He talked of the news—great news for his side—of the Triumph, and, opening his navy list, made a pencil mark.

"She's off!" he said. The book was full of marks. In methodical sailor fashion he had been crossing them off since the war began: British and German—*Blucher, Scharnhorst, Irresistible, Goliath,* and the rest—millions of dollars and hundreds of men at a stroke.

"Where's it going to end?" he demanded. "There's seven hundred good men gone, maybe—how many did the Triumph carry? And we think it's good news! If a man should invent something that would kill a hundred thousand men at once, he'd be a great man. . . Now, what is that?"

The English were hanging on to Sedd ul Bahr—they might try to make another Gibraltar of it. Their aeroplanes came up every day. There was a French-man with a long tail—he only came to the edge of the camp, and as soon as the batteries opened up turned back, but the Englishman didn't stop for anything. He dropped a bomb or two every time he passed—one man must have been square under one, for they found pieces of him, but never did find his head. It wasn't so much the bomb that did the damage; it was the stones blown out by the explosion. If you were standing anywhere within sixty feet when it went off, you were likely to be killed. The captain had had trenches dug all over camp into which they could jump—had one for himself just outside the tent. All you hoped for when one of those fellows was overhead and the shrapnel chasing after him was that the next one would take him fair and square and bring him down. Yet that fellow took his life in his hands every time he flew over. "He's fighting for his country, too!" the captain sighed.

It was our first duty to present ourselves to the commandant of the peninsular forces, Field-Marshal Liman von Sanders—Liman Pasha, as he is generally called in Turkey—and the captain found a carriage, presently, and sent us away with a soldier guard. Our carriage was a *talika*, one of those little gondola-like covered wagons common in the country. There is a seat for the driver; the occupants lie on the floor and adjust themselves as best they can to the bumpings of the hilly roads.

The country reminded one of parts of our own West—brown hills, with sparse pines and scrub-oaks, meadows ablaze with scarlet poppies, and over all blue sky, sunshine, and the breeze from the near-by sea. We passed camel trains, mule trains, horses, and tents masked with brush. Here evidently were the men we had seen marching day after day through the Constantinople streets—marching away to war in the si-lent Eastern fashion, without a waving handkerchief, a girl to say good-by to, or a cheer. Here they were and yet here they weren't, for the brush and tangled hills swallowed them up as thoroughly as armies are swallowed up in the villages of Belgium and France.

We passed even these signs of war and came into pines and open meadows—we might have been driving to somebody's trout preserve. The wagon stopped near a sign tacked to a tree, and we walked down a winding path into a thicket of pines. There were tents set in the bank and covered with boughs, and out of one came a tall, square-jawed German officer, buttoning his coat. He waved aside our passports with the air of one not concerned with such details, asked if we spoke German—or perhaps we would prefer French?—and, motioning down the path to a sort of summer-house with a table and chairs, told an orderly to bring tea.

This was the headquarters of the Fifth Army, and this the commander-in- chief. A bird-man might have flown over the neighbourhood a dozen times without guessing that they were there. We were hidden in the pines, and only an occasional far-off Br-r-rum-m! from the cannons in the south broke the stillness. Some one had brought up a cask of native claret from Chanak, and the field-marshal's staff were helping to put it into the bank in front of the arbour. A professor of chemistry—until the war called him back to the colours—was shovelling and showing the Turkish soldiers how the cask should be slanted; another of the superintendents had lived for ten years in America, and was enthusiastic over the charms and future of Davenport, Iowa. Presently tea came, and thin little sandwiches and cigars, and over these the commander-in-chief spoke with complete cheerfulness of the general situation.

The English and French could not force the Dardanelles; no more could they advance on land, and now that the submarines had arrived, the fleet, which had been bothersome, would be taken care of. He spoke with becoming sorrow of the behavior of Italy, and did not mar this charming little *fete champetre* with any remarks about American shipments of arms. The ex-banker from Davenport also spoke of the

161

Italians, and with a rather disconcerting vigour, considering that they were recent allies. The young aide-de-camp whom we had seen at the wharf declared that the Turkish soldier was the best in the world. It was a very different army from that which had been defeated in the Balkan War, and the endurance and tenacity of the individual soldier were beyond anything he had ever seen. A man would see a dozen of his comrades killed alongside him by a high-explosive shell and only shrug his shoulders and say that now, at any rate, they were all in paradise.

One continually hears similar comments, and there can be no doubt of the Turkish soldier's bravery, and his unusual ability to endure hardship. No one who has wrangled with a minor Turkish official, and experienced the impassive resistance he is able to interpose to anything he doesn't want to do, will underestimate what this quality might become, translated into the rugged physique and impassivity of the common soldier.

Westerners have heard so long of the Sick Man of Europe and his imminent decease that they are likely to associate political with physical weakness, and think that the pale, brooding, official type, familiar in photographs, is the every-day Turk. As a matter of fact, the every-day Turk is tough-bodied and tough-spirited, used to hard living and hard work. The soldiers you see swinging up Pera Hill or in from a practice march, dust-covered and sweating, and sending out through the dusty cedars a wailing sort of chant as they come—these are as splendid- looking fellows as you will see in any army in Europe.

They are dressed in businesslike fashion in dust-coloured woollen tunics and snug breeches with puttees, and wear a rather rakish-looking folded cap—a sort of conventionalized turban not unlike the soldier hats children make by folding newspapers. This protects the eyes and the back of the neck from the sun. They are strong and well made, with broad, high cheek-bones, a black moustache generally, and hawk eyes. Some look as the Tartar warriors who swept over eastern Europe must have looked; some, with their good-natured faces and vigorous compactness, remind one of Japanese infantrymen.

During the early fighting on the peninsula the wounded came up to Constantinople, after days on the way, in wagons, perhaps, over horrible roads, in commandeered ferry-boats and freighters, yet one scarcely heard a sound, a murmur of complaint. Gray and gaunt, with the mud of the trenches still on them, they would be helped into ambulances and driven off to the hospitals, silent themselves and through crowds as silent as those which had watched them march away a few weeks before.

From that little oasis in the pines we drove with a pass, signed by the field-marshal himself, taking us to the heights above Ari Burnu, to a point near the south front, a hill in the centre of the peninsula, from which we could see both the Dardanelles and the Aegean, and to a camp beneath it, where we were to spend the night.

It was dark when our wagon lurched into this camp, and a full hour passed before the baffled Turks could convince themselves that our pass and we were all that they should be, and put us into a tent. Nevertheless, an orderly poked his head in good-naturedly enough at seven next morning with tea and goat's cheese and brown bread, and our captain host, a rather wildish-looking young man from the Asiatic interior, came to say he had telephoned for permission to take us to the heights above Kaba Tepe and Ari Burnu.

The camp was the office, so to speak, of the division commander, with his clerks, telephone operator, commissary machinery, and so on, the commander himself living at the immediate front. It was like scores of other camps hidden away in the hills—brush-covered tents dug into the hillsides, looking like rather faded summer-houses; arbour-like horse-sheds, covered with branches, hidden in ravines; every wagon, gun, or piece of material that might offer a target to an aeroplane covered with brush. They were even painting grey horses that morning with a brown dye. A big 38-centimeter unexploded shell, dropped into a near-by village by the Queen Elizabeth, and with difficulty pushed up on end now by a dozen men, was shown us, and presently we climbed into the carriage with the captain, and went rocking over the rough road toward the Aegean.

The country reminded one of the California foothills in the dry season, and me, particularly, of Honduras and the road from the Pacific up to Tegucigalpa—gravelly brown hills and tangled valleys with sparse pines and scrub-oaks; rocky slopes down which tinkled brown and white flocks of sheep and goats; sunshine and scarlet poppies and fresh wind; and over all a curious, quiet, busy web of war; a long shoulder, sharp against the blue, with a brown camel train ambling down it; a ravine with its arbour-like shelters for cavalry; wounded soldiers in carts, or riding when they were able to ride; now and then an officer on his cranky little stallion—the whole countryside bristling with defence.

Up one of the hot little valleys we climbed, left the carriage, and, walking up a trail, cut into the bank, past men and horses hidden away like bandits, and came at last to the top and several tents dug into the rim of the hill. It was the headquarters of Essad Pasha, defender of Janina in the last war, and division commander in this sector of the front. He received us in his tent beside a table littered with maps and papers—a grizzled, good-natured soldier, who addressed us in German, and might indeed have passed for a German. He apologized for the cramped quarters, explaining that they were likely at any time to be bombarded, and had to live in what was practically a trench, and then at once, in the Turkish fashion, appeared an orderly with tiny cups of sweet coffee.

Things were quiet at the moment, he said. There was nothing but the desultory crack-crack of snipers, coming from one knew not just where, the every-day voice of the trenches—possibly the enemy were dismayed by the loss of the Triumph. He had seen it all, he said, from this very spot—a sight one was not likely to see more than once in a lifetime. The great ship had rolled over like a stricken whale. Her torpedo-nets were out, and as she turned over these nets closed down on the men struggling in the water, and swept them under. He, too, expressed entire confidence in the Turk's ability to stop any farther advance and, calling an aid, sent us to the periscope, which poked its two eyes through a screen of pine branches a few yards away, and looked over the parapet and down on the first-line trenches and the sea.

We were high above the Aegean and opposite the island of Imbros, which lifted its hazy blue on the western horizon, and was used as a base by part of the fleet. To the south rose the promontory of Kaba Tepe, cleared of the enemy now, our Turkish major said, and, stretching northward from it past us and Ari Burnu, the curving rim of beach held by the English.

More than a month had passed since the landing, and the heavy fighting of the next few days, in which the Australians and New Zealanders, under a hail of shrapnel churning up the water between ships and shore, succeeded in getting a foothold; a month and more had passed, and, though they still held their ground, apparently they could do no more. The yellow line of their first trench twisted along the rim of the hill below us, perhaps a quarter of a mile away, and directly behind it lay the blue sea. How much elbow-room they might have between their trenches and the water one could not tell, so completely foreshortened was the space between. Cliffs rise from a narrow strip of foreshore here, however, and apparently they had pushed just over the cliff rim—the first hill above the sea. Their tents, stores and landing-places were out of sight.

Directly in front of the English trenches were the first-line Turkish trenches, in some places not more than fifteen or twenty feet away, so close, indeed, that when there was fighting they must have fought with revolvers, hand-grenades, shovels, anything they could lay their hands on. At the moment it was quiet but for the constant *Crack. . . crack-crack!* of snipers.

We could look down on the backs and heads of the Turkish soldiers; except for a wisp of smoke rising here and there from some hidden camp cook-stove, there was not a sign of life in the English trenches. Snipers were attending to that. Even here, in the second-line trenches on top of the second hill, no one was allowed to show his head, and it was all the more curious to see a squad of Turkish soldiers digging away below as calmly as so many market-gardeners in a potato-field. They were running another trench behind the several that already lined the slope, and must have been hidden by a rise of ground, though looking down from above they seemed to be out in the open.

The position of the English did not seem enviable. They had trenches directly in front of them, and several hundred feet above them a second line (from which we were looking) dominating the whole neighbourhood. The first-line Turkish trenches were too close to their own to be bombarded from the ships, so that that preliminary advantage was cut off; the second-line defences, in the twisting gullies over the hill, could stand bombardment about as well as could trenches anywhere—and behind them was the water. They were very literally between the devil and the deep sea.

With the periscope we worked from Kaba Tepe on the left clear across the ground in front of us to the north. Over in the west, by hazy Imbros, were five or six ships; there was another fleet in the north to-ward the Gulf of Saros, and little black beetles of destroyers crawled here and there across the blue sea floor. The major took us into his tent for cigarettes and another thimbleful of the coffee. He, too, had been educated in Germany, spoke German and French, and with his quick, bright eyes and soft smile, would easily have passed for a Frenchman or Italian.

They had just had a seven hours' armistice to bury the dead and bring in the wounded, some of whom had been lying between the trenches for a week. The English had proposed the armistice; an officer had come out from each side, and they had had a long pow-wow and drawn up a written agreement with meticulous care lest there should be a misunderstanding or danger of breaking the truce. Everything, the major said, had been most good-natured and correct. The English had sent a "diplomat" in addition to their military delegate, a civilian whom he had known well in Constantinople. It was altogether quaint and interesting, meeting and talking with this man, with whom he might, so to speak, have been playing bridge the night before—*"Sehr nett! Sehr nett!"* he said. With his soft smile.

While he was waiting to receive the English delegate, five shrapnel- shells had been fired at him, he said; but he understood that it was a mistake and made no protest, and during the truce a wounded Turk had refused to take the water an English officer had tried to give him, firing at the Englishman instead. A little fanatical, perhaps, but then—and again the major smiled in his charming way—"a little fanaticism in one's soldiers is a good thing!"

No, one didn't care to be hanging on to that strip of beach with those Australians and New Zealanders. We drove back to camp for lunch, which we had in the captain's little brush-covered balcony, set into the hill. He did not eat, but showed us his photograph, very smooth and dapper, compared with his bristling service face, taken with his two children, one a little girl and the other a grave little boy, with a face like a miniature pasha. The captain came from the Asiatic side, near Broussa, on the slopes of Olympus, and was all Turk, without any foreign frills or a word of English, German, or French. He took no lunch, but ate some of the halva left over from Stamboul, and then started with us up the hill behind the camp.

This was about midway in the peninsula, and, facing south from the summit, we looked down over the twisting hills, pockmarked with holes from shells and aeroplane bombs, to the Marmora on the left, and on the right to the Aegean and hazy Imbros, and, in front, almost to the end of the peninsula. The sun was down in the west, and in its track a cruiser steamed a mile or two out from the coast, while from under Ari Burnu, where we had been that morning, a transport put out, rather recklessly it seemed, and went straight across the open water. From the south and west there was the continual *br-r-umr-m. . . br-r-um-m!* of big guns, and over Kaba Tepe way we could see shells bursting. We sat there for an hour or so, waiting for one of the little specks out on the blue sea floor to fire or sink, and then, as nothing happened, returned to camp.

An orderly brought us supper that night—mutton, bread and cheese, haricots, stewed fruit, and coffee—and we dined on a little table outside the tent, with the twilight turning to moonlight and the sheep-bells tinkling against the opposite hill. Soldiers were carrying their suppers from the cook tent—not at all the bread-and-cigarette diet with which one is always being told the hardy Turk is content. He may be content, but whenever I saw him eating he had meat and rice, and often stewed fresh beans or fruit—certainly better food than most Turkish peasants or artisans are accustomed to at home.

I sat outside watching the moon rise and listening to the distant Crack. . . crack-crack! of rifle and machine-gun fire from over Ari Bumu way. Evidently they were fighting in the trenches we had seen that morning. The orderly who had served us, withdrawn a little way, was standing like a statue in the dusk, hands folded in front of him, saying his last prayer of the evening. Beyond, from a bush-covered tent, came the jingle of a telephone and 'the singsong voice of the young Turkish operator relaying messages in German—*"Ja!. . .Ja!. . . Kaba Tepe. . . Ousedom Pasha. . . Morgen frith. . . Hier Multepe!. . .Ja!. . .Ja!"*

And to this and the distant rattle of battle we went to sleep.

CHAPTER 12

Soghan-Dere and the Flier of Ak-Bash

Next morning, after news had been telephoned in that the submarines had got another battleship, the Majestic, we climbed again into the covered wagon and started for the south front. We drove down to the sea and along the beach road through Maidos—bombarded several weeks before, cross-country from the Aegean, and nothing now but bare, burnt walls—on to Kilid Bahr, jammed with camels and ox-carts and soldiers, and then on toward the end of the peninsula.

We were now beyond the Narrows and the Dardanelles. To the left, a bit farther out, were the waters in which the *Irresistible*, *Ocean*, and *Bouvet* were sunk, and even now, off the point, ten or twelve miles away, hung the smoke of sister ships. We drove past the big guns of the forts, past field-guns covering the shore, past masked batteries and search-lights. Beside us, along the shore road, mule trains and ox-carts and camel trains were toiling along in the blaze and dust with provisions and ammunition for the front. Once we passed four soldiers carrying a comrade, badly wounded, on a stretcher padded with leaves. After an hour or so of bumping we turned into a transverse valley, as level almost as if it had been made for a parade-ground.

High hills protected it north and south; a little stream ran down the centre—it might have been made for a storage base and camp. More brush-covered tents and arbours for horses were strung along the hillside, one above the other sometimes, in half a dozen terraces. We drove into the valley, got out and followed the orderly to a brush-covered arbour, closed on every side but one, out of which came a well set-up, bronzed, bright-eyed man of fifty or thereabout who welcomed us like long-lost friends.

It was Colonel Shukri Bey, commander of the Fifteenth Division. We were the first correspondents who had pushed thus far, and as novel to him apparently as he was charming to us. He invited us into the little arbour; coffee was brought and then tea, and, speaking German to Suydam and French to me, he talked of the war in general and the operations at the end of the peninsula with the greatest good humour and apparent confidence in the ultimate result.

Our talk was continually punctuated by the rumble of the big guns over the plateau to the south. "That's ours"... "That's theirs," he would explain; and presently, with a young aide-de-camp as guide, we climbed out of the valley and started down the plateau toward Sedd ul Bahr. The Allies' foothold here was much wider than that at An Burnu. In the general landing operations of April 25 and 26 (one force was sent ashore in a large collier, from which, after she was beached, the men poured across anchored lighters to the shore) the English and French had established themselves in Sedd ul Bahr itself and along the cliffs on either side. This position was strengthened during the weeks of fighting which followed until they appeared to be pretty firmly fixed on the end of the peninsula, with a front running clear across it in a general northwest line, several kilometres in from the point. The valley we had just left was Soghan-Dere, about seven miles from Sedd ul Bahr, and the plateau across which we were walking led, on the right, up to a ridge from which one could look down on the whole battlefield, or, to the left, straight down into the battle itself.

The sun was getting down in the west by this time, down the road from camp men were carrying kettles of soup and rice pilaf to their comrades in the trenches, and from the end of the plateau came continuous thundering and the *Crack... crack... crack!* of infantry fire. The road was strewn with fragments of shells from previous bombardments, and our solicitous young lieutenant, fearing we might draw fire, pulled us behind a bush for a minute or two, whenever the aeroplane, flying back and forth in the west, seemed to be squinting at us. The enemy could see so little, he said, that whenever they saw anything at all they fired twenty shots at it on principle.

For two miles, perhaps, we walked, until from the innocent-looking chaparral behind us there was a roar, and a shell wailed away over our heads out into the distance.

We could see the end of the peninsula, where the coast curves round from Eski Hissariik toward Sedd ul Bahr, and two of the enemy's cruisers steaming slowly back and forth under the cliffs, firing, presumably, as they steamed. Now they were hidden under the shore, now they came in view, and opposite Eski Hissarlik swung round and steamed west again. In front of us, just over the edge of the plateau which there began to slope downward, were the trenches of the Turks' left wing, now under bombardment. The ridge just hid the shells as they struck, but we could see the smoke from each, now a tall black column, like the "Jack Johnsons" of the west, now a yellowish cloud that hung long afterward like fog—and with it the continuous rattle of infantry fire. Several fliers were creeping about far up against the 'blue, looking for just such hidden batteries as that which kept barking behind us, and out in front and to the right came the low Br—r—um—m! of heavy guns.

Fighting like this had been going on for weeks, the ships having the advantage of their big guns by day, the Turks recovering themselves, apparently, at night. They were on their own ground—a succession of ridges, one behind the other—and they could not only always see, but generally looked down on, an enemy who could not, generally, see them. And the enemy's men, supplies, perhaps even his water—for this is a dry country at all times, and after June there are almost no rains—must come from his ships. If English submarines were in the Marmora, so, too, were German submarines off the Dardanelles, and if the Turks were losing transports the English were losing battleships.

The situation held too many possibilities to make prophecy safe—I merely record the fact that on the afternoon of May 27 I stood on the plateau above Sedd ul Bahr, and perhaps five miles from it in an air line, and still found myself a regrettable distance from the Allies' front.

The sun was shining level down the road as we returned to camp, and soldiers were still tramping peacefully up to the front with their kettles of food. Meanwhile the colonel had prepared a little exhibition for us. Six or eight soldiers stood in line, each with a dish and spoon, and in the dish a sample of the food for that night. We started at the top and tasted each: soup, mutton, stewed green beans, new-baked bread, stewed plums, and a particularly appetizing pilaf, made out of boiled whole wheat and raisins. Everything was good, and the beaming colonel declared that the first thing in war was to keep your soldiers well fed. We dined with him in his tent: soup and several meat courses, and cherry compote, and at the end various kinds of nuts, including the cracked hazelnuts, commoner in Turkey than bananas and peanuts at home.

He hoped to come to America some day, and thought we must soon develop the military strength to back our desires for peace, unless there were to be continual wars. New York's climate, the cost of fruit in Germany, and other peaceful subjects were touched on, and the colonel said that it was an honour to have us with him—ours we brilliantly responded—and a pleasant change from the constant talk and thought of war.

He had been six years in the field now, what with the Italian and Balkan campaigns, and that was a good deal of war at a stretch.

After excusing ourselves, though the amiable Turk said that he was in no hurry, we were led to a sort of tent *de luxe*, lined in scarlet with snaky decorations in white, and when the young aid discovered that we had brought no beds with us, he sent out and in a moment had not only cots and blankets, but mattresses and sheets and pillows and pillow-cases. He asked if we had fathers and mothers alive at home, and brothers and sisters, and if we, too, had been soldiers. It surprised and puzzled him that we had not, and that our army was so small. He was only twenty-two and a lieutenant, and he had a brother and father also in the army. With a great air of mystery he had his orderly dig a bottle of cognac out from his camp chest, and after we had drunk each other's health, he gave us his card with his name in Turkish and French. He brought a table and put on it a night candle in a saucer of water, a carafe of drinking water, and gave me a pair of slippers—in short, he did for us in that brush-covered camp in the Gallipoli hills everything that could be done for a guest in one's own house.

You can scarcely know what this meant without having known the difficulties of mere existence once you left Constantinople and got into the war zone, and Colonel Shukri Bey and Lieutenant Ahmed Akif will be remembered by at least two Americans when any one talks of the terrible Turk.

I awoke shortly after daylight, thinking I heard an aeroplane strumming in the distance, and was drowsily wondering whether or not it was fancy, when a crash echoed up the valley. We both hurried out. It was sunup, a delicious morning, and far up against the southern sky the little speck was sailing back toward the west. There was a flash of silver just under the flier—it was an English biplane—and a moment later another crash farther away. Neither did any damage. A few minutes later we were looking at the remains of the bomb and propeller-like wings, whose whirling, as it falls, opens a valve that permits it to explode on striking its mark. Until it had fallen a certain number of metres, we were told, mere striking the ground would not explode it—a device to protect the airman in case of accident to his machine or if he is forced to make a quick landing. In the fresh, still morning, with the camp just waking up and the curious Turkish currycombs clinking away over by the tethered horses, our aerial visitor added only a pleasant excitement to this life in the open, and we went on with our dressing with great satisfaction, little dreaming how soon we were to look at one of those little flying specks quite differently.

We breakfasted with the colonel in his arbour on bread and ripe olives and tea, and walked with him round the camp, through a hospital and into an old farmhouse yard, where the gunsmiths were going over stacks of captured guns and the damaged rifles of the wounded, while the bees left behind in some clumsy old box hives buzzed away as of yore. Wiser than men, the colonel observed. There were English Enfields and French rifles of the early nineties, and a mitrailleuse to which the Turks had fitted a new wooden base. There were rifles with smashed barrels, with stocks bored through by bullets, clean-cut holes that must have gone on through the men who held them—live men like ourselves; quick choking instants of terror the ghosts of——which we were poking and peering into there in the warm sunshine!

We said good-by to the colonel, for our passes took us but to the valley, and he had stretched a point in sending us down the plateau the evening before, and I bumped back to Kilid Bahr. We did not want to leave this part of the world without a sight of Troy, and as we had duly presented ourselves in Gallipoli, and were now by way of coming from it rather than Constantinople, and the Turkish official to whom the orderly took us wrote, without question, a permission to cross to Chanak Kale, we sailed with no misgivings. Alas for Troy and looking down on a modern battle from the heights of Ilium! A truculent major of gendarmes hurried us from the Asiatic shore as if we had come to capture it. We might not land, we might not write a note to the commandant to see if the permission to stop in Chanak, for which we had wired to Constantinople the day before, had arrived; we might not telephone—we must go back to Europe, and write or telephone from there.

So back to Europe, and after consultation and telephoning, back to Asia again, and this time we succeeded in effecting a landing and an audience with the commander of the defences of the Dardanelles, Djevad Pasha. He was sitting under a tree in a garden looking out over the sea gate, which, with the aid of his two German colleagues, Ousedom Pasha and Merten Pasha, it was his task to keep shut—a trim Young Turk, more polished and "European" than the major of *gendarmes*, but no less firm. An American's wish to see the Troy he might never be so near again bored him excessively. We could not stay— we might not even spend the night. There was a boat that evening, and on it we must go.

Gendarmes guarded us while we waited—we who the night before had slept in a scarlet-lined tent!—and gendarmes hung at our heels as we and three patient *hamals* with the baggage tramped ignominiously through Chanak Kale's ruined streets. The boat we went by was the same little side-wheeler we had come down on, crowded with wounded now, mud-stained, blood-stained, just as they had come from the trenches across the water, with no place to lie but the bare deck. The stifling hold was packed with them; they curled up about the engine-room gratings—for it was cold that night—yet there was no complaint. A tired sigh now and then, a moan of weariness, and the soldier wrapped his army overcoat a little closer about him, curled up like a dog on a door-mat, and left the rest to fate. A big, round, yellow moon climbed up out of Asia and poured its silver down on them and on the black hills and water, still as some inland lake.

The side-wheeler tied up at Ak-Bash for the night, and it was not until the middle of the next morning that it was decided that she should cross and leave her wounded at Lap-saki instead of going on up to Constantinople. We lugged our baggage off and hunted up our old friend, the Hamburg-American captain, to see what might be done till some other craft appeared. He finally put us aboard a sort of enlarged tug which might be going up that afternoon or evening.

It was about midday. The sun blazing down on the crowded fiat; on boxes, sacks, stevedores wrapped up in all the variegated rags of the East shuffling in and out of the ships; on gangs digging, piling lumber, boiling water, cooking soup; on officers in brown uniforms and brown lamb's-wool caps; on horses, ox-teams, and a vast herd of sheep, which had just poured out of a transport and spread over the plain, when from the hill came two shots of warning. An enemy aeroplane was coming!

The gangs scattered like water-bugs when a stone is thrown into the water. They ran for the hill, dropped into trenches; to the beach and threw themselves flat on the sand; into the water—all, as they ran, looking up over their shoulders to where, far overhead, whirred steadily nearer that tiny, terrible hawk.

A hidden battery roared and—pop!—a little puff of cotton floated in the sky under the approaching flier. Another and another—all the nervous little batteries in the hills round about were coming to our rescue. The bird-man, safely above them, drew on without flinching. We had looked up at aeroplanes many times before and watched the pretty chase of the shrapnel, and we leaned out from under the awning to keep the thing in view. "Look," I said to Suydam; "she's coming right over us!" And then, all at once, there was a crash, a concussion that hit the ear like a blow, a geyser of smoke and dust and stones out on the flat in front of us. Through the smoke I saw a horse with its pack undone and flopping under its belly, trotting round with the wild aimlessness of horses in the bull-ring after they have been gored. Men were running, and, in a tangle of wagons, half a dozen oxen, on the ground, were giving a few spasmodic kicks.

Men streaked up from the engine-room and across the wharf—after all, the wharf would be the thing he'd try for—and I found myself out on the flat with them just as there came another crash, but this time over by the *Barbarossa* across the bay. Black smoke was pouring from the Turkish cruiser as she got under way, and, with the shrapnel puffs chasing hopelessly after, the flier swung to the southward and out of right.

Officers were galloping about yelling orders; over in the dust where the bomb had struck, a man was sawing furiously away at the throats of the oxen (there were seven of them, and there would be plenty of beef in camp that night at any rate); there was a dead horse, two badly wounded men and a hundred feet away a man lying on his face, hatless, just as he had been blown there: dead, or as good as dead. It appeared that two fliers had come from opposite directions and most of the crowd had seen but the one, while the other dropped the bomb. It had struck just outside the busiest part of the camp, aimed very likely at the stores piled there. It had made a hole only five or six feet wide and two or three feet deep, but it had blown everything in the neighbourhood out from it, as the captain had said. Holes you could put your fist in were torn in the flanks of the oxen by flying stones and chunks of metal, and the tires of some of the wagons, sixty or seventy feet away, had been cut through like wax.

The ground was cleared, the men returned to work, and we even went in swimming, but at every unexpected noise one looked upward, and when about five o'clock the crowd scattered again, I will confess that I watched that little speck buzzing nearer, on a line that would bring him straight overhead, with an interest considerably less casual than any I had bestowed on these birds before. There we were, confined in our little amphitheatre; there was that diabolical bird peering down at us, and in another minute, somewhere in that space, would come that earth-shaking explosion—a mingling of crash and *vohou'*! There was no escaping it, no dodging it, nothing to get under but empty air.

I had decided that the beach, about a hundred yards away from the wharfs, was the safest place and hurried there; but the speck overhead, as if anticipating me, seemed to be aiming for the precise spot. It is difficult under such circumstances to sit tight, reasoning calmly that, after all, the chances of the bomb's not landing exactly there are a good many to one—you demand at least the ostrich-like satisfaction of having something overhead. So I scurried over to the left to get out from under what seemed his line of flight, when what should he do but begin to turn!

This was really rubbing it in a bit. To fly across as he had that morning was one thing, but to pen one up in a nice little pocket in the hills, and then on a vertical radius of three or four thousand feet, to circle round over one's head—anything yet devised by the human nightmare was crude and immature to this. But was it overhead? If behind, and travelling at fifty or sixty miles an hour, the bomb would carry forward—just enough probably to bring it over; and if apparently over, still the bomb would have been several seconds in falling—it might be right on top of us now! Should we run backward or forward: Here was a place, in between some grain-bags. But the grain-bags were open toward the wharf, and the wharf was what he was aiming at, and a plank blown through you— No, the trench was the thing, but—Quick, he is overhead!

The beach, the bags, the ditch, all the way round the camp, and Suydam galloping after. Somewhere in the middle of it a hideous whiffling wail came down the sky: *Trrou. . . trrou. . . trou!*—and then a *crash!* The bomb had hit the water just off the end of the pier. I kept on running. There was another *Trrou. . . trrou!* another geyser of water, and the bird had flown on.

I was on the edge of the camp by this time and that strange afternoon ended, when one of a gang of ditch-diggers, swathed in bright-coloured rags, addressed me in English, a Greek-Turk from the island of Marmora, who, climbing out of the trench in which he and his gang had been hiding, announced that he had lived in New York for five years, in Fortieth Street, and worked for the Morgan Line, and begged that I get, him out of this nerve-racking place and where he belonged, some-where on board ship. There were crowds like him—Greeks, Armenians, Turks, not wanted as soldiers but impressed for this sort of work. They were unloading fire-wood long af-ter dark that night, when our boat at last got under way. We paused till sunup at Lapsaki, crept close to shore through the Marmora, and once through floating wreckage—boards and a galvanized-iron gasoline tank—apparently from some trans-port sunk by a submarine, and after dark, with lights out as we had started, round the corner of Stamboul.

CHAPTER 13

A War Correspondents' Village

The press department of the Foreign Office in Vienna duly presented the application to the press bureau of the Ministry of War; the latter conveyed it to the *"Kaiserliche und Konigliche Armee-Oberkommando Kriegs-Presse-Quartier,"* a day's railroad journey nearer the front; the commandant made his recommendation to the chief of the General Staff. The permission itself percolated back to Vienna presently, and early next morning I took the Teschen express.

It was one of those semi-military trains which run into this region behind the front—officers and couriers, civilians with military passes, just before we started a young officer and his orderly saying good-by to their wives. He was one of those amiable, blue-eyed young Austrians who seem a sort of cross between German and French, and the orderly was much such another man, only less neatly made and sensitive, and there were the same differences in their wives and their good-bys.

The orderly saluted his officer, turned, clicked his heels, and saluted his officer's lady before he embraced his solid wife. The latter, rather proud to be in such company, beamed like a stove as the two men looked down from the car steps, but the girlish wife of the captain bit her lips, looked nervously from side to side, winked faster and faster until the tears began to roll down her cheeks. Then the train started, the orderly waving his hand, but the young officer, leaning quickly forward, drew his wife toward him and kissed her on one of the wet eyelids.

We crossed into Hungary, rolled north-eastward for five or six hours into the Vag valley, with its green hills and vineyards and ruined castles, and finally came to a little place consisting almost entirely of consonants, in the Tatra foot-hills. Two blond soldiers in blue-grey saluted, took my luggage, showed me to a carriage, and drove to a village about a mile away—a little white village with a factory chimney for the new days, a dingy chateau for the old, and a brook running diagonally across the square, with geese quacking in it and women pounding clothes.

It was mid-afternoon, yet lunch had been kept waiting, and the officer who received me said he was sorry I had bothered to eat on the train. He told me where lodgings had been made ready, and that an orderly would take me there and look after my personal needs. They dined at eight, and at five, if I felt like it, I would probably find some of them in the coffee-house by the chateau. Meanwhile the first thing to do was to take one's cholera vaccination—for no one could go to the Galician front without being *geimpft*—and just as soon as I could take the second, a week later, we should start for the Russian front. In this fashion were strangers welcomed to the *"Presse-Quartier,"* or rather to that part of it—this little Hungarian village—in which correspondents lived during the intervals of their trips to the front. The Austrians have pleasant manners. Their court is, next to that of Spain, the most formal in Europe, and ordinary life still retains many of the older courtesies. Every time I came into my hotel in Vienna the two little boys at the door jumped up and extended their caps at arm's length; an assistant porter, farther in, did the same; the head porter behind the desk often followed, and occasionally all four executed the manoeuvre at once, so that it was like a musical comedy but for the music.

The ordinary salutation in Vienna, as common as our "hello!" is "I have the honour" (*Ich habe die Ehre!*). In Hungary—of course one mustn't tell a Hungarian that he is "Austrian"—people tell you that they are your humble servants before they say good morning, and those who really are humble servants not only say "Kiss the hands," but every now and then do it. It was natural, therefore, perhaps, that the Austro-Hungarians should treat war correspondents—often, in these days, supposed to be extinct—not only seriously but with a certain air. They had not only the air but indeed a more elaborate organization than any of the other belligerents.

At the beginning of the war England permitted no correspondents at all at the front. France was less rigid, yet it was months before groups of observers began to be taken to the trenches.

Germany took correspondents to the front from the first, but these excursions came at irregular intervals, and admission to them involved a good deal of competitive wire-pulling between the correspondents themselves. The Austro-Hungarians, on the other hand, prepared from the first for a large number of civilian observers, including news and special writers, photographers, illustrators, and painters, and, to handle them satisfactorily, organized a special department of the army, this *Presse-Quartier*, once admitted to which—the fakirs and fly-by-nights were supposed to be weeded out by the preliminary red tape—they were assumed to be serious workmen and treated as the army's guests.

The *Presse-Quartier* was divided into two sections: an executive section, with a commandant responsible for the arrangement of trips to the various fronts, and the general business of censorship and publicity; and an entertainment section, so to speak, also with its commandant, whose business it was to board, lodge, and otherwise look after correspondents when they were not on trips to the front. At the time I visited the *Presse-Quartier*, the executive section was in Teschen; the correspondents lived in Nagybiesce, two or three hours' railroad journey away.

It was to this village—the most novel part of the scheme—that I had come that afternoon, and here some thirty or forty correspondents were living, writing past adventures, setting forth on new ones, or merely inviting their souls for the moment under a regime which combined the functions of tourists' bureau, rest-cure, and a sort of military club.

For the time being they were part of the army—fed, lodged, and transported at the army's expense, and unable to leave without formal military permission. They were supposed to "enlist for the whole war," so to speak, and most of the Austro-Hungarian and German correspondents had so remained—some had even written books there—but observers from neutral countries were permitted to leave when they felt they had seen enough.

Isolated thus in the country, the only mail the military field post, the only telegrams those that passed the military censor, correspondents were as "safe" as in Siberia. They, on the other hand, had the advantage of an established position, of living inexpensively in pleasant surroundings, where their relations with the censor and the army were less those of policemen and of suspicious character than of host and guest. To be welcomed here, after the usual fretful dangling and wire-pulling in War Office anterooms and city hotels—with hills and ruined castles to walk to, a brook rippling under one's bedroom window, and all the time in the world—seemed idyllic enough.

We were quartered in private houses, and as there was one man to a family generally, he was put in the villager's room of honour, with a tall porcelain stove in the corner, a feather bed under him, and another on top. Each man had a soldier servant who looked after boots and luggage, kept him supplied with cigars and cigarettes from the *Quartier commissariat*—for a paternal government included even tobacco!—and charmed the simple republican heart by whacking his heels together whenever spoken to and flinging back *"Jawohl!"*

We breakfasted separately, whenever we felt like it, on the rolls with the glass of whipped cream and coffee usual in this part of the world; lunched and dined—officers and correspondents—together. There were soldier waiters who with military precision told how many pieces one might take, and on every table big carafes of Hungarian white wine, drunk generally instead of water. For beer one paid extra.

The commandant and his staff, including a doctor, and the officer guides not on excursions at the moment, sat at the head of the long U-shaped table. Any one who came in or went out after the commandant was seated was supposed to advance a bit into this "U," catch his eye, bow, and receive his returning nod. The silver click of spurs, of course, accompanied this salute when an officer left the room, and the Austro-Hungarian and German correspondents generally snapped their heels together in semi-military fashion. All our goings and comings, indeed, were accompanied by a good deal of manner. People who had seen each other at breakfast shook hands formally half an hour later in the village square, and one bowed and was bowed to and heard the singsong ... *"habe die Ehre!"* a dozen times a day.

Nagybiesce is in northern Hungary, and the peasants round about were Slovaks—sturdy, solid, blond people with legs the same size all the way down. Many of them still reaped with scythes and thrashed on the barn floor with old-fashioned flails, and one afternoon there was a curious plaintive singing under my window—a party of harvesters, oldish men and brown, barefooted peasant girls, who had finished their work on a neighbouring farm, and were crossing our village on their way to their own.

The *Quartier* naturally stirred things up a good deal in Nagybiesce. There was one week when we could not go into the street without being surrounded by little girls with pencils and cards asking for our "autogram." The candy shop kept by two girl wives whose husbands were at the front did a vast business, and the young women had somebody to talk to all day long. The evening the news came that Warsaw had fallen, candles were lighted in all the windows on the square, and the band with the villagers behind it came to serenade us as we were at dinner. The commandant bowed from the window, but a young Hungarian journalist leaned out and without a moment's hesitation poured forth a torrent for fully fifteen minutes with scarce a pause for breath. I told him that such impromptu oratory seemed marvellous, but he dismissed it as nothing. "I'm *politiker!*" he explained, with a wave of his hand.

One day a man came into lunch with the news that he was off on the best trip he'd had yet—he was going back to Vienna for his skis, to go down into the Tyrol and work along the glaciers to the battery positions. Another man, a Budapest painter, started off for an indefinite stay with an army corps in Bessarabia. He was to be, indeed, part of the army for the time being, and all his work belonged to the army first. As this is being written a number of painters sent out on similar expeditions have been giving an exhibition in Vienna—portraits and pencil sketches much like those Frederic Remington used to make. Foreigners not intending to remain in Austria-Hungary could not expect such privileges, naturally; but if they were admitted to the *Quartier* at all they were sent on the ordinary group excursions like the home correspondents themselves. Indeed, the wonder was—in view of the comparative ease with which neutral correspondents drifted about Europe: the naivete, to put it mildly, with which the wildest romances had been printed in American newspapers, that we were permitted to see as much as we did.

When a group started for the front, it left Nagybiesce in its own car, which, except when the itinerary included some large city—Lemberg, for instance—served as a little hotel until they came back again. The car was a clean, second-class coach, of the usual European compartment kind, two men to a compartment, and at night they bunked on the long transverse seats comfortably enough. We took one long trip of a thousand miles or so in this way, taking our own motor, on a separate flat car, and even an orderly servant for each man. Each of these groups was, of course, accompanied by an officer guide—several were detailed at the *Quartier* for this special duty—whose complex and nerve-racking task it was to answer all questions, make all arrangements, report to each local commandant, pass sentries, and comfortably waft his flock of civilians through the maze of barriers which cover every foot, so to speak, of the region near the front.

The things correspondents were permitted to see differed from those seen on the other fronts less in kind than in quantity. More trips were made, but there is and can be little place for a civilian on a "front," any spot in which, over a strip several miles wide, from the heavy artillery positions of one side to the heavy artillery of the other, may be in absolute quiet one minute and the next the centre of fire. There is no time to bother with civilians during an offensive, and, if a retreat is likely, no commander wishes to have country described which may presently be in the hands of the enemy. Hidden batteries in action, reserves moving up, wounded coming back, fliers, trenches quiet for the moment—this is about as close to actual fighting as the outsider, under ordinary circumstances, can expect to get on any front. The difference in Austria-Hungary was that correspondents saw these things, and the battle-fields and captured cities, not as mere outsiders, picked up from a hotel and presently to be dropped there again, but as, in a sense, a part of the army itself. They had their commandant to report to, their "camp" and "uniform"—the gold-and-black *Presse-Quartier* arm band—and when they had finished one excursion they returned to headquarters with the reasonable certainty that in another ten days or so they would start out again.

CHAPTER 14

Cannon Fodder

At the head of each iron bed hung the nurse's chart and a few words of "history." These histories had been taken down as the wounded came in, after their muddy uniforms had been removed, they had been bathed, and could sink, at last, into the blessed peace and cleanness of the hospital bed. And through them, as through the large end of a telescope, one looked across the hot summer and the Hungarian fields, now dusty and yellow, to the winter fighting and freezing in the Carpathians.

"Possibly," the doctor said, "you would like to see one of these cases." The young fellow was scarce twenty, a strapping boy with fine teeth and intelligent eyes. He looked quite well; you could imagine him pitching hay or dancing the czardas, with his hands on his girl's waist and her hands on his, as these Hungarian peasants dance, round and round, for hours together. But he would not dance again, as both his feet had been amputated at the ankle and it was from the stumps that the doctor was unwrapping the bandages. The history read: While doing sentry duty on the mountains on March 28, we were left twenty-four hours without being relieved and during that time my feet were frozen.

The doctor spoke with professional briskness. He himself would not have tried to save any of the foot—better amputate at once at the line of demarcation, get a good flap of healthy tissue and make a proper stump. "That scar tissue'll never heal—it'll always be tender and break when he tries to use it; he has been here four months now, and you can see how tender it is."

The boy scowled and grinned as the doctor touched the scar. For our English and those things under the sheet he seemed to have much the same feeling of strangeness: both were something foreign, rather uncomfortable. He looked relieved when the bandages were on again and the white sheet drawn up. "We had dozens of them during the winter—one hundred and sixty-three frozen feet and one hundred frozen hands in this hospital alone. They had to be driven back from the front in carts, for days sometimes. When they got here their feet were black—literally rotting away. Nothing to do but let the flesh slough off and then amputate."

We strolled on down the sunny, clean-smelling wards. The windows were open. They were playing tennis in the yard below; on a bench under a tree a young Hungarian soldier, one arm in a sling, and a girl were reading the same book. Sunday is a very genial day in Budapest. The café tables are crowded, orchestras playing everywhere, and in dozens of pavilions and on the grass and gravel outside them peasants and the humbler sort of people are dancing. The Danube—beautiful if not blue—flows through the town.

Pest is on one bank and Buda on the other, beside a wooded hill climbing steeply up to the old citadel, somewhat as the west bank of the Hudson climbs up to Storm King.

I first came on the Danube at Budapest in the evening after dinner and saw, close in front of me, what looked to be some curious electric-light sign. It seemed odd in war time, and I stared for a moment before I saw that this strange design was really the black, opposite bank with its zigzag streams of lamps.

Few cities have so naturally beautiful a drop-curtain, and, instead of spoiling it with gas-works' and grain-elevators as we should do, the Hungarians have been thoughtful enough to build a tree-covered promenade between the Danube and the string of hotels which line the river. In front of each of these hotels is a double row of tables and a hedge, and then the trees, under which, while the orchestras play, all Pest comes to stroll and take the air between coffee-time and the late Hungarian dinner.

Hundreds of cities have some such promenade, but few so genial and cosy a one as that of Budapest—not the brittle gayety of some more sophisticated capitals, but the simpler light-heartedness of a people full of feeling, fond of music and talk, and ready to share all they have with a stranger.

The bands play tunes from our musical comedies, but every now and then—and this is what the people like best—they swing into the strange, rolling, passionate-melancholy music of the country. Wherever the *tzigany* music comes from, it seems Hungarian, at any rate—fiery and indolent and haphazard, rolling on without any particular rhyme or reason, now piling up and now sinking indolently back as the waves roll up and fall back on the sand. People will listen to it for hours, and you can imagine one of those simpler daredevils—a hussar, for instance—in his blue-braided jacket, red breeches, and big cavalry boots, listening and drinking, and thinking of the fights he has won and the girls he has lost, getting sorry for himself at last and breaking his glass and weeping, and being very happy indeed.

There is a club in Budapest—at once a club and a luxurious villa almost too crowded with rugs and fine furniture. When you go to play tennis, instead of the ordinary locker-room one is ushered into a sort of boudoir filled with Chippendale furniture. It is a delightful place to get exercise, with tea served on a garden table between sets; yet, when I was in Budapest, the place was almost deserted. It was not, it seemed, the season that people came there, although just the season to use such a place. For six weeks they came here, and nothing could bring them back again. They did things only in spurts, so to speak: "They go off on hunting trips to the ends of the earth, bring back animals for the Zoo, then off to their country places and—flop! Then there is a racing season, and they play polo and race for a while, then—flop!"

I have never seen such interesting photographers' show-windows as there are in Budapest. Partly this is because the photographers are good, but partly it must he in the Hungarians themselves—such vivid, interesting, unconventional faces.

These people look as if they ought to do the acting and write the music and novels and plays and paint the pictures for all the rest of the world. If they haven't done so, it must be because, along with their natural talent, they have this indolence and tendency to flop and not push things through.

It was this Budapest, so easy-going and cheerful, that came drifting through the hospital windows, with the faint sound of band music that Sunday afternoon.

On all the park benches and the paths winding up to the citadel, in a hundred shady corners and walks, soldiers, with canes and bandages, were sitting with their best girls, laughing with them, holding hands. The boys, with miniature flower-gardens in their hats, tinselled grass and red-white-and-green rosettes, could sit with their arms round their sweethearts as much as they wanted to, for everybody knew that they had just been called to the colours and this was their farewell.

I looked over more of the histories—not in the ward, where one was, of course, more or less a nuisance, but in the room where they were filed in hundred lots. Some of the men were still in the hospital, some had died, most of them gone back to the front. There were many of these foot cases:

"While on outpost duty in the Carpathians during a snow-storm I felt the lower part of my body becoming powerless. Not being able to walk, was carried back and put on train. Next day we were stopped, because Russians were ahead of us, and obliged to leave train. Waited two days without food or medical attention; then put on train for Budapest."

"My regiment was in the Carpathians, and on or about January 20 my feet refused to obey. I held out for four days and then reported ill. Toes amputated, right foot."

"I belong to German Grenadier Regiment No.——. On February 6, while sleeping in open snow, I felt numbed in feet. Put on light duty, but on 8th reported ill and doctor declared feet frozen."

"March 12, during heavy snowstorm, Russians attacked us. One of my comrades was shot in stomach, and I took off my gloves to bandage him. All at once our regiment sounded 'Storm!' and I had to rush off to attack, forgetting my gloves. I had both my hands frozen."

"I am field-cornet of the——-German Grenadiers. I was, since the beginning of the war, in Belgium and France, and at end of November sent to Russian Poland and January 1 to Carpathians. On February 6, while retiring to prevent the Russians surrounding us, I was shot In thigh at 1,500 yards distance and fell. Within a few minutes I got two more shots."

"That's just like a German," commented the nurse. "They always begin by telling just who they are and what they were doing. A Hungarian would probably just say that he was up in the mountains and it was cold. These soldiers are like big children, some of them, and they tell us things sometimes."

"While in Carpathians on January 20 I reported to my lieutenant, feet frozen. He said dig a hole and when you are quite frozen we will put you in. I stood it another seven days, then we had to retreat. I went myself to the doctor; my feet were then black already. Debreczen hospital six days, then here. Both amputated."

The feet were gone, at any rate, whatever the lieutenant may have said. We returned to the German field-cornet.

"He came in walking—a fine, tall man. We had only one place to bathe the men in, then: a big tank—for everything was improvised and there was no hot-water heater—and one of the doctors told him he could use his own bath upstairs, but he said no, he'd stay with his men. He seemed to be getting on all right, then one morning the doctor touched his leg and he heard that crackling sound—it was gas infection. They just slit his leg down from hip to knee, but it was no use—he died in three hours. Practically all the wounds were infected when the men came in, but suppose he could have picked up something in that bath? He came in walking."

Through most of the German histories one could see the German armies turning now this way, now that, against their "world of enemies," as they say:

"I belong to—Regiment German Infantry and am stationed since March 1 in Carpathians. I am in active service since the start, having done Belgium, France, and Russia."

"While at battle of Luneville, with troop of about forty men stormed battery, capturing them, for which decorated with Iron Cross. Shifted to Carpathians. After march in severe cold, fingers and feet frozen."

"While in France attacking I was hit in head by shrapnel. In hospital fourteen days, then sent to Carpathians on December 7 with Austro-Hungarian troops. Wounded in arm and while creeping back hit five times in fifteen minutes. Lay all afternoon in trenches."

"I think those are the three who came in together one night, all singing 'Die Wacht am Rhein'; they all had the Iron Cross. They were a noisy lot. They all got well and went back to the front again."

Here were three pictures from the Galician fighting:

"Wounded by shrapnel near Przemysl, bandaged by comrade, and helped to house; only occupant old woman. Lay on straw two days, no food. Called to men passing; they had me moved in cart seventy miles to hospital. Stayed eight days; started on train, then taken off for three days, then to Budapest."

"During fighting at Lupkow Pass I was wounded by two pistol-shots. First one, fired by Russian officer, hit me in chest. Ran back to my company and in darkness taken by one of our officers for Russian and shot in arm."

"While digging trenches struck by a rifle-bullet in two places. Lay in trench two hours when found by Russian infantrymen, who hurriedly dressed me and put me out of firing-range on horse blanket in old trench. Later found by our soldiers, carried to base, and dressed there, then to field-hospital, then in cart to railroad station. Went few kilometres by train, but became so ill had to be taken off for two days, then sent to Budapest. Seventeen days. Two months in hospital; returned to front."

"We called that man 'professor,'" said the nurse. "He was a teacher of some sort. There was a boy here at the same time, a Pole, but he could speak English: just out of the university—Cracow, I think. He was in Serbia, and was shot through the temple; he lost the sight of both eyes." Several in the Serbian fighting had struck river mines. One, who had been ordered to proceed across the River Save near Sabac, remarked that he was "told afterward" they had struck a floating mine and that seven were killed and thirteen wounded. The Serbian campaign was not pleasant. The Serbians do not hold up their hands, as the big, childlike Russians sometimes seem to have done. They fight as long as they can stand. Then there was disease and lack of medical supplies and service. "They came in covered with mud and with fractures done up with twigs—just as they had been dressed on the field. Sometimes a fractured hip would be bound with a good-sized limb from a tree reaching all the way from the man's feet to his waist."

Yet the wonder is what nature and the tough constitutions of these young men will do with intelligent help. We came to what they call a "face case."

"Wounded November 4 in Galicia by rifle-fire on right side of face and right hand; dressed by comrade, then lost consciousness until arrived here. ('He probably means,' explained the nurse, 'that he was delirious and didn't realize the time.') Physical examination—right side of face blown away; lower jaw broken into several pieces, extending to left side; teeth on lower jaw loose; part of upper jaw gone, and tongue exposed. Infected. Operated—several pieces of lower jaw removed and two pieces wired together in front."

From the desk drawer the nurse picked out several photographs—X-ray pictures of little round shrapnel bullets embedded in flesh, of bone splintered by rifle-bullets and shot through the surrounding flesh as if they had been exploded; one or two black feet cut off above the ankles; one of a group of convalescents standing on the hospital steps.

"There he is," she said, pointing-to a man with a slightly crooked jaw—the man whose history we had just read. "We saved it. It isn't such a bad face, after all."

The worst wounds, of course, do not come to a hospital so far from the front as this—they never leave the battle-field at all. In Turkey, for instance, where travelling is difficult, very few of those shot through the trunk of the body ever got as far as Constantinople—nearly all of the patients were wounded in the head, arms, or legs. On over a thousand patients in this Budapest hospital the following statistics are based: Rifle wounds, 1,095; shrapnel, 138; shell, 2; bayonet, 2; sabre, 1; hand-grenade, 1; frozen feet, 163; frozen hands, 100; rheumatism, 65; typhoid, 38; pneumonia, 15; tetanus, 5; gas infection, 5. Deaths, 19—septicaemia, 7; pneumonia, tetanus, typhoid, 1. It was dark when I started down-stairs, through that warm, brooding stillness of a hospital at night. The ward at the head of the stairs was hushed now, and the hall lamp, shining across the white trousers of an orderly dozing in his chair within the shadow of the door and past the screen drawn in front of it, dimly lit the foot of the line of beds where the men lay sleeping.

Nothing could happen to them now—until they were sound again and the order came to go out and fling themselves again under the wheels. The doctor on duty for the night, coat off, was stretched on his sofa peacefully reading under a green lamp. And, as I went down-stairs past the three long wards, the only sign of life was in a little circle of light cast by a single lamp over the bed of one of the new patients, lighting up the upturned profile of a man and the fair hair of the young night nurse bending over him and silently changing the cloths on his chest.

We dined late that evening on an open balcony at the top of the house. People in Vienna and Budapest like to eat and drink in the open air. Below us lay the dark velvet of the park, with an occasional lamp, and beyond, over the roofs of Pest, the lights of Buda across the river.

Up through the trees came the voices of men singing. I asked what this might be. They were men, my friends explained, who had had their legs amputated. There were fifty-eight of them, and the people who owned the big, empty garden across the street had set it aside for them to live in. There they could sit in the sun and learn to walk on their artificial legs—it was a sort of school for them.

I went to see it next morning—this Garden of Legless Men. They were scattered about under the trees on benches two by two, some with bandaged stumps, some with crutches, some with no legs at all. They hobbled over willingly enough to have their pictures taken, although one of them muttered that he had had his taken seventy times and no one had sent him a. copy yet. The matron gathered them about her, arranging them rather proudly so that their wounds "would show. One looked to be quite all right—because he had artificial legs, boots and all, below the knee.

"Come," said the matron, "show the gentleman how you can walk." And the obedient man came wobbling toward us in a curious, slightly rickety progress, like one of those toys which are wound up and set going on the sidewalk. At the matron's suggestion he even dropped one of his canes. He could almost stand alone, indeed, like some of the political arguments for which millions of healthy young fellows like him obediently go out to fight.

The Augusta Barracken Hospital is on the outskirts of Budapest—a characteristic product of the war, wholesale healing for wholesale maiming—1,000 beds and all the essentials, in what, two months before, was a vacant lot by the railroad tracks. The buildings are long, one-story, pine barracks, just wide enough for two rows of beds with an aisle down the centre. The space between the barracks is filled, in thrifty European fashion, with vegetable-gardens, and they are set on neat streets through which the patients can be wheeled or carried to and from the operating and dressing rooms without going up or down stairs. Trains come in from the observation hospitals near the front, where all wounded now stay for five days until it is certain they have no contagious disease, and switch right up to the door of the receiving-room.

The men give their names, pass at once to another room where their uniforms are taken away to be disinfected, thence to the bathroom, then into clean clothes and to bed. It is a city of the sick—of healing, rather—and on a bright day, with crowds of convalescents sitting about in their linen pyjamas in the sun, stretcher-bearers going back and forth, the capable-looking surgeons with their strong, kind faces, pretty nurses in nun-like white, it all has the brisk, rather jolly air of any vigorous organism, going full blast ahead.

We had been through it, seen the wards of strapping, handsome, childlike Russians, as carefully looked after by the Hungarians as if they were their own, when our officer guide remarked that in an hour or two a transport of four hundred new wounded would be coming in. We waited in the receiving-room, where a young convalescent had been brought out on a stretcher to see his peasant family—a weather-beaten father, a mother with a kerchief over her head, two solemn, little, round-faced brothers with Tyrolean feathers in their caps. Benches were arranged for those able to sit up, clerks prepared three writing-desks, orderlies laid a row of stretchers side by side for fifty yards or so along the railroad track.

The transport was late, the sun going, and I went down to

the other end of the yard to get a picture of some Russians I had seen two days before. We had walked through their ward then, and I remembered one very sick boy, to whom one of the nurses with us had given a flower she was wearing, and how he had smiled as he put it to his face with his gaunt, white hand. "It doesn't take long," she had said, "when they get like that. They have so little vitality to go on, and some morning between two and five"—and sure enough his bed was empty now.

A troop-train was rushing by, as I came back, covered with green branches and flowers. They went by with a cheer—that cheer which sounds like a cheer sometimes, and sometimes, when two trains pass on adjoining tracks so fast that you only catch a blur of faces, like the windy shriek of lost souls.

Then came a sound of band music, and down the road, outside the high wire fence, a little procession led by soldiers in grey-blue, playing Chopin's "Funeral March." Behind them came the hospital hearse, priests, and a weeping peasant family. The little procession moved slowly behind the wailing trumpets—it was an honour given to all who died here, except the enemy—and must have seemed almost a sort of extravagance to the convalescents crowding up to the fence who had seen scores of their comrades buried in a common trench. Opposite us the drums rolled and the band began the Austrian national hymn. Then they stopped; the soldier escort fired their rules in the air. That ended the ceremony, and the hearse moved on alone.

Then the convalescents drifted back toward us. Most of them would soon be ready for the front again, and many glad of it, if only to be men in a man's world again. One of the nurses spoke of some of the others she had known. One man slashed his hand with his knife in the hope of staying behind. Even the bravest must gather themselves together before the leap. Only those who have seen what modern guns can do know how much to fear them.

"For a week or so after they come in lots of them are dazed; they just lie there scarcely stirring. All that part of it—the shock to their nerves—we see more of than the doctors do. When the word comes to go out again they have all the physical symptoms of intense nervous excitement, even nausea sometimes." The train came at last—two long sections of sleeping-cars. An officer stepped off, clicked his heels, and saluted, and the orderlies started unloading the men. Those who could walk at all were helped from the doors; the others—men with broken hips, legs in casts, and so on—were passed out of the windows on stretchers held over the orderlies' heads. In the receiving-ward they were set down in rows before the three tables, most of them clutching their papers as they came. Each man gave his name and regiment, and such particulars, and the address of some one of his family to whom notice could be sent. It was one clerk's duty to address a post-card telling his family of his condition and that he was in the hospital.

These cards were already ruled off into columns in each of which the words "Lightly wounded," "Wounded," "Severely wounded," "Ill," "Very ill" were printed in nine of the languages spoken in Austria-Hungary. The clerk merely had to put a cross on the proper word. Here, for instance, is the Lightly wounded column, in German, Hungarian, and the other dialects: *"Leicht verwundet, Konnyen megse-besult, Lehce ranen, Lekko raniony, Lecko ranenki, Leggiermente Jcrzto, Lako ranjen, Lahko ranjen, Usor ranit."*

A number were Russians—fine, big, clear-eyed fellows with whom these genuine "Huns" chatted and laughed as if they were their own men. On one stretcher came a very pale, round-faced, little boy about twelve, with stubbly blond hair clipped short and an enchanting smile. He had been carrying water for the soldiers, somebody said, when a piece of shrapnel took off one of his feet. Possibly he was one of those little adventurers who run away to war as boys used to run away to sea or the circus. He seemed entirely at home with these men, at any rate, and when one of the Hungarians brought him a big tin cup of coffee and a chunk of black bread, he wriggled himself half upright and went to work at it like a veteran.

As soon as the men were registered they were hurried out of their uniforms and into the bathroom. At the door two nurses in white—so calm and clean and strong that they must have seemed like goddesses, in that reek of steam and disinfectants and festering wounds—received them, asked each man how he was wounded, and quickly, as if he were a child, snipped off his bandages, unless the leg or arm were in a cast, and turned him over to the orderlies. Those who could walk used showers, the others were bathed on inclined slabs. Even the worst wounded scarcely made a sound, and those who could take care of themselves limped under the showers as if they had been hospital boarders before, and waited for, and even demanded, with a certain peremptoriness, their little bundle of belongings before they went on to the dressing-room.

Discipline, possibly, though one could easily fancy that all this organized kindness and comfort suddenly enveloping them was enough to raise them for the moment above thoughts of pain.

As they lifted the man on the dressing-table and loosened the pillow-like bandage under his drawn-up thigh, a thick, sickening odour spread through the room. As the last bit of gauze packing was drawn from the wound, the greenish pus followed and streamed into the pan. The jagged chunk of shell had hit him at the top of the thigh and ploughed down to the knee. The wound had become infected, and the connecting tissues had rotted away until the leg was now scarcely more than a bone and the two flaps of flesh. The civilian thinks of a wound, generally, as a comparatively decent sort of hole, more or less the width of the bullet itself. There was nothing decent about this wound. It was such a slash as one might expect in a slaughtered ox. It had been slit farther to clean the infection, until you could have thrust your fist into it, and, as the surgeon worked, the leg, partly from weakness, partly from the man's nervousness, trembled like a leaf.

First the gauze stuffed into the cavity had to be pulled out. The man, of an age that suggested that he might have left at home a peasant wife, slightly faded and weather-worn like himself, cringed and dug his nails into the under side of the table, but made no outcry. The surgeon squeezed the flesh above and about the wound, the quick-fingered young nurse flushed the cavity with an antiseptic wash, then clean, dry gauze was pushed into it and slowly pulled out again.

The man—they had nicknamed him "Pop"—breathed faster. This panting went into a moan, which deepened into a hoarse cry, and then, as he lost hold of himself completely, he began a hideous sort of sharp yelping like a dog.

This is a part of war that doctors and nurses see; not rarely and in one hospital, but in all hospitals and every morning, when the long line of men—"'pus tanks' we called 'em last winter," muttered one of the young doctors—are brought in to be dressed, There was such a leg that day in the Barracken Hospital; the case described here was in the American Red Cross Hospital in Vienna.

Such individual suffering makes no right or wrong, of course. It is a part of war. Yet the more one sees of it and of this cannon fodder, the people on whom the burden of war really falls, how alike they all are in their courage, simplicity, patience, and long-suffering, whether Hungarians or Russians, Belgians or Turks, the less simple is it to be convinced of the complete righteousness of any of the various general ideas in whose name these men are tortured. I suspect that only those can hate with entire satisfaction and success who stay quietly at home and read the papers.

I remember riding down into Surrey from London one Sunday last August and reading an editorial on Louvain—so well written, so quivering with noble indignation that one's blood boiled, as they say, and one could scarcely wait to get off the train to begin the work of revenge. Perhaps the most moving passage in this editorial was about the smoking ruins of the Town Hall, which I later saw intact. I have thought occasionally since of that editorial and of the thousands of sedentary fire-eaters and hate-mongers like the writer of it—men who live forever in a cloud of words, bounce from one nervous reaction to another without ever touching the ground, and, rejoicing in their eloquence, go down from their comfortable breakfasts to their comfortable offices morning after morning and demand slaughter, annihilation, heaven knows what not—men who could not endure for ten minutes that small part of war which any frail girl of a trained nurse endures hour after hour every morning as part of the day's work.

If I had stayed in London and continued to read the lies of but one side, I should doubtless, by this time, be able to loathe and despise the enemy with an entire lack of doubt, discomfort, or intelligence. But having been in all the countries and read all the lies, the problem is less simple.

How many people who talk or write about war would have the courage to face a minute, fractional part of the reality underlying war's inherited romance? People speak with pleasant excitement of "flashing sabres" without the remotest thought of what flashing sabres do. A sabre does not stop in mid-air with its flashing, where a Meissonier or a Detaille would paint it—it goes right on through the cords and veins of a man's neck. Sabre wounds are not very common, but there was one in the Vienna hospital that morning—a V-shaped trench in which you could have laid four fingers fiat, down through the hair and into the back of the man's neck, so close to the big blood-vessel that you could see it beat under its film of tissue—the only thing between him and death. I thought of it a day or two later when I was reading a book about the Austrian army officer's life, written by an English lady, and came across the phrase: "'Sharpen sabres!' was the joyful cry."

Be joyful if you can, when you know what war is, and, knowing it, know also that it is the only way to do your necessary work. The absurd and disgusting thing is the ignorance and cowardice of those who can slaughter an army corps every day for lunch, with words, and would not be able to make so trivial a start toward the "crushing" they are forever talking about as to fire into another man's open eyes or jam a bayonet into a single man's stomach. Among the Utopian steps which one would most gladly support would be an attempt to send the editors and politicians of all belligerent countries to serve a week in the enemy's hospitals.

CHAPTER 15

East Of Lemberg

We left Nagybiesce in the evening, climbed that night through the high Tatras, stopped in the morning at Kaschau long enough for coffee and a sight of the old cathedral, rolled on down through the country of robber barons' castles and Tokay wine, and came at length, in the evening, to Munkacs and the foot of the high Carpathians.

This was close to the southernmost point the Russians touched when they came pouring down through the Carpathian passes, and one of the places in the long line where Germans and Austro-Hungarians joined forces in the spring to drive them back again. Munkacs is where the painter Munkacsy came from. It was down to Munkacs, through Silesia and the Tatras, that the troop-trains came in April while snow was still deep in the Carpathians. Now it was a feeding-station for fresh troops going up and wounded and prisoners coming down.

The officers in charge had no notion we were coming, but no sooner heard we were strangers in Hungary than we must come in, not only to dinner, but to dine with them at their table. We had red-hot stuffed paprika pods, Liptauer cheese mixed salmon-pink with paprika, and these and other things washed down with beer and cataracts of hospitable talk. Some one whispering that a bit of cheese might come in handy in the breakfastless, cholera-infested country, into which we were going that night, they insisted we must take, not merely a slice, but a chunk as big as a small trunk. We looked at the soup-kitchen, where they could feed two thousand a day, and tasted the soup. We saw the dressing-station and a few wounded waiting there, and all on such a breeze of talk and eloquent explanation that you might have thought you had stepped back into a century when suspicion and worry and nerves were unknown.

The Hungarians are like that—along with their indolence and romantic melancholy—lively and hospitable and credulous with strangers. Nearly all of them are good talkers and by sheer fervour and conviction can make almost any phrase resemble an idea and a real idea as good as a play. Hungarians are useful when trenches must be taken by storm, just as the sober Tyrolean mountaineers are better for sharp-shooting and slow resistance.

One of the interesting things about the Austro-Hungarian army, as well, of course, as an inevitable weakness, is the variety of races and temperaments hidden under these blue-grey uniforms—Hungarians, Austrians, Croatians, Slovaks, Czechs. Things in universal use, like post-cards and paper money, often have their words printed in nine languages, and an Austro-Hungarian officer may have to know three or four in order to give the necessary orders to his men. And his men cannot fight for the fatherland as the Germans do; they must rally round a more or less abstract idea of nationality. And one of the surprises of the war, doubtless, to many people, has been that its strain, instead of disintegrating, appears to have beaten this loose mass together.

At the table that evening was a middle-aged officer and his aid on their way to a new detail at the front. They were simple and soldier-like and, after the flashing bosoms of the sedentary hinterland, it was pleasant to see these men, who had been on active service since the beginning, without a single medal. The younger Hungarian was one of those slumbering daredevils who combine a compact, rugged shape—strong wrists, hair low on the forehead—with the soft voice and shy manners of a girl. He spoke a little German and English in the slow, almost plaintive Hungarian cadence, but all we could get out of him about the war was that it had made him so tired—so *'mude'*. He had gone to school in Zurich but could not tell our Swiss lieutenant the name of his teacher—he couldn't remember anything, any more, he said, with his plaintive smile. He had a little factory in Budapest and had gone back on furlough to see that things were ship-shape, but it was no use, he couldn't tell them what to do when he got there. Common enough, our captain guide observed. He had been in the fighting along the San until invalided back to the *Presse-Quartier*, and there were times, then, he said, when for days it was hard for him to remember his own name.

We climbed up into the mountains in the night and he had us up at daylight to look down from creaking, six-story timber bridges built by the Austro-Hungarian engineers to replace the steel railroad bridges blown up by the Russians. We passed a tunnel or two, a big stockade full of Russian prisoners milling round in their brown overcoats, and down from the pass into the village of Skole. Here we were to climb the near-by heights of Ostry, which the Hungarians of the Corps Hoffmann stormed in April when the snow was still on the ground, and *"orientiren"* ourselves a bit about this Carpathian fighting.

I had looked back at it through the "histories" and the amputed feet and hands in the hospital at Budapest—now, in the muggy air of a late August morning we were to tramp over the ground itself. There were, in this party of rather leisurely reporters, a tall, wise, slow-smiling young Swede who had gone to sea at twelve and been captain of a destroyer before leaving the navy to manage a newspaper; a young Polish count, amiably interested in many sorts of learning and nearly all sorts of ladies—he had seen some of the Carpathian fighting as an officer in the Polish Legion; one of the Swiss citizen officers—one can hear him now whacking his heels together whenever he was presented, and fairly hissing *"Oberleutnant W—, aw Schweiz!"* and a young Bulgarian professor, who spoke German and a little French, but, unlike so many of the Bulgarians of the older generation who were educated at Robert College, no English. The Bulgarians are intensely patriotic and there was nothing under sun, moon, or stars which this young man did not compare with what they had in Sofia. German tactics, Russian novels, sky-scrapers, music, steamships—no matter what—in a moment would come his *"Bei uns in Sofia"*—(With us in Sofia) and his characteristic febrile gesture, thumb and forefinger joined, other fingers extended, pumping emphatically before his face.

Then there was our captain guide from the regular army, a volunteer automobile officer, a soldier servant for each man—for the Austrians do such things in style—and even, on a separate flat car, our own motor. The Carpathians here are in the neighbourhood of three thousand five hundred feet high—a tangle of pine-covered slopes as steep as a roof sometimes, and reminding one a bit of our Oregon Cascades on a much-reduced scale. You must imagine snow waist-deep, the heights furrowed with trenches, the frosty balsam stillness split with screaming shells and shrapnel and the rat-tat-tat of machine guns; imagine yourself floundering upward with winter overcoat, blanket, pack, rifle, and cartridge-belt—any one who has snow-shoed in mountains in midwinter can fancy what fighting meant in a place like this. Men's feet and hands were frozen on sentry duty or merely while asleep—for the soldiers slept as a rule in the open, merely huddled in their blankets before a fire—the severely wounded simply dropped in the snow, and for most of them, no doubt, that was the end of it.

Puffing and steaming in our rain-coats, we climbed the fifteen hundred feet or so to the top of the mountain, up which the Russians had built a sort of cork-screw series of trenches, twisting one behind the other. We reached one skyline only to find another looking down at us. Barbed-wire entanglements and "Spanish riders" crossed the slopes in front of them—it was the sort of place that looks to a civilian as if it could hold out forever.

The difficulty in country like this is, of course, to escape flanking fire. You fortify yourself against attack from one direction only to be enfiladed by artillery from some ridge to right or left. That was what the Austrians and Germans did and, following their artillery with an infantry assault, captured one of the upper Russian trenches. From this it was only a matter of a few hours to clear out the others. Except for the visits of a few peasants the battle-field had scarcely been touched since the snow melted. The hillside was peppered with shell holes, the trenches littered with old hand-grenades, brown Russian over-coats, the rectangular metal cartridge clip cases——about like biscuit tins—which the Russians leave everywhere, and some of the brush-covered shelters in which the Russians had lived, with their spoons and wet papers and here and there a cigarette box or a tube of tooth-paste, might have almost been lived in yesterday.

The valley all the way back to Skole was strung with the brush and timber shelters in which the Russians had camped—the first of thousands of cut-up pine-trees we were to see before we left Galicia. All the drab and dreary side of war was in that little mountain town—smashed houses; sidewalks, streets, and fences splashed with lime against cholera; stores closed or just keeping alive, and here and there signs threatening spies and stating that any one found carrying explosives or building fires would be shot. I went into one fairly clean little cafe, where it seemed one might risk a cup of tea—you are not supposed to drink unboiled or unbottled water in such neighbourhoods—and the dismal old Jew who kept the place told me that he had been there since the war began. He made a sour face when I said he must have seen a good deal. A lot he could see, he said, six months in a cellar *"gesteckt."*

There was a certain amount of cholera all through eastern Galicia, especially among the peasants, not so well housed, often, as the soldiers, and not nearly so well fed and taken care of. Every one who went into Galicia had to be vaccinated for cholera, and in the army this had all but prevented it. In a whole division living in a cholera-infected neighbourhood there would be only one or two cases, and sometimes none at all. The uncomfortable rumour of it was everywhere, however, and one was not supposed to eat raw fruit or vegetables, and in some places hand-shaking, even in an officers' mess, was prohibited.

Russian prisoners were working about the station as they were all over eastern Austria-Hungary—big, blond, easy-going children, apparently quite content. Our Warsaw Pole talked with one of them, who seemed to mourn only the fact that he didn't have quite so big a ration of bread as he had had as a soldier. He had come from Siberia, where he had left a wife and three children—four, maybe, by this time, he said; some rascally Austrian might have made another one.

Beyond Skole we left the mountains—looking back at that imposing wall on the horizon, one could fancy the Russians coming down from the north and thinking, "There we shall stand!"—and rode northward through a pleasant, shallow, valley country, past Ruthenian settlements with their three-domed churches and houses steep-roofed with heavy thatch. Some of these Ruthenians, following the Little Russians of the south, Gogol's country, were not enthusiastic when the Russians came through. Among others, the Russian Government had made great propaganda, given money for churches and so on, so that the apparently guileless peasants occasionally revealed artillery positions, the Austrians said, by driving their cattle past them or by smoke signals from cottage chimneys. We stopped for dinner at Strij, another of those drab, dusty, half-Jewish towns filled now with German and Austro-Hungarian soldiers, officers, proclamations, and all the machinery of a staff headquarters, and the next morning rolled into Lemberg. The Russians captured it in the first week of the war, held it through the winter, and then, after the Czar had, from a balcony in the town, formally annexed it to the empire forever and a day, in April, the Austro-Hungarians retook it again in June.

There were smashed windows in the railroad station, but otherwise, to a stranger coming in for the first time, Lemberg seemed swinging along, a big modern city of some-two hundred thousand people, almost as if nothing had happened.

With an officer from General Bom-Ermolh's staff, and maps, we drove out to the outlying fortifications, where the real fighting had taken place. The concrete gun positions, the permanent infantry protections with loopholes in concrete, and all the trenches and barbed wire, looked certainly as if the Russians had intended to stay in Lemberg. The full explanation of why they did not must be left for the present. What happened at one fortified position, a few miles southwest of Lemberg, was plain enough.

Here, in pleasant open farming country was a concrete and earth fort, protected by elaborate trenches and entanglements, in front of which, for nearly a mile across the fields, was an open field of fire. Infantry might have charged across that open space until the end of the war without getting any nearer, but the offensive did not, of course, try that. Over behind distant clumps of trees and a wooded ridge on the horizon they planted their heavy batteries. On a space perhaps three hundred yards long some sixty of these heavy guns concentrated their fire. The infantry pushed up under its protection, the fort fell, and the garrison was captured with it.

It is by such use of artillery that herds of prisoners are sometimes gathered in. Just before the charging infantry reaches the trench, the cataract of artillery fire, which has been pouring into it, is suddenly shifted back a few hundred yards, where it hangs like a curtain shutting off escape. The success of such tactics demands, of course, finished work from the artillerymen and perfect co-ordination between artillery and infantry. At lunch a few days later in Cracow, a young Austrian officer was telling me how they had once arranged that the artillery should fire twenty rounds, and on the twenty-first the infantry, without waiting for the usual bugle signal to storm, should charge the trenches. At the same instant the artillerymen were to move up their range a couple of hundred yards. The manoeuvre was successful and the Russians caught, huddled under cover, before they knew what had happened.

Though Lemberg's cafes were gay enough and the old Jews in gaberdines, with the orthodox curl dangling before each ear, dozed peacefully on the park benches, still the Russians were only a few hours' motor drive to the eastward, and next morning we went out to see them. All of the country through which we drove was, in a way, the "front"—beginning with the staff head-quarters and going on up through wagon-trains, reserves, horse camps, ammunition-stations, and so on, to the first-line trenches themselves.

Sweeping up through this long front on a fine autumn morning is to see the very glitter and bloom of war. Wounds and suffering, burned towns, and broken lives—all that is forgotten in the splendid panorama—men and motors and fliers and guns, the cheerful smell of hay and coffee and horses, the clank of heavy trucks and the jangle of chains, all in beautiful harvest country; in the contagion of pushing on, shoulder to shoulder, and the devil take the hindmost, toward something vastly interesting up ahead.

Every one is well and strong, and the least of them lifted up and glamoured over by the idea that unites them. All the pettinesses and smallness of every-day existence seem brushed aside, for no one is working for money or himself, and every man of them may be riding to his death.

Flippant young city butterflies jump to their feet and gravely salute when their elders enter, the loutish peasant flings up his chin as if he would defy the universe. What a strange and magic thing is this discipline or team-work or whatever you choose to call it, by which some impudent waiter, for instance, who yesterday would have growled at his tips, will to-day fling his chin up and his hands to his sides and beam like a boy, merely because his captain, showing guests through the camp, deigns to peer into his mess-can and, slapping him affectionately on the cheek, ask him if the food is all right!

209

We whizzed into the village of Kamionka, on the upper Bug, across which the Russians had been driven only a few days before. Their trenches were just within the woods a scant mile away, and the smoke of their camp-fires curled up through the trees. Across the much-talked-of Bug, which resembles here a tide-water river split with swampy flats, were the trenches they had left. They trailed along the river bank, bent with it almost at a right angle, and the Austro-Hungarian batteries had been so placed that a crisscross fire enfiladed each trench. From the attic observation station into which we climbed, the officers directing the attack could look down the line of one of the trenches and see their own shells ripping it to pieces. "It was a sight you could see once in a lifetime," said one of the young artillerymen, still strung up with the excitement of the fight—exactly what was said to me at Ari Bumu by a Turkish officer who had seen the Triumph go down.

That attic was like a scene in some military melodrama, with its tattered roof, its tripod binoculars peering at the enemy, the businesslike officers dusty and unshaven, the field-telegraph operator squatting in one corner, with a receiver strapped to his ear. We walked across the rafters to an adjoining room, where there were two or three chairs and an old sofa, had schnapps all round, and then went out to walk over the position.

In front was the wobbly foot-bridge run across by the pioneers, and on the swampy flats the little heaps of sod thrown up by the first line as they pushed across—wading up to their necks part of the way—under fire.

On the near bank the Austro-Hungarian trenches had run between the tombs of an old Jewish burying-ground, and from the earth walls, here and there, projected a bone or a crumbling skull. The Russian trenches on the other bank wound through a farmyard in the same impersonal way—pig-pens, orchard, chicken-coops, all thought of merely as shelter. It was just to the left of a pig-pen that a Russian officer had held his machine gun until the last minute, pouring in a flank fire. "He did his work!" was the young officer's comment.

We lunched with a corps commander and dined with a genial old colonel and his staff, and between times motored through level farming country to a position to the northward on the Rata, a tributary of the Bug. Both sides were watching each other here from their sausage-shaped captive balloons, and a few aeroplanes were snooping about but at the moment all was quiet. The Austro-Hungarians had been waiting here for over a fortnight, and the artillerymen had polished up their battery positions as artillery-men like to do when they have time. Two were in a pasture, so neatly roofed over with sod that a birdman might fly over the place until the cows came home without knowing guns were there. Another, hidden just within the shadow of a pine forest, was as attractive as some rich man's mountain camp, the gun positions as snug as yacht cabins, the officer's lodges made of fresh, sweet-smelling pine logs, and in a little recess in the trees a shrine had been built to St. Barbara, who looks out for artillery-men.

The infantry trenches along the river, cut in the clean sand and neatly timbered and loopholed, were like model trenches on some exposition ground. Through these loopholes one could see the Russian trenches, perhaps a mile away, and in between the peasant women, bright red and white splashes in the yellow wheat, were calmly going ahead with their harvest. All along the Galician front we saw peasants working thus and regarding this elaborate game of war very much apparently as busy farmers regard a drag hunt or a party of city fishermen. At one point we had to come out in the open and cross a foot-bridge. "Please—Lieutenant," one of the soldiers protested as the officer with us stepped out, standing erect, "it is not safe!" The officer crouched and hurried across and so did we, but just before we did so, up out of the field where they had been mowing, straight through this gap, came a little company of barefooted peasant women with their bundles of gleanings on their heads, and talking in that singsong monotone of theirs, as detached as so many birds, they went pat-

patting across the bridge. If one of these women could but write her impressions of war!

They had done their part, these peasant women and old men and children. All over Galicia, round the burned villages, right through barbed-wire entanglements up to the very trenches, stretched the yellow wheat. Somehow they had ploughed and sowed and brought it to harvest, and now with scythes, with knives even, sometimes, they were getting it under cover. At home we know gleaners generally only in rather sentimental pictures; here we saw them day after day, barefooted women and children going over the stubble and picking up the forgotten wheat heads and arranging them in one hand as if they were a bouquet. There will be no wheat wasted this year.

And with them everywhere were the Russian prisoners, swinging scythes, binding grain, sometimes coming down the road, without even a guard, sprawled in the sun on a load of straw. It would be hard to find a place where war seemed more a vast theatricalism than in some of these Hungarian and Galician neighbourhoods. There seemed to be no enmity whatever between captors and prisoners. Everywhere the latter were making themselves useful in the fields, in road-making, about railroad yards, and several officers told me that it was surprising how many good artisans, carpenters, iron-workers, and so on, there were among them. The Russians got exactly the same food as the Hungarian soldiers, and were paid a few cents a day for their work. You would see men in the two uniforms hobnobbing in the open freight-cars as the work-trains rolled up the line, and sometimes a score or so of husky Russians working in the wheat, guarded by some miniature, lone, *Landsturm* man. Of all the various war victims I had seen, these struck me as the most lucky—they could not even, like the wounded, be sent back again.

We drove back through the dark that night, and in the bright, waving circle of an automobile search-light, with the cool breath from the pines in our faces, saw that long "front" roll back again. Now and then a soldier would step into the white circle and, holding up his arm, struggle between his awe of this snorting motor with its imperial double-eagle flag and its sharp-voiced officers muffled in grey coats—between his peasant's habit of taking off his hat and letting such people blow by, and his soldier's orders to stop every-thing that passed. He stopped us, nevertheless, and the pass was laboriously read in the light of his electric lamp before we went on again.

In the dark and quiet all the countless joints and wheels of the vast organism were still mysteriously turning. Once, in a cloud of dust, we passed troops marching toward the front—tired faces, laughing faces—the shout "Man in the road!" and then the glimpse of a couple of Red Cross men kneeling by a soldier who had given out on the way; once, in the black pines, cows driven by two little frightened peasant children; once a long line of bearded Jews, bound, with packs on their backs, for what was left of their homes; a supply-train, a clanking battery, and now and then other motors like ours with shrouded grey figures, streaking by in a flashing mist of dust.

Next day, swinging southward into another sector of the front, over beautiful rolling hills, rather like the Genesee Valley, we drummed up a hill and came out at the top in a village square. It had once been a white little village clinging to the skirts of an old chateau—the village of Swirz and Count Lavasan's chateau—and both were now black and tumbled walls.

In the centre of the square people were singing—a strange little crowd and strange, mournful singing. We thought at first it was a funeral service, for the women were weeping as they sang, but as the auto-mobile swept up beside them, we saw that it was men the women were crowding round—live men, going away to war.

They were men who had not been called out because the Russians held the country, and by one of fate's ironies, now that the enemy had been beaten and driven home, they must go out and fight. At a little table by the side of the square sat the recruiting officer with his pen and ledger, and the village schoolmaster, a grave, intelligent-looking young man, who must have held such a place in this half-feudal village as he would have done a hundred years ago, was doing his best to glamour over the very realistic loss of these wives and sweethearts with patriotism's romance. He sang and obediently they all wailed after him the old song of scattered Poland—"Poland is not lost" *"Yeszcze Polska me Zginela Poki my zygemy. . ."*

The song stopped, there was a word of command, and the little squad started away. The women clung to their men and cried aloud. The children hanging to their skirts began to wail, too. There was something creepy and horrible, like the cries of tortured animals, in that uncontrolled crying there in the bright morning sunshine. The schoolmaster spoke to them bluntly, told them to go back to their homes and their work, and obedient, and a little quieter now, they drifted away, with aprons to their faces and their little children clinging to their skirts—back to their cottages and the winter ahead.

This picture did not fit in very well with our rollicking military panorama, but we were soon over the hills, and half an hour later were breakfasting on *pate-de-foie-gras* sandwiches and champagne, with a charming old corps commandant, at a round table set outdoors in a circle of trees that must have been planted for that very purpose. Cheered and stiffened by many bows and heel clickings and warming hospitality, we hurried off to an artillery position near the village of Olszanica.

Just under the brow of a hill we were stopped and told that it was dangerous to go farther, and we skirted off to the right under cover, to the observation station itself. More little Swiss chalets, more hospitable officers, and out in front, across a mile of open country, the Russian trenches. Through a periscope one could see Russians exercising their horses by riding them round the circle—as silent and remote and of another world as a picture on a biograph screen.

"You see that clump of trees," said the young officer, "one of their batteries is just behind there. Those aren't real trees, they were put there by the Russians." I swung the glass to the left, picked up a company of men marching. "Hello, hello," he whispered, then after a moment's scrutiny: "No—they're our men." After all, war isn't always so different from the old days, when men had a time for fighting and a time for going in to powder their wigs! The division commander, standing a little behind us, remarked: "We shall fire from the right-hand battery over behind the hill and then from the left—the one you passed near the road." Then turning to an officer at the field telephone he said; "You may fire now."

There was a moment's pause, from over the woods behind us came a *"Whr-r-rong!"* and out over the sunny fields a shell went milling away to send back a faint report and show a puff of cotton above the trenches to the right. It was a bit short—the next fell better. Another nod, another *"Whr-r-row?"* from somewhere behind us, and this time the cottony puff was just short of the clump of trees where the Russians had concealed their battery. I picked up the spot through the glass and—one might have known!—there was One of those eternal peasants calmly swinging his scythe about fifty yards short of the spot where the shrapnel had exploded. I could see him straighten up, glance at it, then go on with his mowing again.

There was a certain elegance, a fine spaciousness about these artillery-men and their work which made one more content with war again. No huddling in muddy trenches here, waiting to be smashed by jagged chunks of iron—everything clean, aloof, scientific, exact, a matter of fine wires crossing on a periscope lens, of elevation, wind pressure, and so on, and everything in the wide outdoors, and done, so to say, with a magnificent gesture.

People drive high-power motor-cars and ride strong horses because of the sense of power it gives them—how about standing on a hill, looking over miles of splendid country to where a huddle of ants and hobby-horse specks—say a battalion or two—are just crawling around a hill or jammed on a narrow bridge, and then to scatter them, herd them, chase them from one horizon to another with a mere, "Mr. Jones, you may fire now," and a wave of the hand!

215

The division commander took us back a mile or so to his headquarters for lunch, the Russians slowly waking up and sending a few perfunctory shells after us as we went over the hill, and here was another genial party, with three *"Hochs"* for the guests at the end. Even out here in empty Galicia the soldiers got their beer. "We're not quite so temperate as the Russians," the general smiled. "A little alcohol—not too much—does 'em good."

A young lieutenant who sat next me regaled me with his impression of things in general. The Russians had squandered ammunition, he said, in the early days of the war—they would fire twenty rounds or so at a single cavalryman or anything that showed itself. They were short now, but a supply would come evidently every now and then, for they would blaze away for a day or so, then there would be a lull again. They were short on officers, too, but not so much as you might think, because they kept their officers well back of the line, generally. Their artillery was better than the infantry, as a rule; the latter shot carelessly and generally too high.

Both he and the officer at my left—a big, farmer-like commissary man—spoke most amiably of the Russians. The latter told of one place where both sides had to get water out of the same well. And there was no trouble. "No," he said, in his deep voice, "they're not hose," using the same word "bad" one would apply to a naughty boy. They were a particularly chipper lot, these artillerymen, and when I told the young lieutenant, who had been assigned to speak French to me under the notion that I was more at home in that language, that I had stopped at Queens Hotel instead of the St. Antoine in Antwerp, and that the Belgian army had crossed the Scheldt, and the pontoon bridge had been blown up directly in front of the hotel, he said that he would "certainly engage rooms there for the next bombardment," as he waved good-by.

We were presented, while in Lemberg, to General Bom-Ermolli, and lunched at the headquarters mess. We also met Major-General Bardolf, his chief of staff, and chief of staff of the assassinated Crown Prince. The latter described to us the campaign about Lemberg, and it was interesting to hear the rasping accent he gave to a word like *"Durchbrechung,"* for instance, as if he were a Prussian instead of an Austrian, and to observe the frankness with which he ascribed the difference that had come over the spirit of the Austro-Hungarian army to the coming of Mackensen and the Germans.

West of Lemberg the pleasant country lost its war-time air and in Przemysl the two or three lonely *Landsturm* men guarding the wrecked fortifications, twice taken and twice blown up by retreating armies, lit candles to take us through the smashed galleries, and accepted a few *Hellers* when we came out, with quite the bored air of professional museum guides.

The town of Przemysl itself was untouched. The greater part of the visible damage to the forts, some distance outside the town, was done by the dynamite of the retreating army. In one place, however, we saw the crater of one of the 42-centimetre shells which have been talked about oftener than they have been used. The Austrian "thirty-point-fives" have done much of the smashing ascribed to the "forty-twos," and ordinary work, like that of bombarding a city or infantry trenches, by cannon of smaller calibre. A genuine forty-two had been dropped here, however, we were told, on a building used by the Russians to store ammunition, and the building had simply disappeared. There was nothing left but a crater sixty or seventy feet across and eighteen to twenty feet deep.

We trailed westward, through Tarnow, where the great drive first broke through, and on to the pleasant old university city of Cracow on the frontier of the Poland of which it was once the capital, and to which it belonged until the partition of 1795. It was toward Cracow that the Russians were driving when they first started for Berlin, and they were but a stone's throw away most of the winter. We got to Cracow on the Emperor's birthday and saw a military mass on the great parade-ground with the commandant of the fort standing uncovered and alone facing the altar, behind him his staff, and perhaps a hundred yards behind them and stretching for a quarter of a mile down the field, the garrison. At the intervals in the mass the whole garrison fired salutes, the volleys going down the field, a battalion at a time, now and then reinforced by the cannon on Kosciusko Hill.

Cracow is Polish in atmosphere and feeling, and even in the few hours we were there one heard a good deal of Polish hopes and ambitions. The independence which Russia was to grant must come now, it would appear, from some one else. The Poles want a king of their own, but apparently they preferred to be under the wing of Austria rather than of Germany. The Germans, who had laid rather a firm hand on the parts of Poland they had occupied, might not fall in with this notion and one could detect here one of those clouds, "no bigger than a man's hand," which dramatists put in the first act, and which often swell to interesting proportions before the final curtain goes down.

CHAPTER 16

In the Dust of the Russian Retreat

Warsaw had fallen, and Ivangorod, and the centre of the German and Austro-Hungarian armies, sweeping across eastern Europe like beaters across a prairie, was now before Brest-Litovsk. This was the apex of this central triangle of Russian forts, a city and a rail-road centre as well as a fortress, and the last strongly fortified place on the direct road to Moscow. It seemed as if the Russians must make a stand here, and even though we were four or five days getting there, the heavy artillery was not yet up, and there might still be time.

We wound through the green hills and under the ruined castles of northern Hungary in the afternoon, rolled slowly up across Silesia and into Russian Poland in the night, and came at noon to Radom, only sixty-five miles south of Warsaw. Hindenburg had been here in October, 1914, when he invaded Poland to draw off the Russians from Galicia, then the Russian offensive had rolled over the place. The Russians had held it all the winter; now they were a hundred and fifty miles eastward—beyond the Vistula and the Bug—*"boog,"* not *"bug,"* by the way—and just hanging to the edge of Poland.

The war had scarcely touched Budapest and Vienna—scarcely touched the ordinary city surfaces, that is to say. In hotels and cafes, streets and parks, life flowed on almost as brightly as ever. Farther north, in the Hungarian towns and villages, life still went on as usual, but one felt the grip of war—you might not go there nor move about without a military pass. Beyond Radom, where now in the pleasant park the very literary Polish young people were strolling, reading as they walked, there was, so to speak, no ordinary life at all—only the desert of war and the curious, intense, and complicated life of those who made it. Our car was hitched to a long transport-train—for it would be another two days before the automobiles would come back for us from the front—and we rode into this deserted Polish country toward Ivangorod.

It had all been fought over at least twice—railroad stations and farm buildings burned, bridges dynamited, telegraph-poles cut down. The stations now were mere board shelters for a commandant and a soldiers' lunch-room; the bridges, timber bridges flung across by the pioneers; and the sawed-off telegraph-poles, spliced between railroad rails to save cutting new ones, were stuck back into the ground like forks. The Russians had a rather odd way of burning stations and leaving the rails, the important thing, intact, but here and there they had neatly destroyed them for miles by exploding a cartridge under the end of each.

The country is level here—fields interspersed with dark pine forests, planted in the European fashion, to be grown and harvested like any other crop—parks of living telephone-posts, thick as the quills of a porcupine. And through these pines and across the fields were the eternal Russian trenches, carefully built, timber-lined, sometimes roofed and sodded over, with rifle holes under the eaves. Barbed-wire entanglements, seven rows deep sometimes, trailed in front of them, through timber, through the long grass and flowers of marsh-land, a wicked foggy band against the green as far as one could see. Along the Galician front and in the Carpathians I had seen mile after mile of such trenches, timber-work, wires, and Spanish riders left behind, good as new, until it began to seem as if war were a peculiarly absurd game, consisting principally in chopping down good trees and digging ditches, and then going somewhere else.

In front of Ivangorod great preparations had been made. There was no town here, but the great fortress, with its citadel, barracks, machine-shops, gardens, church, and protecting forts, was almost a city in itself. It had a garrison of twenty thousand, and its gigantic concrete walls, covered over with earth and grass, its, moat and barbed wire, looked formidable enough. It had no modern heavy artillery, however, and even if it had, artillery in a fixed, known spot is comparatively helpless against the mobile guns, screened by hills and timber, besiegers can bring against it. Elaborate earthworks had, therefore, been thrown up several miles to the west of the fortress, but these became useless when the enemy, crossing the Vistula to north and south, swung round to cut off the one way out—the railroad to Brest-Litovsk.

The Russians might have shut themselves in and waited—not very long, probably—until the big "thirty-point-fives" smashed the fort to pieces. They chose to get out in time, blew up the railroad bridge across the Bug, burned the barracks, and, with enough dynamite to give a good imitation of an earthquake, tumbled the walls and galleries of the fortress into melancholy heaps of rock.

It was dusk when we rolled into Ivangorod and into the thick of that vast and complicated labour which goes on in the rear of an advancing army—all that laborious building up which follows the retreating army's orgy of tearing down—bridge builders, an acre or two of transport horses, blacksmiths and iron-workers, a semi-permanent bakery, the ovens, on wheels, like thrashing-machine engines, dropping sparks and sending out a sweet, warm, steamy smell of corn and wheat. It never stopped, this bakery, night or day, and the bread was piled up in a big tent near by like cord-wood.

And here you could see the amount of trouble that can be made by blowing up a railroad bridge. First, of course, a new timber bridge has to be flung across, and the Vistula is a good two hundred yards wide here and the river was high. Up ahead the army was fighting forward, dependent, for the moment, on what came across that bridge. A train arrives, hundreds of tons of freight which normally would roll across the river in a few puffs of a cigarette. The cars must be opened, each box and sack taken out by hand, carried down a bank, loaded into a wagon; the wagons creep over the pontoons, struggle through the sand on the other side, then each piece must be unloaded and put on a train again.

An axle breaks, the returning line waits an hour for the other to cross, a sixty-foot pine log for the new railway bridge wedges fast in turning a corner and stops everything—you must imagine them at it all day, sweating and swearing in all the dialects of the dual monarchy—all night, with fagged horses and drivers dazed with sleep, in the blaze of a search-light reaching out over the river. Meanwhile a tall timber railroad bridge was creeping across. There was no pile-driver engine, and at each cluster of piles fifteen or twenty Russian prisoners, in their brown service uniforms, hung to as many ropes—"Heave. . . whack! Heave. . . whack!"—in quaint retribution for what a few sticks of dynamite had done a fortnight before.

A thousand fresh Hungarian troops had just come in next morning, and were waiting for their coffee, when the word came by field-telephone that a Russian flier was dropping bombs about twenty kilometres away. It was fine hunting-ground—men, horses, stores, and the new bridge—but he sailed away, and we drove a dozen miles up the Vistula to New Alexandria, burned during the enveloping movement on Ivangorod.

All along the way were trenches, telltale yellow lines of sand winding among the pines, gun positions, barbed wire, and every now and then a big plane-tree, with ladders running up to an artillery observation platform. I climbed up one of them on cleats worn by Russian boots for a look at the Vistula and the string of Red Cross barges, filled with wounded, going up the river. The children hereabout, at any rate, will revere the Russians, for their pioneers had carried that winding stairway up to the very tip-top of the tree in a manner only seen in dreams or picture-books.

All the farmhouses had been burned, and the peasants were just returning. We passed several tired mothers with babies in shawls hanging from their shoulders and little boys trudging behind with some rusty kettle or coffee-pot, and once a woman, standing in the ruins of her house, of which only the chimney was left, calmly cooking her dinner.

New Alexandria, a pleasant little town, grown up round an old chateau, and used as a sort of summer resort by Warsaw people, was nothing but blackened chimneys and heaps of brick. The Russians had burned everything, and the inhabitants, who had fled into the pines, were just now beginning to straggle back. Some had set up little stands in front of their burned houses and were trying to sell apples, plums, pears, about the only marketable thing left; some were cleaning brick and trying to rebuild, some contented themselves with roofing over their cellars. And while we were observing these domestic scenes, the army, which had taken the outer forts by assault the preceding night, was marching into burning Brest-Litovsk.

It was another day before the motors came and we could get under way and whirl through such a cross-section of a modern army's life as one could scarcely have seen in the west of Europe since the Germans first came rolling down on Paris. No suburban warfare this; none of that hideous, burrowing, blowing up, methodically squashing out yard after yard of trenches and men. This was war in the grand old style—an army on the march, literally, down roads smoky with dust and sunshine, across bridges their own pioneers had built, a river of men and horses, wagons and guns, from one hazy blue horizon to another.

And all these men had come from victory and knew they were marching to it. How far they were going none could tell, but the gods were with them—so might the Grand Army have looked when it started eastward a hundred years ago. Men and horses had been pouring down that road for weeks—on each side of the macadam highway the level, unfenced fields were trampled flat. It was fully one hundred and twenty miles, as the motor road ran, to Brest-Litovsk, and there was scarce a moment when, if we were not in the thick of them, we were not at least in sight of wagons, motors, horses, and men. And, of course, this was but the rear of the army; the fighting men proper were up in front. The dust hung like fog in the autumn sunshine. Drivers were black with it; in the distance, on parallel roads, it climbed high in the still air like smoke from burning villages. And out of this dust, as we whizzed on, our soldier chauffeur, whistle in mouth, shrieking for room, appeared pontoon trains—big steel scows on top, beams underneath, cut, numbered, and ready to put together; trains of light farm wagons, wide at the top, slanting toward the middle, commandeered from all over Austria-Hungary at the beginning of the war and driven, some by soldiers, but oftener by civilians with the yellow Austrian bands on their arms; heavy ammunition wagons drawn by four horse; with a soldier outrider astride one of the leaders, and from time to time columns of reserves, older men for the most part, bound for guard duty, probably, shuffling along in loose order. Round and through these wagon-trains, in a swirl of dust, rumbled and swayed big motor-trucks, and once or twice, scattering everything with a lilting *"Ta-te. . . Ta-da"* the grey motor, the flash of scarlet, pale blue, and gold, and the bronzed, begoggled, imperial visage of some one high in command.

Once we passed a big Austrian mortar, covered with tarpaulin, by the side of the road, and again two big 20-centimetre guns, which had not had time to get up to Brest-Litovsk. This is where you find the heavy artillery nowadays, quite as likely as in a fort, on some hard highway, where it can easily be moved and sheltered, not behind concrete, but some innocent-looking apple-tree. Each fence corner was chalked with letters and numbers intelligible to the drivers, who passed that way; each bridge, down to the few boards across a ditch, had been examined by the pioneers, rebuilt if necessary, and a neat little sign set up on it, telling whether or not the heavy artillery could safely cross. Flowing back toward this huge, confident, onrushing organism, the peasants—timid, halting, weary, and dust-covered, with wagons heaped with furniture, beds, hay for the horses, with the littlest children and those too old to walk—were returning to the charred ruins of their homes. They, too—like the grass—had their unconquerable strength.

The same patience and quiet courage which had struck me in Antwerp as peculiarly Belgian, was here again in these Poles, Slovaks, and Ruthenians, whose boys, perhaps, were fighting with the armies which had driven the Belgians out. You would see peasant mothers with their children hanging from their shoulders—women who had been tramping for days, perhaps, and might have days yet to tramp before they reached the heap of charred bricks that had once been a home. Nearly all had a cow, sometimes pulling back on its halter and filling the air with lamentation, sometimes harnessed with the horse to the family wagon. They had their pet dogs and birds, the little girls their kittens; from the front of one wagon poked the foolish head of a colt. Babies scarcely big enough to sit up crammed their little fingers into their eyes to shut out the dust; bigger children, to whom the ride would be, no doubt, the event of their lives, laughed and clapped their hands, and old men on foot took off their caps, after the fashion of the country, and bowed gravely as we whirled past. It seemed as if it were we who should do the saluting.

From the fields, as we whirled into and out of layers of air, sharply, as one does in a motor, came now the odour of ripe straw, now a whiff of coffee from a "goulash cannon," steaming away behind its troop like the calliope in the old-fashioned circus, and now and then, from some thicket or across a clover field, the sharp, dismaying smell of rotting flesh. The countryside lay so tranquil under the August sun that it was only when one saw a dead animal lying in an open field that one recalled the fire that, a few days before, must have crisscrossed this whole country, as now, doubtless, in constant cavalry fights and rearguard skirmishes, it was crisscrossing the country up ahead.

Half an hour short of Brest-Litovsk an unfinished bridge turned us off into a potato field. The soft ground had long since been pounded flat, as the army, swinging round to the north, had crossed on a pontoon a mile or two lower down. The motor plunged, snarled, and stopped, and again, as we shovelled in front and pushed behind, we knew why armies burn bridges behind them.

Past us, as we sweated there, the slow but surer wagon-trains ploughed forward. One, a German train, stopped beside us to bait their horses—officers of the *Landwehr* or *Landsturm* type, who looked as if they might be, as doubtless they were, lawyers, professors, or successful business men at home. They were from a class who, with us, would generally be helpless in the field, yet these bronzed, bearded, thoughtful-looking men seemed just as familiar with the details of their present job as with the work they had left behind.

Ever since we had crossed into Poland this sober, steel-grey stream had been mingling with and stiffening our lighter-hearted, more boyish, blue-grey stream of Austrians and Hungarians. Here were men who knew what they were doing, believed in it, and had the will to put it through. One thought of Emerson's "Earnest of the North Wind" whenever they came in sight.

Those who talk of "frightfulness" and get their notions of German soldiers from the vapourings of sedentary publicists, who know no more of them than may be seen through the pipe smoke of their own editorial rooms, are destined to a melancholy awakening. You may prefer your own ways, but you cannot make them prevail by blackguarding the other man's weaknesses; you must beat him where he is strong.

Lies and the snobbish ridicule with which our magazines and papers have been full, run off men like these like water off a duck. These men are in earnest. They have work to do. No one who has heard them singing the *"Wacht am Rhein"* through the starlight of garrisoned towns all the way from the Channel to the Carpathians, will talk of their being "stolid";

but they have, it is true, no coltishness. They are grown up. And this discipline of theirs does not mean, as so many people seem to think it does, being compelled to do what you don't want to do. It means doing what you are told to do as well as it possibly can be done, no matter how small it is nor who is looking on—a sense of duty which makes every switchman behind the lines act as if he were Von Hindenburg. The thing of theirs, this will-power and moral earnestness, is one of the things that last—something before which the merely frivolous has always gone down and always will.

The road down which we were going was, in a general way, the path already taken by the Austrian and Hungarian troops which had stormed the outer works at Kobilany two days before and been the first to enter the town. What happened was much like what had happened at Ivangorod. A German corps crossed the Bug to north and south and closed in on the railroad, the Sixth Austro-Hungarian Corps under Corps General of Infantry Arz attacked the centre. The Russians sent the entire civil population eastward, removed their artillery and everything of value they could take, and set fire to the city. There was a brief artillery preparation to which the Russians, who all through this retreat appeared to be short in ammunition and artillery, replied for a time; then the outer forts were stormed, and when the Sixth Corps entered the burning city the Russians, except for the rear-guard prisoners, were gone.

We swung past a freight yard littered with over-turned cars, through a tangle of wagons—army wagons pushing one way and distracted peasants the other—over a pontoon across the narrow Bug and on into the town.

A city of sixty-five thousand people, with the exception of a church or two and houses that could almost be counted on one's fingers, was a waste of gaping windows and blackened chimneys. The Russians' purpose was not altogether clear, for the town was their town, and its destruction at this time of the year could not seriously embarrass a well-provisioned, confident enemy, but they had, at any rate, wiped it off the map. Not a woman, a child, a glimmer of peaceful life; only smouldering ruins, the occasional abandoned rifles and cartridge-boxes of the army that had retired, and the endless wagon-trains of the army pursuing them.

All the dust through which we had ridden since morning seemed to have gathered over that dismal wreck. It was a fog in the streets, on which darkness was already settling—streets without a lamp or a sound except that from the on-flowing trains. Through this dust we tried to find the headquarters of the Sixth Army Corps. To its commander our passes took us and without him we had no reason for being in Brest-Litovsk. Nobody knew where the Sixth was. Two Hungarian officers, hurrying by in a commandeered carriage, shouted back something about the "church with a blue cupola"; somebody else said "near the schnapps factory"; a beaming young lieutenant, helping to disentangle wagon-trains at the main street comers, said that the Sixth had marched at three that morning. We had driven all day with nothing to eat but a bit of war bread and chocolate, we were black with dust, there was not a crumb in the place that did not belong to the army, and we sat there in the thickening dusk, almost as much adrift as a raft in mid-ocean,

The two armies—wagon-trains, that is to say—were crossing each other at that corner. The Germans were going one way, the Austro-Hungarians the other—tired, dust-covered horses and men, anonymous cogs in the vast machine, which had been following the man ahead since the day before, like enough, and might go on into another day before they could make camp.

Young Hungarian officers greeted one another gaily, and exchanged the day's adventures and news; young Germans rode by, slim, serious, and self-contained. Now the stream would stop as one line tried to break through the other, puzzled drivers would yank their horses back, then some determined section commander would come charging back, fling his horse into the tangle—wagon tongues jammed into the canopy in front, protestations in German, Hungarian, Polish, Slovak, goodness knows what, until at last one line gave way and the other shot forward through the dust again.

I had been in another captured city, with the besieged then, and when I think of Antwerp it is of the creepy, bright stillness during the bombardment—the autumn sun, the smell of dead leaves, the shuttered streets, without a sound except when a shell came screaming in from the country or, a block or so away, there was a detonation and some facade came rumbling down. But when I think of Brest-Litovsk it will be of dust—dust like fog and thickened with the smoke and twilight—and that strange, wild, creaking stream of wagons fighting through it as they might have fought in the days when Europe was young and whole races of men came pouring over the frontiers.

We started off finally on foot through streets silent as the grave—not a person, not a lamp, not so much as a barking dog, as queer and as creepy as some made-up thing in a theatre. Once we stumbled past a naked and dismembered trunk set up beside a doorway—a physician's manikin that chance or some sinister clown had left there. Once—and one of the strangest sounds I ever heard—behind the closed up-stair shutters of an apothecary's shop, whose powders and poisons were strewn over the sidewalk, a piano haltingly played with one finger.

At last a light, an open door, a sentry—and this was, indeed, theatrical—a lighted room and a long table set with candles, flowers, and wine. The commander of the Sixth Corps had just been decorated with the order *"Pour le mérite"* and he and his officers were dining before taking up the march. He welcomed us in the true Hungarian style, grabbed me by the arms and asked if I was hungry, apologized for their frugal war-time fare, told how splendidly his men had behaved, had a word and a place for every-body, as if we were all old friends.

There were three rooms full of officers, and every-one half rose and bowed in military fashion as we made our way between the tables to our seats at the end of the third. An amiable young signal-officer who had been at his telephone some thirty kilometres away when the city was taken and was off at three next morning, sat opposite me and told with great spirit how the only common language between him and some of his polyglot men was the English he had learned in school and they had picked up in America.

We slept on commandeered mattresses that night on the floor of a vacant house, with a few Hungarian hussars still singing over the victory in the back yard, and got up to find the crowded town of the night before as empty as the old camp-ground the day after the circus.

We strolled through some of the empty streets and into the citadel, where a handful of German soldiers were guarding a placid, tan-coloured little herd of Russian prisoners; recrossed the pontoon bridge, as crowded as it had been the afternoon before, and then stopped at Kobilany fort on the way back to Ivangorod.

The brief Austrian fire had been accurate. There were shell holes inside the fort, along the parapet, and one frightful bull's-eye, which had struck square on the inner concrete rim and blown chunks of concrete, as well as its own steel, all over the place. The rifle-men left in this embrasure were killed at a stroke, and their blood remained freshly dried on the stones. Of various uncomfortable places I have seen in the war this was one—left behind in an open concrete fort to cover the retreat of artillery, and wait with a pop-gun rifle until the enemy decided that his artillery had "silenced" you and that it was time to storm.

One outer angle of the fort had been blown up and the rest was to have been dynamited, but a nimble Pole, fearing that he might be blown up, too, before the order came to retire, had, so we were told, cut the electric wire. Just why Brest-Litovsk was given up must be left for those who have had a more comprehensive view of all the causes behind the Russian retreat. It was plain to any one, however, that although this outer fortress had been taken by storm and a certain amount of damage done to the attacking force by mines laid in front of it, scarcely more than nominal resistance, considering the original preparations, had been made.

Again we whirled down the Ivangorod road, through a stream of wagons and peasants' carts almost as thick as the day before. We took a new road this time, but the deserted trenches still crossed the fields, and creeping up toward them, behind trees, through the greasy, black mud of pasture-land, were those eloquent little shelters, scarcely more than a basketful of earth, thrown up by the skirmishers as they ran forward, dropped and dug themselves in.

We came to Radom and turned southward again. There were people, smoke coming from cottage chimneys, goose-girls with their spotless and absurdly peaceful geese, once a group of peasants—young men and barefooted girls—sitting on the grass resting from their work in the fields. As the train passed one of the boys flung his arm round the neck of the tanned young nymph beside him, and over they rolled, fighting like good-natured puppies. They were the very peasants we had seen dragging through the dust of the Brest-Litovsk road and this the same country, though it looked so strangely bright and warm and full of people. War had blown over it, that was all, and life, which is so much stronger than the strongest field-marshal, which can be bent, beaten down, and crushed some-times, like the grass, was growing back again.